Dee Brown's
Civil War Anthology

BOOKS BY DEE BROWN

NON-FICTION

Grierson's Raid — 1954

The Gentle Tamers: Women of the Old Wild West — 1958

The Bold Cavaliers: Morgan's 2nd Kentucky Cavalry Raiders — 1959

Fort Phil Kearny: An American Saga — 1962

The Galvanized Yankees — 1963

The Year of the Century: 1876 — 1966

Bury My Heart at Wounded Knee: An Indian History of the American West — 1970

Andrew Jackson and the Battle of New Orleans — 1972

Tales of the Warrior Ants — 1973

The Westerners — 1974

Hear That Lonesome Whistle Blow: Railroads in the West — 1977

The American Spa: Hot Springs, Arkansas — 1982

Wondrous Times on the Frontier — 1991

When the Century Was Young (A Writer's Notebook) — 1993

The American West — 1994

WITH MARTIN F. SCHMITT

Fighting Indians of the West — 1948

Trail Driving Days — 1952

The Settlers' West — 1955

WITH MORT KUNSTLER

Images of the Old West — 1996

EDITED BY DEE BROWN

Pawnee, Blackfoot and Cheyenne — 1961

EDITED BY STAN BANASH

Best of Dee Brown's West — 1998

FICTION

Wave High the Banner — 1942

Yellowhorse: A Novel of the Cavalry in the West — 1956

Cavalry Scout — 1958

They Went Thataway — 1960 (republished as Pardon My Pandemonium — 1984)

The Girl from Fort Wicked — 1964

Showdown at Little Big Horn — 1964

Action at Beecher Island — 1967

Tepee Tales of the American Indian — 1979

Creek Mary's Blood — 1980

Killdeer Mountain — 1983

Conspiracy of Knaves — 1987

The Way to Bright Star — 1998

BOOKS EDITED BY STAN BANASH

Best of Dee Brown's West — 1998

Dee Brown's Civil War Anthology

DEE BROWN

Edited by STAN BANASH

Clear Light Publishers
Santa Fe, New Mexico

Clear Light Publishers, 823 Don Diego, Santa Fe, N.M. 87501
WEB: www.clearlightbooks.com

First Edition
10 9 8 7 6 5 4 3 2 1

Library of Congress Cataloging-in-Publication Data

Brown, Dee Alexander.
  [Civil War anthology]
  Dee Brown's Civil War Anthology / Dee Alexander Brown;
edited by Stan Banash.
      p.   cm.
  Includes index.
  ISBN: 1-57416-009-5 (cloth) — ISBN: 1-57416-010-9 (pbk.)
    1. United States—History—Civil War, 1861–1865. 2. United
States—History—Civil War, 1861–1865—Sources.
  I. Banash, Stan, 1940–. II. Title.
  E468.B78 1998
  973.7—dc21   98-5448
                                                          CIP

Cover Photograph: Meade Statue, Cemetery Ridge, Gettysburg, Pennsylvania
© David Muench

Typographical Design/Production: Vicki S. Elliott

Articles comprising the chapters in this publication appeared in *Civil War Times
Illustrated Magazine*, and in *The Bold Cavaliers* and *The Galvanized Yankees*, both by
Dee Brown.

Contents

Editor's Acknowledgments

The content for this book was already provided in the Civil War writings of Dee Brown; consequently, there was very little original research that needed to be completed. My role, therefore, consisted of organizing the articles into chapters that portrayed a progressive development as events unfolded between 1861 and 1865. This was followed by researching and assembling a "Reference Identification Guide," locating illustrations and writing descriptive captions, preparing a bibliography and suggested reading list, and penning an introduction. This effort is affectionately dedicated to: The loving memory of my sister Anita Banash-Arlen, who abhorred war as a means of resolving disputes, believed in peace, and worked to advance understanding among all peoples of different races, nationalities, and religions.

Along the way, there were many people who made it possible for this book to be completed. Once again, I must acknowledge the cooperation of Dee Brown's literary agent, Peter Matson, Sterling Lord Literistic, and Cynthia Cooper, permissions coordinator, Cowles History Group. Deserving of equal special thanks are the staff at Clear Light Publishers—publishers Harmon Houghton and Marcia Keegan, who also provided creative and layout design; my editor Sara Held; and typographer Vicki Elliott—all of whom believed in this project from its inception and provided ongoing guidance, considerable prodding, and wholehearted support.

Deserving of thanks for suggesting research facilities, lending their guidance, and providing other forms of assistance are Howard Bryan, Bruce Herrick, Anne Lunde, Irwin Reynolds, Susan Staley, and Larry Underwood.

Research libraries and museums along with their staffs were extremely cooperative and helpful. To those whom I contacted or visited repeatedly, I apologize for taking advantage of your gracious assistance and excellent facilities. In acknowledgment, I extend a special thank you to: Lyle Benedict and Ellen O'Brien, librarians, Municipal Reference Collection, Harold Washington Chicago Public Library; Leslie H. Blythe, interpretive specialist, Natchez Trace Parkway in Tupelo, Mississippi; Jan Brooks and Lynne Kiviluoma, librarians, Government Publications, Harold Washington Chicago Public Library; John Chalmers, curator of special collections, Connie Gordon, librarian, and Andrea Telli, senior archival specialist, all of the Harold Washington Chicago Public Library; Chicago Historical Society Library; Raymond Collins, reference librarian, Illinois State Library in Springfield; John M. Coski, curator and historian, Museum of the Confederacy in Richmond; Sean Eads, librarian assistant, Lexington Public Library in Kentucky; Mathew Aron, Government Publications, Matthew Frankel, security, Soon Koo Kwon and Zhifeng Li, both students in Newspaper and Microtext, and Mary Pinnard, student in Periodicals, all of Northwestern University Library; Douglas Keller, interpretive specialist, Pea Ridge National Military Park; Jeff Patrick, park ranger, and David Edie, volunteer librarian, Wilson's Creek National Battlefield Park; Reference Department, Crawfordsville District Public Library in Indiana; Reference Department, Park Ridge Public Library in Illinois; Arnold Schofield, staff historian, and Alan Chilton, museum aide, Fort Scott National Historic Site; Michael Smith, chief curator, and William Johnson, curator, both of the State Historical Society of Iowa in Des Moines; Joann Spragg, museum coordinator/historian, and Gregory R. Schneider, assistant museum coordinator, General Lew Wallace's Study in Crawfordsville, Indiana; and Terrence J. Winschel, historian, Vicksburg National Military Park.

I would be remiss if I did not extend my gratitude and appreciation to my friend Dee Brown whose writings made this endeavor possible. His personal interest and prolific works continue to serve as a beacon, guiding the way for others with similar inquisitiveness and desire to visit the historic sites and understand the cataclysmic events that shaped our nation over a century ago.

STAN BANASH

Foreword
by Dee Brown

Thirty-five years or so ago, the nation was celebrating the centennial of the great Civil War. With many of my contemporaries I attended reenactments of the battles. On a warm spring afternoon, in company with a serious Civil War buff, I was watching the playing out of one of the last of the scheduled reenactments.

"What are we going to do next?" my friend asked suddenly. "It's 1965 and the war is almost over. Will the Civil War now vanish from the national memory?"

"Probably so," I said. "All the books surely have been published now, and the audiences for Civil War memorabilia must be dying out. The sons and daughters and even the grandchildren of veterans are passing from the scene."

We were both utterly wrong in our suppositions.

Civil War Roundtables still flourish everywhere. Civil War books, magazines, and movies are as popular as ever. A book that was set in the time of the Civil War was the best-seller of 1997–98.

How can we account for this—with descendants of veterans of that war comprising an ever-diminishing percentage of the population?

Some time ago I was visited by two Civil War enthusiasts from Illinois. On their vacations through the years they had studied first-hand all the larger battlefields, and now they were determined to see all the smaller scenes of action. Obviously both had read widely in various aspects of a war that had become perhaps the keenest interest in their lives.

I asked if veterans were among their ancestors. They both laughed.

They were second-generation Europeans, German and Russian, whose forebears arrived in America half a century after the war. But that bloody conflict, it seems, held a strong appeal for many who came to America to escape the incessant wars of their countries. Our Civil War had a beginning and an ending. Theirs went on and on forever.

Nor will interest in that war come to an end when old codgers such as I shuffle off the planet. The last roundtable that I attended had an audience well-sprinkled with attentive teen-agers of both genders, well armed with books and notebooks. Presumably they came voluntarily.

Of the fourteen episodes selected by editor Stan Banash for inclusion in this volume, all but three or four are from what is known as the Western Theater of the Civil War. The reason for this is that I am a westerner and know the terrain and atmosphere of the action far better than in the Eastern Theater. Perhaps I better understand the participants' attitudes, behavior, and manners of thought and speech. After all, several of the survivors were still around while I was a young boy. While going through the letters, diaries, and memoirs of participants in Grierson's Raid, for example, I felt as if I knew well the men on both sides. This made the writing of the incidents much simpler.

Therefore, for accounts of Gettysburg and the great battles of Virginia, readers must go elsewhere.

DEE BROWN

Introduction

ortherners called it "The Civil War," while southerners referred to it as "The War Between the States." However defined, it was a devastating conflict in terms of lives lost, property destroyed, and families torn asunder. After more than 130 years, it continues to retain the interests of academic historians, history buffs, students, and military collectors.

What is the magnetism that attracts so many to search out roads taken by marching armies, gun emplacements that quelled cavalry charges or shattered the ranks of disciplined troops, the site of a general's death in battle, the streams that ran with blood of friend and foe, the buildings and homes that once served as makeshift hospitals and headquarters, and the battlefields and skirmish sites where thousands perished while following rigid orders of unit commanders?

I am pleased to have the opportunity to draw attention to some of the major battles in the western theater—the stepchildren of this great conflict. They have not received the attention they deserve, and I am hopeful this book will rekindle interest in their significance.

Dee Brown's Civil War Anthology is a natural sequel to my first book, *Best of Dee Brown's West*. It brings to closure the feature article writings of Dee Brown during the period following the centennial of the Civil War and development of the Trans-Mississippi West.

Most commemorative tributes and memorials had concluded between 1961 and 1965, the end of the centennial observance. But Brown had already been smitten by this conflict. His original contribution came earlier in three books: *Grierson's Raid* (1954), *The Bold Cavaliers* (1959), and *The Galvanized Yankees* (1963). Believing that there was more to be said, he wrote shorter pieces about regions and subjects of which he knew, focusing primarily on the western theater of the war.

Rarely do weeks pass during the summer months when reenactment groups are not seen staging mock battles, many of which draw attention to major engagements in the east and occasionally provincial battles in the west. These reenactments fulfill a valuable need for those who seek a greater visual appreciation and understanding of these events. But for many readers, including myself, who follow the maneuverings of Civil War armies, there is always a layer of confusion that permeates the naming of rank and units and descriptions of troop movements. For example, references to an individual of general rank was often misleading when he officially held the rank of brigadier general or major general. Other times, mention was made of an officer's brigade or division when in fact he did not have direct command of that unit but oversaw it as part of a larger force. To avoid this mix-up, I introduced a new device to help readers and students understand the participants named in a specific engagement. For this book, I researched and prepared a reference identification list of participants named in each chapter. Consequently, readers will find the specific ranks and units of command at the time of the engagement listed by chapter in the back of this book.

Unfortunately, the record keeping of this period was not as precise as a researcher of today would like. Yes, information was often more complete in Union camps than in those of the Confederates. But when focusing on a cavalry unit whose success was often measured by surprise advancements, as well as rapid and continuous movements, the filing of reports and updating of personnel records were not done regularly. This is where shortcomings surface and, for our purposes, it occurred primarily with the regiments under the command of Brigadier General John Hunt Morgan in his raid through Indiana and Ohio and again in the role some of his men played in escorting President Jefferson Davis in his retreat southward. As regiments became decimated through death, woundings, drownings, capture, and desertion, many were consolidated with little or no paper trail. Nevertheless, my research resulted in 381 of 388 identifications completed to my satisfaction.

The Bibliography refers to books used in identifying participants and not in the research for each article. (*Civil War Times Illustrated* did not publish a bibliography of Brown's research sources.)

Dee Brown's prodigious writings about the Civil War and development of the West can only be described as monumental over more than fifty years. This book seeks to perpetuate that immense contribution so that future students of American history may be drawn as I was to this difficult period of our nation's growth.

STAN BANASH

Brigadier General Nathaniel Lyon, who, as a captain, played a significant early role in preserving Missouri for the Union, was among the first to be killed at the Battle of Wilson's Creek. From Frank Leslie's Illustrated History of the Civil War, 1861–65, page 86.

1

Wilson's Creek

*"This battle, the 'Bull Run of the West,' left Missouri
open to the Confederacy and gave the Union another
graphic lesson that this would be no easy war."*

On February 6, 1861, a short, spare, red-bearded captain of
infantry reported for duty with an understrength company of
troops at the St. Louis, Missouri, arsenal. He was forty-two-
year-old Nathaniel Lyon, one of the few confirmed aboli-
tionists in the United States Army. Not long after his arrival in St.
Louis, Lyon set forces in motion which made inevitable the second
great battle of the Civil War. This battle followed Bull Run by less
than three weeks and was much the same kind of amateur action—
confused, blundering, indecisive, and very bloody. The Confederates
named it Oak Hills. For the Union soldiers it was the Battle of
Wilson's Creek, and it is now best known by that name.

Nathaniel Lyon was a West Point professional who had served
with distinction in the Mexican War. Prior to his transfer to St.
Louis, he spent six years at posts in Kansas where he developed an
intense dislike for the pro-slavery element. To Lyon's dismay he found
St. Louis and much of Missouri, including its governor, leaning
toward the South. When the war began his ire was aroused by an
encampment of pro-Confederate state militia just outside the city.
Suspecting that the militia planned to capture the vital arsenal, Lyon
surrounded the camp with a force of Regular troops and pro-Union

volunteers and informed the militiamen that they were prisoners. As the captives were being taken back to the city, a riot broke out in the streets and Lyon's men fired into a mob of civilians, killing twenty-eight of them. The incident immediately widened the breach between pro-Union and pro-Confederate Missourians. Men such as former Governor Sterling Price, who had opposed the state's secession, now became fully committed to the Southern cause. Price soon took command of the Confederate state troops, and Lyon, who was promoted from captain to brigadier general on May 31, began moving up the Missouri River in pursuit of Price. After winning easy victories at Jefferson City and Boonville, Lyon established a base at Springfield from which he hoped to drive Price's Confederates completely out of Missouri.

By the end of July 1861, however, Lyon was in a precarious position. Terms of service of his three-months volunteers were nearing expiration, and his commander, General John Frémont, seemed unwilling to send reinforcements or supplies. "God damn General Frémont," Lyon shouted in exasperation after receiving a final curt refusal of aid from St. Louis. "He is a worse enemy to me and the Union cause than Price and the whole damned tribe of Rebels!"

Early in August, after an indecisive fight at Dug Springs, Lyon fell back on Springfield, fully aware that he must either withdraw from southwestern Missouri or defeat Price in a quick victory before too many reinforcements reached him from Arkansas. From scouts and spies, Lyon learned that Confederate troops under Generals Ben McCulloch and N. Bart Pearce had already joined Price's Missourians, forming an army of more than 10,000 men, and they were now camped ten miles southwest of Springfield. Lyon had only about 5,000 ready for battle, but on August 9 he informed his officers that he intended to attack the Confederates before they attacked him.

During the council of war, Colonel Franz Sigel proposed that the Union force be divided; he would take his regiment of St. Louis Germans, a few Regular cavalrymen, and six pieces of artillery by side roads and attack the Confederates from the rear while Lyon attacked simultaneously from the front. All officers present were

Brigadier General Ben McCulloch, a veteran of the War for Texas Independence and the Mexican War, led the victorious Confederate troops at Wilson's Creek. From Frank Leslie's Illustrated History of the Civil War, 1861–65, page 86.

opposed to dividing 5,000 men to attack a superior force of 10,000, but for some reason Lyon accepted Sigel's plan.

Perhaps Lyon had fallen under the spell of the Sigel myth—the German's haughty manner, his thick-accented allusions to intricate military tactics, and boasts of his superior European military training and experience. Sigel had been a mathematics teacher in St. Louis, but somehow in his uniform he looked more like an officer than anybody else. (During the next three years, Franz Sigel would humbug far more experienced men than Lyon and not until 1864 would the Sigel myth explode in a final bloody fiasco in the Shenandoah Valley.)

Late in the evening of August 9, the two columns moved out of Springfield by separate roads. Rain began drizzling on Lyon's regiment about midnight, and not long afterward advance scouts sighted the campfires of the Confederates. Lyon ordered a halt until first daylight, and then after borrowing a rubber coat from his adjutant, Major John M. Schofield, he stretched out between two corn rows and went to sleep.

At 4:15 A.M. Lyon's column was moving again in gray light under broken clouds with the 1st Missouri Volunteers in advance, Company H deployed forward as skirmishers. The grass was wet from the night drizzle, and as they began marching up a slope their formations were broken by stunted oaks and underbrush. From the summit, the men in the first ranks could see the Confederate camps, smoke hanging over them, in the half-mile-wide valley of Wilson's Creek, "a thousand tents, stretching off into the distance, and partially screened from view by a hill jutting into an angle of the creek." The hill would later be called Bloody Hill, and Lyon made it his immediate objective.

At 5:10 the forward skirmishers of the 1st Missouri opened fire on Confederate pickets, and Lyon began deploying his troops for battle. Off to the left and across the creek into a cornfield went Captain Joseph Plummer with his 1st U.S. Infantry, supported from the hill slope by Lieutenant John Du Bois' four pieces of light artillery. To the right went Major Peter Osterhaus and a battalion of the 2nd Missouri. Charging up through the blackjacks of Bloody Hill, the 1st

Kansas at left and the 1st Missouri at right center quickly took the high ground, but they were separated by sixty yards of broken ravine. Behind them bounced the six light guns of Captain James Totten's battery of 2nd U.S. Artillery.

A cloud was passing over the rising sun when Totten's gunners fired their first shot. It was a signal to Sigel, who was supposed to be at the other end of the valley, and artillery somewhere off to the southwest replied immediately. In the creek bottom below, Confederates from the nearest camp (Brigadier General James S. Rains' 2nd Division, Missouri State Guard) were scattering southward on foot and on horseback. A St. Louis newspaper reporter, who had just reached the crest of Bloody Hill, observed the flight and said: "We have completely surprised them."

"General Lyon attacked us before breakfast," Lieutenant W. P. Barlow, one of the Missouri Confederates later reported. "We were surprised completely." The main reason for this apparent carelessness on the part of the Confederates was the loose chain of command which existed in their hastily combined army. On July 28 at Cassville, Missouri, General Price had joined his forces with those of Generals McCulloch and Pearce. McCulloch, a former Texas Ranger, had been commissioned a brigadier by President Jefferson Davis, and his C.S.A. command consisted of well-trained soldiers from Texas, Louisiana, and Arkansas. Pearce's troops were Arkansas Volunteers who were "cooperating" with McCulloch.

During the week between July 28 and August 4, McCulloch let Price know that he was planning to take his troops back into Arkansas in order to be closer to his supply base. Price was so dismayed that he offered to put himself and all his forces under McCulloch's command, provided the latter would help him defeat Lyon. "If you refuse to accept this offer," Price said, "I will move with the Missourians alone, against Lyon." At first McCulloch declined Price's offer, but on August 4 he changed his mind and agreed "to take the command and march upon the enemy." On the sixth, this loosely organized army reached Wilson's Creek. For three days the Confederates camped there while McCulloch waited for his scouts to bring him reliable information on the strength and exact location of Lyon's army. Finally, on the morning of the ninth, General Price confronted McCulloch. "Are you going to attack Lyon or not?" he demanded. When Mc-Culloch refused to commit himself, Price bluntly asked for the Missouri troops to be returned to his command so that he could lead them into battle. Knowing that Price meant what he said, McCulloch issued an order for the army to move out for Springfield at nine P.M.

Just before time for the march to begin, a summer storm threatened. Horses were already saddled and pickets had been called in, but when a light rain began falling, McCulloch conferred with Price. Fewer than a fourth of the soldiers had ammunition boxes, and if the twenty to twenty-five rounds which they carried in their cotton sacks became wet, they would have no ammunition to fire. McCulloch sent orders to all troop commanders to see that their men took special care to keep their ammunition dry and be prepared to move at a moment's notice when the rain ceased. It continued falling until eleven o'clock, slacked to a drizzle, and then stopped about midnight, but McCulloch issued no order to march. A few commanders sent pickets back out to their camp perimeters; most did not. For this reason, Lyon was able to secure his position on Bloody Hill before the Confederates knew he had even left Springfield.

McCulloch, Price, and Colonel James McIntosh were breakfasting in Price's tent on roasted green corn when a horseman galloped in from General Rains' camp to warn that Lyon's army was approaching. McCulloch and McIntosh were skeptical. Neither man had much respect for the Missouri Volunteers, especially Rains' division which had over 1,000 mounted men unarmed or poorly armed and with little military training. McIntosh referred to them as "Price's stupid fools," and McCulloch despaired of their discipline and complained that "instead of being a help, they are continually in the way." Not long after the messenger arrived, however, the distant rattle of rifle fire was unmistakable, and to the northwest a confused mass of retreating horsemen and wagons was plainly visible. McCulloch quickly devised a counterattack: Colonel McIntosh would lead the trained Louisiana and Arkansas troops to the right along the creek and strike for Lyon's flank while Price and his Missourians would drive to the left, straight up through the underbrush on Bloody Hill.

McCulloch and McIntosh, who were in uniform, mounted to ride back to their troops. Price, in a suit of rough linen, was buttoning his suspenders as he ran for his horse. "A stout farmer-looking old gentleman," one of the soldiers there described him. In his haste, Price forgot his hat, but later in the morning, someone gave him a black plug hat to shield his head from the August sun. An Arkansas artilleryman said that throughout the battle that tall black headpiece "ranged over the field like an orriflamme to the Missourians."

Meanwhile, the first troops ordered into battle were tying pieces of white cloth around their left arms to distinguish them from the enemy. (Lack of distinguishable uniforms caused more confusion at Wilson's Creek than in any other Civil War battle. Many men on both sides had no uniforms; others wore state militia uniforms of varying colors, including blues and grays on both sides. Most of the 3rd Louisiana companies wore new bluish-gray uniforms, while the 1st Iowa Volunteers on the Union side wore uniforms of a similar shade of gray.)

When General McCulloch came galloping along the slope where Colonel Louis Hébert's 3rd Louisiana was camped he found the men scurrying about in search of their uniform coats. McCulloch reined his horse and stood in his stirrups; he was a wiry man of about fifty with piercing blue eyes. "Colonel Hébert," he shouted, "why in hell don't you lead your men out!" Hébert immediately started his columns, and many of the infantrymen marched off without their coats, tying strips of white canvas over their shirtsleeves.

To the left across the creek, Price was positioning four small "divisions" (about 2,000 men altogether) under Brigadier Generals William Slack, J. H. McBride, John B. Clark, and Mosby M. Parsons. With Captain Henry Guibor's battery in support, the infantrymen rushed up through the hazel and blackjack at Bloody Hill. Because of the full-leafed cover their old short-range rifles and shotguns were as effective as the longer-ranged rifles of their Union opponents. On the left of the crescent-shaped line of battle it was Missourian against Missourian as McBride's Ozarkers stopped Lyon's 1st Missouri Volunteers; on their right Slack's division tangled with the 1st Kansas.

On the opposite side of the creek Colonel McIntosh was forming a battle line with his 2nd Arkansas Mounted Rifles, Lieutenant Colonel Dandridge McRae's Arkansas infantry battalion, and Hébert's 3rd Louisiana. The cornfield into which Captain Plummer's U.S. Regulars were advancing was McIntosh's objective. As the Louisianans moved off the open slope where they had been camped, Major Totten's Union artillerymen saluted them with a blast of shot. By this time Captain William Woodruff's Arkansas battery was ready to reply, and the Arkansans' cannon fire helped check the advance of Lyon's forces on Bloody Hill. Ironically, young Woodruff had been drilled and instructed by none other than the man with whom he was dueling. Major Totten as commander of the Little Rock arsenal had trained the local militia, but when Arkansas seceded he had been forced to surrender the arsenal and the very guns that Woodruff was now firing upon him.

McIntosh's infantrymen pushed on through shoulder-high bottomland brush toward the cornfield fence. Most of the grain had already been harvested and the stalks were trampled down. "We could see the enemy's line advancing in beautiful order," said Sergeant William Watson of the 3rd Louisiana, "with skirmishers in front."

Along one section of the fence, the opponents came together before a shot was exchanged. Two U.S. Regulars climbed upon the rails to confront the raised rifle of a Confederate who was wearing a blue uniform. "Don't shoot!" cried one of the Union infantrymen. "We are friends." To his surprise he learned a moment later that he and his comrade were prisoners of the Confederates. When firing began, the lines were so close together that officers on either side could hear the others' commands. By coincidence the opposing leaders, McIntosh and Plummer, had been classmates at West Point. Also, Major Samuel Sturgis, who was in the field as Lyon's second-in-command, had been McIntosh's commander only a few months earlier.

At first the old-style phalanx formation of the U.S. Regulars made them easy targets for the Confederates kneeling in the brush, but in a short time powder smoke became so thick in the humid air that the Confederates could see no targets until the advancing ranks were almost upon them. Fearing that Plummer's Regulars would overrun his troops, McIntosh ordered a bayonet charge. Superior numbers forced the Regulars back across the field, but as soon as the Confederates were in the open, Lieutenant Du Bois' flanking artillery checked them. "The ground was black with their dead," Du Bois later reported, but he should have added that many of the casualties were Union soldiers. His artillery bombardment split McIntosh's troops apart, half of them taking cover in woods to the right of the creek, the others crossing the stream into a brushy hollow. As soon as Captain Plummer withdrew his Regulars up Bloody Hill, a company of determined Louisianans made a quick thrust at Du Bois' battery. When Du Bois saw their bluish-gray uniforms through the thick underbrush he thought they might be Union soldiers from one of Sigel's regiments trying to break through the Confederate lines. At twenty yards, however, they opened fire on the artillerymen with rifles and pistols. "They nearly carried my guns," Du Bois said. "This only lasted ten minutes, but it was very bloody."

To Du Bois' right along the crest of Bloody Hill, heavy fighting was now in progress, the lines moving back and forth in the blackjack woods. Sometimes the contending Missourians came so close together they recognized the faces of former friends and acquaintances, and Price and Lyon could hear each other's commands. After almost two hours of hard fighting, the lines drew apart like two winded, bloodied, but undefeated animals. "The most remarkable of the battle's characteristics," said one of the participants, "was the deep silence which now and then fell upon the smoking field—while the two armies, unseen to each other, lay but a few yards apart, gathering strength to grapple again in the death struggle for Missouri."

During the first long pause in the fighting, Lyon brought up the gray-uniformed 1st Iowa to relieve the 1st Kansas, and the 2nd Kansas to relieve the battered 1st Missouri. On the Confederate side, McCulloch ordered Pearce's Arkansas Volunteers and some of

Members of the 1st Iowa Regiment are urged onward during a charge at the Battle of Wilson's Creek. From Frank Leslie's Illustrated History of the Civil War, 1861–65, *page 31.*

McIntosh's troops into Price's front ranks on Bloody Hill. Forming into three ranks, the Confederates began moving upward through the bullet-shattered blackjack. "On they came in overwhelming numbers," said the New York *Herald* correspondent. "Not a breath was heard among the Iowans till their enemies came within thirty-five or forty feet." Then there was the sharp click of 1,000 rifles and the battle was resumed. The time was now between nine and ten o'clock in the morning.

From his Confederate battery across the creek, Captain Woodruff noted the gray-clad Iowans moving into a position which gave him an excellent opportunity to enfilade the regiment. "We opened on it with the effect of breaking its beautiful line and scattering it its full length." At the same time, Major Totten sent a section of Union artillery forward to open at close range upon the Confederate infantry. A Confederate officer afterward described this action as "the most terrific storm of grape and musketry ever poured out upon the ranks of any American troops."

General Lyon on horseback was dashing recklessly about, trying to rally his outnumbered troops. He kept asking: "Where is Sigel? What has happened to Sigel?" Blood flowed from surface wounds in his head and leg. When he galloped to the rear to give an order to Totten, the major offered him some brandy, but he declined. As he turned toward the front again, his horse was shot and fell dead. While his adjutant, Major Schofield, was obtaining another mount for him, Lyon wiped blood from his face and remarked despondently: "Major, I fear the day is lost." Schofield tried to reassure him, but it was evident that the Iowa and Kansas regiments were beginning to break apart. Without Sigel's troops, they could not long contain the mass of attacking Confederates. "Everything," Lieutenant Du Bois noted tersely, "was covered with blood." The 1st Iowa had lost thirteen of its twenty-seven officers, and its entire color guard was cut down. As companies fell back to re-form ranks, they became mixed with retreating companies of the 2nd Kansas.

In a desperate move to save the day, Lyon hurried to the front. "Swinging his hat in the air," Major Schofield reported, "he led forward the troops, who promptly rallied around him." A few seconds later a bullet tore into Lyon's chest and killed him. Some accounts of his death say that he dismounted and then fell into the arms of his orderly. Others say that his horse was felled first and that he was standing upon the animal's prostrate body, waving his sword and cheering his men on, when he was shot. Most pictorial representations of the event show him dying in the saddle. Major Schofield was convinced that Lyon, despairing of victory without Sigel's missing troops, threw away his life in desperation. Moments after Lyon died, Schofield was at his side; the major had to catch a loose "secesh" horse to ride to Major Sturgis and inform him that he was now in command.

What *had* happened to Colonel Franz Sigel? Exactly as the haughty German had planned, he arrived at the southwest end of the Confederate camps just as dawn was breaking. His forward cavalry units cut off forty Confederate soldiers who were getting water from Wilson's Creek. After passing the prisoners to the rear, Sigel placed his battery of six guns on a hill and sent his infantry across the creek. At 5:30, upon hearing the rattle of Lyon's first rifle attack, he ordered his battery to begin firing into the tented camps of Thomas J. Churchill's 1st Arkansas Mounted Rifles and Colonel Elkanah Greer's Texas Rangers. While the Confederates were taking cover in the woods to the north, Sigel sent his infantry in pursuit of them—but only as far as the Springfield-Fayetteville road. As soon as he heard Major Totten's opening artillery signal, he brought his own battery across the creek and placed it on low bluffs overlooking Skeggs Branch.

With his troops and guns astraddle the Fayetteville road, Sigel was now in perfect position to strike the Confederates from the rear while Lyon was attacking in front. Instead of pushing forward, however, Sigel formed a line and waited for Lyon to drive the Confederates to him. While he waited, his idle troops wandered through the abandoned Confederate tents along the creek collecting souvenirs. Sigel himself obtained a Texas Ranger's hat. All that he had accomplished thus far was to drive several hundred Arkansas and

Texas troops to the base of Bloody Hill, where McCulloch promptly added them to the force that was cutting Lyon's regiments to pieces.

During the nine o'clock lull in the fighting on Bloody Hill, Sigel's men sighted a column of troops approaching along the Fayetteville road. Through the dust and smoke their uniforms appeared to be a shade of gray. Because of the silence which had fallen over the battlefield Sigel assumed that the Confederates had fled the fighting in disorder and that these oncoming troops must be the Iowa regiment in their militia gray. Sigel ordered his men to hold their fire and wave their flags so that the Iowans would not fire upon them.

The approaching soldiers were not Union, however. They were led by General McCulloch, who had observed Sigel's threatening presence in his rear and had hastily collected some scattered units of cavalry and three companies of infantry from the 3rd Louisiana to launch an attack. Because he met with no challenging fire all the way to the base of the low bluff where Sigel's battery was placed, McCulloch began to wonder if the guns and men above him were Union. He knew that two light Confederate batteries were supposed to be somewhere in the area.

"Whose forces are those?" he demanded of a soldier posted beside a huge oak.

"Sigel's," the soldier replied in a German accent.

McCulloch's shaggy eyebrows lowered in a questioning frown. "Whose did you say?" he shouted.

"Union. Sigel," the man replied and raised his rifle.

Before the soldier could fire, Corporal Henry Gentles of the Pelican Rifles dropped him with a quick shot. McCulloch turned and glanced at Gentles. "That was a good shot," he said, and then quickly shouted an order to Captain John Vigilini: "Take your company up, captain, and give them hell!" Even as the Louisianans swarmed over Sigel's batteries, the Union artillerymen were still shouting: "Don't shoot! We're friends!" But a few minutes later, Sigel's entire command was shaken by the realization that a Confederate force had penetrated their lines and captured the artillery.

At the sight of Confederate bayonets, most of Sigel's artillerymen abandoned their guns and fled with their caissons, lashing the horses down the road, away from the battlefield. Panic quickly spread through the infantry and they also took flight, leaving only two small units of Regular cavalry on the flanks. Many of the fleeing men circled around to the rear of Lyon's line of battle, where they were badly needed, but there was no one to stop them. As they fled toward Springfield, they left small arms, blankets, coats, and knapsacks strewn along the road. Colonel Sigel himself took flight, donning the yellow slouch hat taken from the abandoned Confederate camp and throwing a blanket over his uniform so he would not be recognized as an enemy by pursuing Confederates. He was completely out of the fight by ten o'clock, and reached Springfield before the main battle was ended. The Confederates had captured five of his six guns, a regimental standard, and more than 200 prisoners.

On Bloody Hill, meanwhile, McCulloch had unloosed a cavalry thrust at his enemy's right flank. Assembling in woods cover on the west side of the hill, the horsemen startled Union rear support units with their sudden appearance. "The enemy tried to overwhelm us," Major Totten reported, "by an attack of some 800 cavalry, which unobserved, had formed below the crests of the hills to our right and rear." Totten wheeled a section of artillery upon them and Major Osterhaus's Missouri Union infantry soon checked the cavalry charge. In his official report, Totten was most uncomplimentary toward the Confederate cavalry: "It was so effete and ineffectual in its force and character as to deserve only the appellation of child's play. Their cavalry is utterly worthless on the battlefield." He made no allowance for the terrain, the dense brush and trees which made it impossible for horsemen to ride through in formation. Some of these Texas and Arkansas cavalrymen would later serve with Forrest and Morgan to disprove Major Totten's estimate of their prowess.

Between 10:30 and 11:00 A.M., the battlefield once again lay silent. "An almost total silence," Major Schofield described it. "As soon as the enemy began to give way and it became apparent that the field was at least for the present ours, the principal officers of the command were informed of General Lyon's death, and Major

The death of Brigadier General Nathaniel Lyon at Wilson's Creek was a severe loss to the Union forces in Missouri and deprived them of his energy, ability, and command leadership in the West. From Frank Leslie's Illustrated History of the Civil War, 1861–65, page 71.

Sturgis assumed command. He at once called together the chief officers in his vicinity and consulted with them as to the course that should be pursued."

While the Union officers were discussing whether or not they should push forward and resume the battle, the Confederates settled the question for them by launching their third massive attack of the day. It proved to be the fiercest of the entire battle, and it began with a wild Rebel yell. In the forefront of the Confederate line was Colonel John Gratiot's 3rd Arkansas Infantry, which had been supporting Woodruff's battery most of the morning. Upon receiving orders to enter the battle, the Arkansans marched up Bloody Hill in columns of fours. "I advanced them until we came near the enemy," Gratiot reported. "We then faced toward them, and marched in line of battle about fifty paces, when we were attacked by a large force of the enemy in front and on the left flank."

During the next few minutes Gratiot's men were in the vortex of the final struggle for Bloody Hill. While they were fighting almost muzzle to muzzle with Kansas infantrymen, they were caught in enfilading fire from Lieutenant Du Bois' artillery. At the same time the 5th Arkansas coming up through thick powder smoke fired into them from the rear. In the very few minutes they were in action, the men of the 3rd suffered 109 casualties. "It was," said one of the participants, "a mighty mean-fowt fight."

At one time, attacking Confederates almost overran Totten's battery. To prevent disaster, Captain Gordon Granger of the Regulars rallied scattered units of Kansans, Iowans, and Missourians and led them against the Confederate right flank. This surprise attack blunted the Confederates' forward motion, and Granger had pushed their right ranks halfway down Bloody Hill when Sturgis called him back. "Most of our men had fired away all their ammunition," Sturgis explained in his report. "Nothing, therefore, was left to do but to return to Springfield."

The Confederates also had expended most of their ammunition, and they were as bloodied and weary of the fighting as their opponents. "We watched the retreating enemy through our field-glasses," said General Bart Pearce of the Army of Arkansas, *"and were glad to see him go."*

After the Union forces withdrew toward Springfield with their wounded, the Confederates took over the contested ground of Bloody Hill. Among the many dead who lay there they found the body of General Lyon. At the last moment, hospital orderlies evidently had removed Lyon's dead body from an army wagon and replaced it with a wounded man. Under a flag of truce, Confederate officers took the dead commander's body into Springfield and were received in a friendly manner by Union officers. "We gave the Confederates a good dinner and some whiskey," Lieutenant Du Bois recorded, "and when we sat on the ground afterwards, chatting gaily over our segars, one would not have supposed that we had been trying to take each others' lives only a few hours ago."

Like Bull Run in the East, Wilson's Creek in the West was acclaimed as a victory by Confederates because they had forced Union soldiers to leave the field. Neither battle was decisive, of course, and many of Lyon's junior officers always looked upon Wilson's Creek as a standoff. Some believed that they would have been victorious had the men with Sigel been on Bloody Hill. Nine officers were so disgusted with Sigel's lack of leadership and his flight into Springfield that they signed a statement addressed to General H. W. Halleck requesting that he be removed from command. The statement was ignored, however, and General Frémont cited Sigel "for gallant and meritorious conduct in the command of his brigade."

Casualties at Wilson's Creek for the Union were 223 killed, 721 wounded, 291 missing, for a total of 1,235; for the Confederates, 257 killed, 900 wounded, 27 missing for a total of 1,184. Considering the lesser number of men engaged, Wilson's Creek was a far bloodier battle than Bull Run. One-fourth of the Federal soldiers were killed, wounded, or missing. The 1st Missouri Union Infantry marched on the field with 720 men and left it with but 420; the 1st Kansas lost 300 of 800. More than half of the Confederate casualties were from Price's Missouri regiments, but the 3rd Louisiana and two Arkansas regiments also took heavy losses.

So far as the war in the West was concerned, Wilson's Creek changed almost nothing. In or out of the Union, Missouri was doomed by geography to suffer four years of guerrilla fighting. Many of those who would be involved in that border terror—men such as William Quantrill, Frank James, Cole Younger, Wild Bill Hickok—were there at Wilson's Creek.

Brigadier General Samuel R. Curtis led the Union forces to victory at the Battle of Pea Ridge (Elkhorn Tavern), March 7–8, 1862. Courtesy of National Archives [Brady Collection], III-B-2204.

2

Pea Ridge

*"Here, near Elkhorn Tavern, on March 7 and 8, 1862,
was fought 'the Gettysburg of the West,' a seesaw battle
whose outcome secured Missouri for the Union and led
to the Federal occupation of Arkansas."*

When the Butterfield Company opened a stagecoach line between St. Louis and San Francisco in 1858, a shrewd Arkansas farmer who lived on the route converted his home into a tavern. His name was Jesse Cox, and his large two-story frame house stood just below the Missouri border at the east end of a swell of ground called Pea Ridge. To make certain that travelers would recognize and remember his tavern, Cox mounted the horns and skull of a huge elk at the center of the ridgepole. Elkhorn Tavern with its overhanging roof, wide porches, and big fireplaces soon became known as a place where "good cheer was most ample."

Three years later, war was raging northward in Missouri, and the transcontinental coaches were no longer running on that route. During 1861 the Confederates won some victories in Missouri, but after Brigadier General Samuel R. Curtis took command of Union forces on Christmas Day, the tide began to turn. Jesse Cox watched anxiously as Confederate Brigadier General Ben McCulloch slowly withdrew from Missouri with his Texas, Louisiana, and Arkansas troops. In February 1862, Brigadier General Sterling Price's Missouri

Confederates also began retreating into the Boston Mountains of Arkansas, with Curtis's pursuing Federals not far behind.

Cox sympathized with the South, but he was also concerned over the safety of his fine cattle herd. Thousands of soldiers foraging through the countryside could soon make short work of livestock without payment to the owner. Leaving his tavern in the care of his wife Polly and his young son Joseph, Cox set out for Kansas with the cattle herd. Before he returned, Elkhorn Tavern would become the vortex of one of the bloodiest battles fought west of the Mississippi River.

On March 3, Major General Earl Van Dorn, a handsome and flamboyant veteran of the Mexican War, arrived in the Boston Mountains to take command of the combined Confederate forces of Price and McCulloch. Responding to a forty-gun salute, Van Dorn promised his troops a victory, after which they would sweep across Missouri to St. Louis. They numbered 16,000 men, including 1,000 Cherokees fresh from Indian Territory under command of Brigadier General Albert Pike.

Van Dorn immediately set this army in motion northward, confident that he could smash the 10,500 Federals strung out across seventy miles of northwest Arkansas. He overlooked the fact that thousands of his men were without battle experience. Many were recent Arkansas volunteers, incensed by the invasion of their state. "Very few of the officers," General Price's adjutant noted, "had any knowledge whatever of military principles or practices." As for the Cherokees, they knew nothing of discipline or firing by command.

For three days the Confederates marched through rain and melting snow, subsisting on scanty rations. On March 6, near Bentonville, Van Dorn's cavalry struck hard at one end of the Federals' extended line. General Curtis, however, had been alerted by his scouts and had already begun concentrating his forces along Little Sugar Creek, two miles below Elkhorn Tavern. When the Confederates attacked at Bentonville, Brigadier General Franz Sigel's two divisions under Peter Osterhaus and Alexander Asboth were moving into their new positions. Sigel himself directed the rear guard withdrawal until nightfall

Brigadier General Franz Sigel, who commanded two divisions at the Battle of Pea Ridge, was promoted to major general on March 21, 1862. From Frank Leslie's Illustrated History of the Civil War, 1861–65, *page 86.*

of the sixth, fighting off slashing attacks from Joseph Shelby's Missouri cavalrymen, giving Osterhaus and Asboth time to prepare defenses.

In the extreme rear of Curtis's main line of defense was Elkhorn Tavern, still occupied by Polly Cox, her son Joseph, and his teenage wife, Lucinda. They were somewhat crowded by the addition of the Union army's provost marshal and his staff; the adjacent storehouses and barn were filled with army rations, and all about the grounds were wagons and tents containing ordnance and other supplies. Curtis's headquarters was a mile to the south. Nearby was Colonel Eugene Carr's division; several details from Colonel Grenville Dodge's 4th Iowa regiment were out along the roads felling trees to slow any Confederate night approach. On the bluffs above Sugar Creek, Colonel Jefferson C. Davis's division of Indiana and Illinois regiments was well dug in. West of Davis's position, Sigel's men were building fortifications and emplacing guns, facing southward.

All preparations anticipated an attack from the south. As darkness deepened, a light snow began falling. Four miles away to the southwest, the campfires of the Confederate bivouac began twinkling; by eight o'clock they were burning in a wide arc.

About three o'clock the following morning (March 7) Private Thomas Welch of the 3rd Illinois Cavalry was patrolling the road west of Elkhorn Tavern. Snow had stopped falling but the weather was bitter cold, and Private Welch was confident that he would meet neither friend nor foe in that extreme rear area. Then suddenly a party of Rebel cavalry loomed out of the night, and Private Welch was a prisoner. As he was hustled back down the road under guard he could scarcely believe what he saw—company after company of marching Confederate infantry, troops of cavalry, caissons, and numerous artillery pieces (Van Dorn had sixty-five guns against Curtis's fifty). To Welch it seemed that he was passing through the entire army of the C.S.A. Escape was uppermost in his mind, and at the first opportunity he turned into a side road and plunged into the icy undergrowth. As rapidly as he could, Welch made his way back through the woods to Elkhorn Tavern, awakened his commanding officer, and told him what he had seen.

Welch's story reached Curtis's headquarters at five o'clock in the morning, about the same time that reports were coming in from Sigel's camp that the enemy was moving in strength along the Bentonville road. By first daylight the entire Federal camp was alerted; the hundreds of Rebel campfires were still smoking but the Confederates had vanished.

The plan for bypassing the Union army during the night and attacking in the rear was General McCulloch's. Van Dorn approved it, and soon after nightfall of the sixth he started Price's Missourians moving north along the Bentonville detour, an eight-mile road which circled the Federal positions and then entered Telegraph Road, two miles north of Elkhorn Tavern. Ill with a cold, Van Dorn rode in an ambulance with the advance units. He left one division at the bivouac camp to guard the baggage train and keep campfires burning brightly for the benefit of the watchful Yankees.

Around midnight the Confederates were delayed by trees which Colonel Dodge's Iowans had felled across the road. According to plan, Van Dorn should have been astride Telegraph Road, positioned for an attack by daylight, but he was three hours late getting there. Soon after dawn, advance cavalry units were already skirmishing along the Federal flank, and from Curtis's encampments came the sounds of blaring bugles, drums beating the long roll, and the rumble of artillery wheels.

As soon as Curtis realized that Van Dorn had tricked him, he began turning his army around. "I directed a change of front to the rear," Curtis wrote in his report of the battle, "so as to face the road upon which the enemy was still moving. At the same time I directed the organization of a detachment of cavalry and light artillery, supported by infantry, to open the battle."

It was Sigel's division under Osterhaus that moved out toward the Bentonville road to challenge McCulloch's army. At that time of the morning McCulloch should have been five miles farther east, massed along Pea Ridge in close communication with Price's army, which was beginning to cannonade the Federals near Elkhorn Tavern. This five-mile separation between Price and McCulloch would prove to be crucial before the day ended. Instead of attacking with two coordinated wings, Van Dorn was forced to fight two separate battles, one of them screened from his headquarters by hills and woods and too far away for any unity of direction.

Osterhaus's regiments marched northwestward across fields filled with withered cornstalks, passing around Leetown, where yellow hospital flags were already fluttering from the scattered houses of the hamlet. The night's coating of snow was melting rapidly. Along the south edge of a field, Osterhaus deployed infantrymen of the 36th Illinois and 12th Missouri, supporting them with a battery of the 4th Ohio. With bugles blowing and pennons flying, a squadron of the 3rd Iowa Cavalry under Lieutenant Colonel Henry Trimble then crossed the fields and advanced into a brushy wood. Confederate infantry waiting in concealment caught them in short musket range. During the next five minutes a large number of Iowans became casualties, including Trimble with a severe head wound. The survivors broke ranks and retreated.

For the next two hours McCulloch's 10,000 Confederates dominated the field. At one time early in the fighting confused Union artillerymen shelled their own troops, and Sigel was so dismayed by the way the battle was going that he was on the verge of advising Curtis to retreat or surrender.

Around noon, a charge by McCulloch's Texans, supported by Pike's Cherokees under Stand Watie, broke through the Federals' forward lines. The Indians attacked with rifles, shotguns, knives, and arrows, and their war whoops were more terrifying than the Texans' Rebel yells. Union cavalrymen went tearing back in retreat, some without hats or arms, riding through the infantrymen with shouts of "Turn back! Turn back!" Stand Watie's Cherokees swept over a battery, killing the gunners, but they were so excited by their success that instead of pressing the Federal retreat into a rout, they milled around the guns. General Pike later described them as "all talking, riding this way and that, and listening to no orders from anyone."

Taking advantage of this momentary lull, Sigel unlimbered his rear batteries, and at the first artillery fire the Indians scurried back into the woods, as frightened as the Union cavalrymen had been of their scalping knives. At the same time, Osterhaus sent the 22nd Indiana and 36th Illinois Infantry regiments charging across the field to retake the battery.

By 1:30 McCulloch's advance had been stalled. Pike and Stand Watie had finally restored order among the Cherokees, but it was evident that the undisciplined Indians would be of no use in a frontal charge; they wanted to fight individually behind trees and boulders. McCulloch brought up one of his crack infantry regiments, the 16th Arkansas, and sent skirmishers forward. Mounting, he rode out ahead of the Arkansans' advancing lines. When the skirmishers moved into a brushy area, McCulloch went in with them. His black velvet coat and white felt hat made a good target for a squad of infantrymen from the 36th Illinois waiting behind a rail fence. He was struck in the breast and soon expired. Peter Pelican of Aurora, Illinois, fired once, leaped over the fence, and secured the dead general's gold watch before the advancing Arkansans drove him back to cover.

The time was two o'clock, a decisive hour in the contest between Curtis and Van Dorn. Carr (at Elkhorn Tavern) and Osterhaus (at Leetown) had both been calling urgently for reinforcements. Curtis decided to send his reserve division under Colonel Jefferson C. Davis to aid Osterhaus. Davis led off with his two Illinois regiments and two batteries of artillery. At this same hour Sigel and Asboth, who had been guarding the Bentonville road flank, started moving toward the Leetown area.

General Price meanwhile had been giving Colonel Carr a severe mauling north of Elkhorn Tavern, and Van Dorn was confident that a coordinated attack by Price and McCulloch would bring a quick victory. He sent messengers racing to McCulloch with orders to attack in full force about two o'clock.

McCulloch, however, was dead before the orders reached him. His successor, Colonel James McIntosh of the Arkansas Mounted Rifles, rallied the Confederates and led a charge against Federal infantry concealed in dense woods. Fifteen minutes later McIntosh was killed, shot from his horse.

Brigadier General Alexander Asboth (second from left) and members of his staff—Acting Brigadier General Anselm Albert, Brigade Quartermaster Captain James H. McKay, Colonel George E. Waring, Jr., Commanding, 4th Missouri Calvary Regiment, Aide-de-Camp Lieutenant Peter Gillen, and Aide-de-Camp Second Lieutenant George F. Kroll, along with General Asboth's dog, York—at the Battle of Pea Ridge. From Frank Leslie's Illustrated History of the Civil War, 1861–65, page 119.

Less than half a mile to the east, Colonel Louis Hébert's Louisianans had become entangled in a thick brushwood and were taking a severe shelling from Davis's batteries. Davis's 59th Illinois was on the edge of this same thicket. "The underbrush was so heavy," Lieutenant Colonel George Currie recorded, "we could not see twenty feet from us." Hébert's men finally surged out, fighting hand-to-hand with the Illinois infantrymen. A few minutes later the 18th Indiana, moving to the front in double-quick time, found the 59th Illinois retiring in disorder. Sure of victory, Hébert led his men out into the open, only to be flanked and then surrounded by fresh Illinois and Indiana troops. At 2:30 P.M., Colonel Hébert's brigade fell apart and he was captured.

With their leaders gone, the units of Van Dorn's right wing collapsed. Demoralized soldiers retreated in confusion—divisions, regiments, and companies becoming intermixed. Batterymen and cavalrymen along the Bentonville road—most of whom had seen no action—waited impatiently for orders, but none came.

About three o'clock General Pike learned of the loss of the army's leaders. He tried to rally the troops near Leetown, but it was too late. He began riding about the rear areas—an odd-looking figure in frontier buckskins—ordering his Indians and other scattered units to move toward the high ground of Pea Ridge and try to make their way to Van Dorn's position near Elkhorn Tavern. When Sigel reached Leetown about four o'clock to bring the full power of his artillery to bear on the Confederates, he found no one there to fight.

Around Elkhorn Tavern that day, however, it was a different story.

At about the same time that McCulloch's cavalry began their early morning skirmishing with the Federals near Leetown, Price's army of 6,200 men reached the Telegraph Road junction two miles north of Elkhorn Tavern. Very few Union soldiers were in that deep rear area, and the Confederates moved rapidly southward along Telegraph Road, meeting scattered resistance from the 24th Missouri Union Infantry. This regiment had been placed on light guard duty in the rear because its term of service had ended and the men were awaiting orders to be sent home. Two companies of Missouri and Illinois cavalry came to their aid.

In an enveloping movement, Price sent his first and second brigades down the west side of the road, while he led a third brigade down the east side. A mile north of the tavern, Colonel Elijah Gates led his Missouri Confederate cavalry in a sweeping charge across the fields, fell back before heavy fire, dismounted his men, attacked, and was again driven back.

To meet this thrust at his rear supply area, Curtis chose Colonel Eugene Carr, a born horse soldier with piercing eyes and a jutting black beard. Carr rode hurriedly up to Elkhorn Tavern, ordered his staff to establish division headquarters there, and immediately began forming a battle line. To the east of the road went Colonel Grenville Dodge's brigade; to the west Colonel William Vandever's brigade.

When Carr first saw the advancing masses of Confederates he was amazed at the size of the force that had got in the Union army's rear. He sent an urgent call for reinforcements back to Curtis and ordered Dodge and Vandever to take defensive positions and hold fast. Union artillery was already emplaced along both sides of the road facing southward; the pieces had scarcely been turned about when the Confederates opened a bombardment.

For thirty minutes the big guns dueled, with Elkhorn Tavern in the midst of the exchange. A New York *Herald* correspondent, who had counted on the relative safety of Carr's division headquarters, reported a shell bursting upon a company of infantry beside the tavern; another fell among horse teams in the rear yard; a solid shot struck the building and passed completely through. Polly Cox, her son, and his wife were not injured; at the first shriek of an overhead shell they had taken refuge in the cellar.

As dense clouds of smoke began covering Pea Ridge, a few reserve companies of infantry and cavalry and a battery of mountain howitzers reached Carr's headquarters. At that stage of the fighting, Curtis dared send no more troops to his right because of McCulloch's fierce assault against his left. "Colonel Carr," Curtis later wrote, "sent me

The Union forces at the Battle of Pea Ridge, Arkansas, although outnumbered nearly two to one, were able to repulse the Rebel attack following the death of Brigadier General Ben McCulloch, and defeated the Confederates on March 8, 1862. From Frank Leslie's Illustrated History of the Civil War, 1861–65, page 197.

word that he could not hold his position much longer. I could then only reply by sending him the order to 'persevere'."

With almost uncanny accuracy, Price's gunners now began blasting the 3rd Iowa Battery from the ridge. A cavalry charge followed up the shelling, but was forced back by Vandever's 9th Iowa Infantry. In a succession of attacks and repulses that continued through the morning, both sides suffered heavy casualties, among them Price's most trusted brigadier, William Slack, mortally wounded. Both Carr and Price also were painfully wounded, but refused to leave the field.

About two o'clock, as though by mutual agreement, the exhausted troops of both armies drew apart for the first lull of the day. During this period Carr, still awaiting reinforcements, consolidated his defense positions, while Van Dorn prepared to mount a massive attack, hoping for a coordinated action from McCulloch's army to the west.

By three o'clock the battle was raging furiously again, Price attacking Dodge's 4th Iowa and 35th Illinois with such force that Dodge's left collapsed. When Vandever saw what was happening, he ordered his brigade to shift rightward and close the gap. As Vandever was executing this change of front, Colonel Henry Little's Confederates swarmed out of the brush with wild yells, breaking through Vandever's 9th Iowa, capturing men and guns. "With a shout of triumph," Colonel Little reported, "Rive's and Gates's regiments dashed onward past the Elkhorn Tavern, and we stood on the ground where the enemy had formed in the morning."

Bringing batteries forward, the Confederates quickly enfiladed Dodge's regiments, forcing them back to a rail fence opposite Vandever's hastily re-formed line. "At this time the ammunition of the 4th Iowa was almost entirely given out," Dodge reported, "and I ordered them to fall back, which they did in splendid order in line of battle, the enemy running forward with their batteries and whole force."

As an early dusk fell over the smoky battlefield, Captain Henry Guibor unlimbered a Confederate battery directly in front of the tavern and began dueling with Carr's harried gunners, who had fallen back almost to Curtis's headquarters. About five o'clock Curtis himself came up with Asboth's division and found Carr still persevering, doggedly holding his line across Telegraph Road almost a mile below the tavern.

Weariness from eleven hours of continuous fighting and loss of blood from three wounds had brought Carr near to collapse. Curtis immediately relieved him, ordered the troops to bivouac in position, and then asked for a report of casualties. The 4th and 9th Iowa regiments had paid heavily for their stubborn resistance. The men of the 24th Missouri, whose terms of service had ended, but who had to bear the first shock of Price's attack, had taken 25 percent casualties.

Elkhorn Tavern, which had served as a Union headquarters in the morning, now became a Confederate headquarters. "My troops," said Sterling Price, "bivouacked upon the ground which they had so nobly won almost exhausted and without food, but fearlessly and anxiously awaiting the renewal of the battle in the morning." The tavern cellar served as a hospital, one of the first patients being Price himself. By the light of a candle, Mrs. Cox cleaned his wounded arm and bandaged it with one of her aprons.

Van Dorn was pleased to learn that Price's troops had captured seven cannons and 200 prisoners, but as the night wore on and the full story of the rout of McCulloch's troops began to come in, he realized that victory on the left had been nullified by defeat on the right. General Pike arrived to report the loss of McCulloch, McIntosh, and Hébert; he had placed Stand Watie's mounted Cherokees on Pea Ridge and was hopeful the Indians would fight better on the morrow. Hours later Van Dorn heard from Colonel Elkanah Greer; the Texas cavalryman had collected remnants of McCulloch's scattered regiments and was awaiting orders. Van Dorn ordered Greer to march his force up to Telegraph Road and prepare for another day of fighting.

Outside the tavern, troops built fires against the night chill. Although orders were issued to extinguish these blazes, many continued to burn long after midnight. From the darkened Federal lines only a short distance away, sounds came clearly on the frosty air. "Their artillery and baggage wagons," noted Colonel Henry Little, "seemed to be continually moving."

General Curtis's artillery and wagons were indeed moving that night—into positions selected by Franz Sigel, who had been given the responsibility for preparing a massive artillery attack at dawn. Sigel studied campfires along the ridge, estimating the location of Confederate troops, and disposed his guns accordingly. He also ordered his own troops to keep silent and build no fires.

At midnight, Union division commanders and staff officers met in Curtis's tent. Carr, Dodge, and Asboth were wounded and depressed. Only Curtis and Sigel were optimistic. Curtis pointed out that for the first time in the fighting the Union army had four infantry divisions massed for attack; Sigel was confident that his artillery would stop Van Dorn's drive.

In their lines facing Elkhorn Tavern, the Union troops shivered and tried to catch a few winks of sleep. Some angrily discussed the Indians' way of fighting, their barbarous use of scalping knives. They also could hear the sounds of their enemy, "the tread of their sentinels and the low hum of conversation but a few yards away."

Dawn came early on March 8, with a reddish sun in a pale blue sky. Because there had been no wind to drive away the previous day's battle smoke, it still hung in folds over woods and fields. On both sides of the battlefield artillerymen were making last-minute changes in positions. They unlimbered their guns, led horses fifty paces to the rear, and awaited orders.

Most of the Confederate batteries were in open woods along the base of the ridge, the Federals facing them from a crest of high ground below Elkhorn Tavern. About seven o'clock a cannon blast from the Confederates opened the second day of fighting. Sigel, who was commanding Curtis's left wing, accepted the challenge with alacrity, and soon had forty guns in action. "A brisk cannonade was kept up for upward of two hours," reported the New York *Herald* correspondent. "The sharp booming of the six-, twelve- and eighteen-pounders followed each other in rapid succession." This was probably the most concentrated artillery duel ever fought west of the Mississippi River; the muffled roar of guns was heard for forty miles across the Ozark hill country.

Sigel's well-placed guns scored hits on the Confederate batteries, and quickly scattered Stand Watie's Cherokees along Pea Ridge. When he was confident that he had his enemy off balance, Sigel ordered the 12th Missouri and the 25th and 44th Illinois to throw forward a strong force of skirmishers. With drums beating and flags waving, the Federal infantry regiments moved out in perfect alignment. "The rattling of musketry," Sigel later wrote, "the volleys, the hurrahs, did prove very soon that our troops were well at work in the woods, and that they were gaining ground rapidly."

Meanwhile Curtis's right wing had fallen back before the Confederate artillery fire, but as soon as Sigel's regiments began advancing, Curtis ordered Carr and Davis to attack with extended lines, maneuvering so as to get on Van Dorn's left flank. At the same time additional regiments from Osterhaus's and Asboth's divisions joined in the general attack upon the ridge. "The upward movement of the gallant 36th Illinois," Curtis noted, "with its dark-blue line of men and its gleaming bayonets, steadily rose from base to summit, when it dashed forward into the forest, driving and scattering the rebels from these commanding heights. The 12th Missouri, far in advance of the others, rushed into the enemy's lines, bearing off a flag and two pieces of artillery." It was a classical pincers movement, and in a matter of minutes the Confederates were caught in a concentrated crossfire.

By ten o'clock Van Dorn knew that he was beaten. All morning he had been waiting for ammunition wagons from his temporary base camp near Sugar Creek; they had been delayed because of a mix-up in orders and were still a mile from the battle ground when the federals opened their flanking attacks. Confederate gunners used stones in their cannons when their shot gave out; infantrymen threw away their useless rifles and fired short-range shotguns at advancing Yankees.

Van Dorn started his ambulances moving eastward from Elkhorn Tavern down a side road that led to Huntsville, and for the next half hour the Confederates were fighting to cover a general withdrawal. "The enemy advanced," said Colonel Henry Little, who was in the midst of this engagement. "On, on they came, in overwhelming numbers, line after line, but they were met with the same determined courage which this protracted contest had taught them to appreciate . . . Their intention of turning our flanks . . . being now clearly evident, we slowly fell back from our advanced position, disputing every inch of ground which we relinquished."

In this last fighting Confederate losses mounted sharply and included many of the South's most promising young officers. Among them was nineteen-year-old Churchill Clark, a battery commander, grandson of William Clark, the famous Western explorer. While covering the withdrawal, young Clark was decapitated by a round shot.

A soldier of the 36th Illinois who was among the first to reach the top of the ridge described the scene: "The mangled trunks of men lay thickly scattered around, and so close as to require the utmost care to avoid stepping on their cold remains. From each tree or sheltering nook the groans of the wounded arose, while muskets, saddles, horses, blankets, hats and clothes hung in shreds from every bush or in gory masses cumbered the ground. . . . Federal soldiers shared the contents of their canteens with thirsty wounded Confederates. The fierce passions which animated them an hour before, while panting for each other's blood, had subsided, and pity for the maimed supplanted the feelings of hate and fury."

By noon all artillery fire had ceased. In the mistaken belief that they were close on the heels of Van Dorn's army, Sigel's infantrymen poured northward up Telegraph Road in pursuit of fleeing Confederates. The main army, however, had slipped away southeastward on the road to Huntsville, with Shelby's cavalry covering the rear.

After the fighting ended and Colonel Carr was moving his division out to find forage for his horses, he stopped briefly at Elkhorn Tavern. Polly Cox, her son, and daughter-in-law had already departed; twenty-one hours under fire had been enough of war for them. Carr glanced at the ridgepole of the abandoned, shell-torn tavern, then ordered the huge elkhorns brought down as a souvenir of the battle. (Years later the horns were returned and are now in a museum at Garfield, Arkansas.)

Carr's division had suffered more casualties than the other three

Federal divisions combined. Total for the Union forces was 1,384. The Confederates lost about the same number, but they lost three good generals and too many line officers who could never be replaced, and they had lost the crucial battle for control of the Missouri border. Missouri was now secure for the Union, and Arkansas was open for eventual Federal occupation.

For some reason the fortunes of the Civil War did not favor the leaders who fought at Pea Ridge. Both Curtis and Sigel became major generals, but Curtis fell into disfavor in Missouri and was shunted off to Kansas; Sigel went to Virginia and was twice relieved of command for poor generalship. Carr and Dodge had to wait until after the war to establish their reputations on the Western frontier—Carr as an Indian fighter, Dodge as a railroad builder. Van Dorn returned to Mississippi, was defeated at Corinth and charged with dereliction of duty; although exonerated he was soon afterward shot to death off the battlefield by a jealous husband. Price also lost his Mississippi battles, invaded Missouri in 1864, was defeated at Westport, and would have been brought before a Confederate court of inquiry had the war not ended.

As for the two private soldiers who achieved the fame of being mentioned in dispatches—Thomas Welch who brought the warning of a Confederate attack in the rear and Peter Pelican who killed General McCulloch—a few months after the battle both men took leave without permission and never returned to their companies.

On the other hand, there was Curtis's chief quartermaster, a thirty-year-old captain who had gone north the day before the battle to collect grain and rations for the Federal troops. His name was Phillip H. Sheridan.

Captain Henry Van Sellar, photographed at the time of his marriage on February 18, 1864, was promoted to lieutenant colonel the following day. From an unknown source.

Sallie Pattison as she looked on her wedding day in Springfield, Illinois. From an unknown source.

3

A Civil War Love Story

*"From their first notice of each other, through their courtship, and
the early days of their marriage, the letters between Captain Henry
Van Sellar and Sallie Pattison tell a touching tale."*

er name was Sallie Pattison and he was Henry Van Sellar,
Captain, 12th Illinois Volunteer Infantry. She saw him
first, in church at Paris, Illinois, on a Sunday in 1862.
"Miss Sis Connelly and I were sitting back of you," she
wrote him afterward. "We could only see the back of your head. Sis
remarked to me during prayer, 'He is my sweetheart.' I told her it was
useless for her to put in a claim, for he belonged to me. Do you know
what we were in love with? It was your hair and the neatness of your
collar . . . We came to the conclusion that you were a married gentleman and that it was your neat little wife's taste displayed in adjusting
your collar. I left the next day for Cincinnati, was gone three months
and entirely forgot our stranger. When I returned Sis met me at the
train. Almost her first words were, 'Oh, Sallie, our gentleman is not
married!' But alas it was all the same as I failed to make his acquaintance before he left our little town. But seems to have improved it
slightly since."

The "improvement" of their acquaintance gained considerable
headway during the spring of 1863 when the dashing, black-haired,
black-eyed bachelor of twenty-four returned to Illinois on recruiting
duty. They exchanged formal notes, and Captain Sellar made his first

call at the Pattison home. During the hour between the time she met him on the front steps and the time they stood by the parlor mantel looking at an album of photographs, he fell in love with her.

From St. Louis a few days later the captain mailed her a copy of a new novel which everyone was talking about, Victor Hugo's *Les Miserables,* signing it "A Soldier Friend." As he had hoped, Sallie penetrated his concealed identity and sent him a note of thanks: "Very much to my surprise I received a package from St. Louis which proved to be *Les Miserables.* No name was attached but that of a *Soldier Friend.* Though written in an unknown hand, upon examination I thought it to be the same as a note I received containing a photograph. Allow me to thank you very kindly for both. The photograph will always have a place in my album and the book I will read with interest . . . I shall ever remember my Soldier Friend. If convenient I would be pleased to hear from you."

This was the beginning of a courtship and romance by mail that was to move back and forth from the home front with its anxieties, joys, and sadnesses to the fighting fronts of Kenesaw Mountain, Chattahoochee River, the Siege of Atlanta, Sherman's March to the Sea, and the last battles in the Carolinas.

Back with his regiment in northern Mississippi, Captain Sellar replied to "Miss Sallie" on May 23: "I am a very clumsy epistolarian . . . I can't write a readable letter to a lady." He asked her to send one of her photographs "to a soldier friend way down South in Dixie," and assured her that he had enjoyed his visit with her in Paris.

She complied with the request for a photograph and informed him that she had "whiled away many pleasant hours perusing *Les Miserables.*" She continued: "Did you ever hear Poe's 'Raven' chanted? I had some gentlemen friends from Terre Haute who chanted it beautifully. I have an Indiana friend who has such a sweet voice. He has read it repeatedly for me. Words are inadequate to express my admiration for it." In this way she let the captain know that she was as interested in literature as he, and also that she had other suitors.

Captain Sellar responded by sending her a volume of Poe's poetry, and for several weeks continued his correspondence on the literary front, extolling his favorite author, Charles Dickens, and mailing her copies of *Godey's Lady's Book* and *Harper's*, which he obtained from the well-stocked sutlers who followed the Union Army everywhere.

During the summer of 1863, the 12th Illinois was a very busy regiment with General William T. Sherman's XV Corps in Tennessee, but Captain Sellar found time to write "Miss Sallie" about the beautiful starry evenings in Dixieland. "One is prompted to read some rare, romantic book," he wrote, adding hopefully that he expected to be home for good in another year. "The faint prestige the Confederacy enjoyed is gone." Occasionally he noted his military responsibilities: "My family is a large one—a company of 66 soldiers present for duty . . . This is not all romance, Sallie, but earnest, chivalrous, *earnest purpose."*

With these preliminaries out of the way the earnest young captain expressed his warm feelings for his correspondent. Miss Pattison replied by promising to be his "Lady Love," but warned him that she called herself "Cautious Sallie." His reply from Pocahontas, Tennessee, in October 1863 came close to being a proposal by mail: "When a young lady writes she will be my 'Lady Love' I believe it literally, especially in this case. And now I will go further than perhaps I ought and confess I am *in love* with *Sallie.* I am proud to be your 'Knight' in this best and truest cause in which any man ever 'took arms': and don't fear, please, that I shall ever prove ungallant, or untrue to my *Lady Love."*

She responded to this by granting him permission to address her as "Sallie, though a homely name," and promised to be his "Guardian Angel." He now changed the salutation in his letters from "Miss Sallie" to "My Dear Sallie."

One difficulty with this courtship by correspondence was the irregularity of the wartime mails. Letters from the far-flung Army of Tennessee were collected and taken to Chattanooga or Nashville for posting, and most of Captain Sellar's envelopes bear postmarks dated about a week after he wrote them. When his regiment was in motion, letters from home arrived in delayed batches, some three or four weeks old—all of which made it awkward for lovers to carry on any meaningful exchange.

In the late autumn of 1863 General Grant, who was now in command in the West, began massing his divisions around Chattanooga. The 12th Illinois left its old base near Shiloh, and on November 21 Henry wrote Sallie from Pulaski, Tennessee, informing her that he had been there a week, but had heard nothing from her since October 30. His regiment had marched 200 miles in fifteen days; Pulaski was a pretty town in the best part of Tennessee; he was encamped "on a young mountain; very high, very airy."

By the time communications between Pulaski and Paris were matched again, the Christmas season was approaching. On December 15, Sallie wrote: "I don't believe in long continued engagements, still not too brief. I would be afraid a gentleman would get tired of me unless he knew me pretty well. I believe I am too fickle to be trusted long. I am sure I would get out of the notion. We will have to have an additional newspaper for the publication of weddings in the Spring. The girls all say 'I would rather send a husband than a lover to war.' "

Apparently this letter had a profound effect upon Captain Sellar. In January, while his regiment was being re-enlisted as veterans, he arranged for extended leave. On January 30, 1864, Sallie Pattison was surprised to receive a note delivered by hand: "Henry sends compliments and requesting to 'call round' to see Sallie this evening, please." No record exists of their ensuing meetings, but on February 1 she received a package with an enclosed note: "Accept please this album from me and believe me, ever, Henry."

During the following two weeks, Henry convinced Sallie that he also did not believe in "long continued engagements." They journeyed to Springfield, Illinois, and were married there at nine o'clock in the morning, February 18. Next day he was commissioned a lieutenant colonel.

Not long afterward he was back on duty at Pulaski, more love-smitten than ever, writing to "Sallie of the blue eyes and brown hair, who is my ideal of *beauty*, *sense*, *propriety*, and *everything* else that's

The "march through Georgia" by the Union forces of Major General William T. Sherman caused many citizens of Atlanta to gather their possessions and flee southward. From an unknown source.

nice. I lay on my buffalo robe with my face to the moon, and smoked a cigar, thinking of you, *my darling,* until midnight ere my peepers were closed by the 'sleep god' . . . I wish you sat on my lap this evening, *Dearest*—wouldn't there be some talkin' n kissin' and kissin' n talkin' and *caressing!* Guess there would! . . . Our wedding is full of romance, surely—a few meetings, a few letters during a few months."

On March 26, 1864, General James B. McPherson took command of the Army of the Tennessee, which was preparing to move against Atlanta under General Sherman's supreme command. As a part of this campaign, the 12th Illinois was alerted for a march into Georgia.

From Adairsville, Georgia, on May 18, Sellar wrote optimistically: "We are pushing General Johnston very hard. [Joseph E. Johnston, commanded the Confederate forces defending Atlanta.] I guess we will yet beat him into Atlanta." Three weeks later he was writing from battlefield headquarters, heading his letter "In the Woods, Ga." The 12th Illinois, he said, was the left regiment of the corps, positioned on a hill with a line of rifle pits almost completed. "The folks have almost all gone from this part of Georgia further south and in a great

& affrighted hurry, leaving everything except what they could carry in their haste."

He described an abandoned house where he had spent the previous night. "The yard gate was thrown down as was the fence; the garden was stripped of all edibles, the furniture was broken and scattered and the floor torn up and the door broken from its hinges. Articles of clothing and bedding were trodden in the mud & dirt and tableware lay where it had been thrown, in pieces . . . Sallie Dear, my heart grew sick at the sight and I rode away querying, Are they thus guilty O Lord? Or why does this punishment light upon them? If the deluded creatures would remain at home their rights to all except 'subsistence' would be sacred. We are ordered to subsist on the people as much as possible and we take corn and meat, leaving them only a present supply."

From Big Shanty on June 20, Henry complained bitterly of the daily drenching rains and the tenacity of the Confederates. "We have thought it certain all the time that the Rebels were retreating on Atlanta, but yesterday they seem to have changed their notion and their course to some point farther east. And when McPherson began to advance his lines he found them yet in force . . . therefore after getting quite ready to chase 'em we began to 'don't' and are yet in camp as before."

When Sallie complained about delays in receiving Sellar's letter, he explained: "General Sherman did prohibit the mails from their usual regularity & promptness but everything mailed was sure to go and without any molestation—for instance, just previous to an important movement he suppressed the mails for a week perhaps and then sent all." He assured her that this was "necessary for success of our grand campaign . . . We think Gen'l Sherman is the next best Gen'l to our Grant and whatever he does is right."

As the summer of 1864 wore on and the campaign before Atlanta bogged down, Henry lost some of his earlier optimism and enthusiasm. "How weary I become of this army life! There's nothing congenial in it. I would were it not for honor and country leave it tomorrow." He complained of Georgia heat, insects, and reptiles.

"Too warm for even a salamander's endurance . . . In this country are thousands of insects, tormentors of the 'genus homo.' Among others is a tiny thing no larger than the eye of a cambric needle—color a 'flushed pink.' We call it by the name it goes by among the natives—'Chigua.'" He used iodine against the chiggers, but could find nothing to stop lizards from waking him every night by slithering across his face on their cold bellies. "More lizards here than there ought to be in the world I think."

Late in June, the 12th Illinois marched by night to Kenesaw Mountain. Thus far, Sherman had fought a campaign of maneuver, avoiding frontal assaults on entrenchments, but he believed a battle would have to be fought here to dislodge Johnston's army from its anchor post. Lieutenant Colonel Sellar spared his wife the details of the bloody fighting on Kenesaw Mountain, a futile assault which cost the Union army 3,000 men but left the Confederates still holding their lines.

By the end of June, Sherman had decided to try to dislodge Johnston by outflanking him and threatening his line of communications with Atlanta. The tactics worked, and the Confederates withdrew to the Chattahoochee. On July 2 Lieutenant Colonel Sellar had his first opportunity in days to trim his beard. After glimpsing himself in a mirror he wrote: "I do look rough, my dear beauty, too rough to be your mate. But when this campaign is over I will 'fix up' I guess . . . My hair is untrimmed, but it will not be shorn yet awhile." He had lost thirty pounds during the Atlanta campaign. "I am now about my fighting weight, 163."

After a week of fighting along the Chattahoochee, the 12th Illinois camped at Roswell, and Lieutenant Colonel Sellar drew a special assignment. "Roswell is a beautiful village—a manufacturing town. The mills were burned before our arrival by our cavalry. They were cotton mills and the operatives were chiefly females. Three hundred of them were moved by us to Marietta. I don't know what they will do. The Gov't will provide for them I suppose." He went on to describe the march of thirty miles, with only two hours for sleep or refreshment.

In letters to his beloved Sallie, Lieutenant Colonel Henry Van Sellar spared the horrific details of war depicted in this illustration of the attack of the XIV, XVI, and XX Army Corps during the Battle of Kenesaw Mountain on June 22, 1864, as part of Sherman's campaign in Georgia. From Frank Leslie's Illustrated History of the Civil War, 1861–65, page 422.

At last the battle for Atlanta began in earnest. On July 22 General McPherson was killed, General Oliver O. Howard replacing him. Very early on the morning of August 1, "a dull morning, cloudy and damp," a weary Henry Sellar managed to pen a few lines from the outskirts of Atlanta. "Both sides are exhausted with the fighting of all day and almost all night," he wrote. He was homesick for Sallie. "I love you more and dearer every day."

Sallie did not have long to wait until she saw her husband in person. Late in September he arranged a brief furlough, part of which they spent in Cincinnati so they would have a few more hours together. As Henry expressed it, he was "haunted with the idea of the brevity of the time we are to be together."

Not long after rejoining his regiment in Georgia, his letters began hinting at an important new military movement, warning Sallie that she might not hear from him again for some time. "Gen'l Sherman keeps his own counsel and don't allow his soldier boys to tell his 'doin's' to their correspondents up north. We never expect our mail to go when any movement is imminent until it has transpired too far for the revelation to do any harm." He could tell her only that "we are going through the Confederacy . . . and will turn up somewhere (?) Lord knows 'whar'."

Then for almost two months, neither heard from the other. Lieutenant Colonel Sellar and his 12th Illinois were marching with General Sherman to Savannah and the sea. The key to Savannah was Fort McAllister. It fell on December 13, and a few days later Henry could mail a letter to Sallie: "The campaign is over and Savannah is ours. . . . I am writing in my tent and am very comfortable without fire. My house is floored and carpeted with unthreshed rice—nice, clean and agreeable floor . . . beside the desk is a small box in which is a small present for 'you'ns.' I could send lots of things but I will not pilfer nor appropriate pilfered property & curiosities. The wine is some Maj. Anderson, the Rebel commandant of Ft. McAllister, gave me. He buried a lot as we neared Savannah, and because I treated him 'kindly,' as he said, he told me where to find three dozen of it. The Yankees had exhumed several hundred of it before, but this was so well concealed no one could find it . . . Savannah fell with little resistance. Some artillery practice on each side but very little harm done. I had two men slightly wounded. . . . My camp is just in the edge of the city towards Thunderbolt Battery and the Savannah River . . . this army of 50,000 or 60,000 men admire W. T. Sherman and entirely confide in his skill—'the best Conductor on the Road.' We have a string band that plays very well. Occasionally in passing through the city I hear a piano and the music almost enchants me after hearing for so long the drums 'n fife with their scream & noise."

After conducting prisoners to Hilton Head Island, Lieutenant Colonel Sellar led his regiment on a parade through Savannah. "As we marched through the city on the 19th [January 1865] we halted a while and as I stood beside Fannie I saw a very beautiful little girl on the walk looking at the soldiers. I approached and asked her name. 'Lizzie,' she said. 'Only Lizzie,' said I. 'Yes, Lizzie Hood, but no kin to the General,' she replied. I talked to her and gave her an apple, and she was so intelligent & sprightly I almost fell in love with the little Miss Hood though I'm sure she wasn't above six years of age. Pretty child! The embodiment of beauty & innocence! Little does she realize the terrible & big meaning of the sights she sees each day! Little did she suspect the horse & equipage, the uniform & saber she admired so much were significant of cruel war. God bless the pretty children of Savannah and elsewhere and make a quick work of this rebellion for their sakes! I did pray this as I thought of Lizzie. She told me where she lived and that her Pa was dead. I feared to question her of him. I thought perhaps he was slain in the army and she might like me less if I discovered to her that the Yankees were her enemies. Oh! Cruel, cruel war!" Like many of his comrades, Henry Sellar was torn between compassion for the people of the South and a desire to deal a final crushing blow that would end the fighting. On February 1, he was waiting impatiently for the rain to stop so that his regiment could cross into South Carolina.

February 18, 1865, was a special day for both Sallie and Henry, the anniversary of their wedding. Sallie spent a miserable day of remembrance, and that evening made no attempt at her usual cheeriness when she wrote Henry: "Who so happy and light hearted as I was then and who so sad and lonely tonight . . . I opened all the windows and had fires lighted in each room to have it look a little cheerful but all to no effect. More than one time today I have stolen to *our* room alone and been as near *you* as possible. . . . All day tears would unbidden start and now I cannot see to write."

At last on April 28, from Raleigh, North Carolina, Henry began a letter with the words he had been wanting to write since his wedding day: "We start homeward tomorrow . . . Gen'l Joe Johnston capitulated two days since and the close of the war is announced by every one, none doubting peace now that the capital & two chief armies of the Rebs are in our hands." And then he went on to tell of his sorrow "occasioned by Mr. Lincoln's death . . . I confess I can't even read of the affair without tears—a little grief I can control but such mighty grief controls me . . . No one speaks his name now irreverently—the feeling is worthy—he was the gentle parent of the nation."

Writing from Paris on April 16, Sallie described how a small town in Lincoln's home state was affected by the news of the assassination: "Such gloom as it caused, almost utter despair was depicted on almost every countenance. . . . All the bells tolled over an hour this morning. Dear, words fail to express our feelings. What next will befall us, I wonder. All my thoughts are given to the interests of the Army now my Darling is there and with him are all my hopes of happiness."

From that day the correspondence of Sallie and Henry was concerned mainly with the question of when the 12th Illinois would return home for mustering out. "We may be citizens by the 4th of July, Darling," Henry declared optimistically in April, but he also cautioned his wife that it would require some weeks to march from North Carolina to Washington and then on to Illinois. "We can't be mustered out in a day." Lieutenant Colonel Sellar, like many other Union officers faced with the sudden realization of becoming civilians again, now began considering making a career of military service.

On May 24, the 12th Illinois marched in the grand review down

Pennsylvania Avenue in Washington, departing soon afterward for Louisville, Kentucky. On May 30, Sallie wrote: "I was delighted to have a letter once more, but was not so much delighted when I read perhaps *June* would not find you at home. I began looking down my nose and feeling dreadful bad."

A month later Henry reported that he was momentarily expecting orders to move his regiment to Illinois. He had had second thoughts about remaining in the Army. "Tired doing nothing," he confessed. "Today I decided to not remain in the U.S. Service."

Their wartime love letters were all written now. On July 18, 1865, at Camp Butler, Illinois, the 12th Regiment was mustered out. Free of military duty at last, Henry hastened to Paris to join his beloved Sallie, and presumably they lived happily ever afterward.

Brigadier General John Hunt Morgan and his bride, Martha Ready. The picture may have been taken on their wedding day, December 14, 1862, in Murfreesboro, Tennessee. Courtesy Library of Congress, LC-USZ62-13688.

4

Morgan's Christmas Raid

"Dashing northward around Union-occupied Nashville, John Hunt Morgan's cavalry set out on a daring mission to starve Rosecrans' army."

At Alexandria, Tennessee, on December 21, 1862, Brigadier General John Hunt Morgan reviewed the 4,000 cavalrymen of his brigade, a command which within a few months had grown from his original 2nd Kentucky Cavalry to seven regiments. With Morgan as he watched his regiments pass in review was the young wife he had married only a week before, twenty-one-year-old Martha Ready. Although some members of the general's staff looked upon her as a child bride who might diminish the spirited audacity of their thirty-seven-year-old leader, the wedding had been a gala affair in Murfreesboro—almost outshining the visit of President Jefferson Davis to the headquarters of Braxton Bragg's Army of Tennessee.

Jefferson Davis's presence was coincidental with a hurried tour of the western theater of war where two Federal armies were massing large numbers of men. On the Mississippi, Grant threatened Vicksburg. At Nashville, Major General William Rosecrans' Army of the Cumberland evidently was preparing a thrust southward toward Chattanooga. Neither Union commander appeared willing to wait out the winter before opening their campaigns; consequently there was an air of urgency in all the Confederate camps in middle

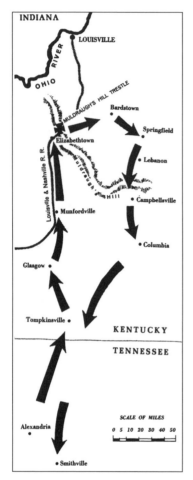

Map of Brigadier General John Hunt Morgan's Christmas Raid on the Muldraugh's Hill trestles along the Louisville & Nashville Railroad, in Kentucky. From Civil War Times Illustrated staff.

Tennessee. President Davis undoubtedly sat in on the planning at Bragg's headquarters which committed heavy use of cavalry to the early winter strategy. Forrest would operate in west Tennessee to harass Grant's supply lines; Morgan would sweep north around Rosecrans' base at Nashville in an effort to sever the Union supply line by destroying railroad bridges in Kentucky.

Morgan and the Army of Tennessee's staff officers knew that Union soldiers had built a chain of almost impregnable stockades from Bowling Green, Kentucky, southward to Nashville. Bridges were under full guard, rail towns strongly garrisoned. After studying a map of the Louisville & Nashville Railroad, the Confederate leaders selected the weakest point, a pair of trestleworks just north of Elizabethtown where the road cut through Muldraugh's Hill. Each of these trestles was about 500 feet long and 100 feet high, and if destroyed would effectively cut Rosecrans' rail supply line for most of the winter. The uncertain factor in this plan was that Muldraugh's Hill was only a few miles below Louisville. With the best of luck a Confederate cavalry brigade might reach the trestles, but something more than luck would be required to overcome the defenders, burn the structures, and then march out safely through swarms of aroused Federal troops.

After receiving his orders, Morgan divided his brigade into two parts to permit greater flexibility of movement. Colonel Basil Duke, Morgan's brother-in-law, commanded the 2nd, 3rd, 8th, and 9th Kentucky Cavalry regiments, while Colonel William C. P. Breckinridge led the 10th and 11th Kentucky and the 14th Tennessee regiments. On December 20 they moved from their camps around Murfreesboro to Alexandria, where farriers completed shoeing of horses, and the men cleaned their arms and equipment for final inspection. Next day was Sunday, the weather clear and autumnlike.

A future governor of Kentucky, Lieutenant James McCreary, noted in his diary: "As company after company moved into line with horses prancing, firearms glistening, bugles blowing, and flags waving, and with our artillery on the right flank, and finally halted in a beautiful valley with bright eyes and lovely faces gaping at us, it formed a grand and imposing scene." Never again would John Morgan command such a splendid body of cavalrymen, the majority seasoned veterans mounted on the best Kentucky and Tennessee horseflesh left in the South.

Before daybreak on the twenty-second, reveille sounded in the Alexandria camps. Horses were fed, watered, and saddled, and breakfast fires lighted. The march out was set for nine o'clock. It was a soft, mild morning, the sun bright in a cloudless sky, winter birds twittering in the cedars. The first to ride out were Tom Quirk's scouts. Several of these sixty men had been with Morgan since organization of his first company at Lexington. Their leader, Irish-born Tom Quirk, had kept a candy store in Lexington before the war; his favorite command was "Double quick! Forward!"

Except for the regimental commanders none of the men knew exactly where they were going, but all were sure they would be in Kentucky for Christmas and that was enough. For two hours, columns of fours marched out of the frost-browned, cedar-fringed meadows until regiments were strung out over seven miles. Suddenly above the steady hoofbeats and the creak of leather, tremendous cheers broke out far back down the column. The men in the advance knew what the cheering meant; Morgan had bid his bride farewell and was coming up front to join Colonel Duke. "Alongside the column," said Bennett Young, "with a splendid staff, magnificently mounted, superbly dressed, riding like a centaur, bare-headed, with plumed hat in right hand, waving salutations to his applauding followers, the general came galloping by." Just before the early winter dusk the column reached Sand Shoals ford on the Cumberland. The men crossed without incident and went into camp on the north side.

At daylight they were moving again, Morgan aiming for Tompkinsville, but the plodding artillery held the columns back. When they crossed the Kentucky line, the short December day was closing, a full moon lighting the sky. "Cheer after cheer and shout after shout echoed for miles toward the rear of the column, breaking the stillness of the night," Lieutenant McCreary noted in his journal. "Tonight we are camped on the sacred soil of old Kentucky and it fills my heart with joy and pride to know that I am once more on my native heather. . . . Campfires illuminate every hill and valley and the fires burn brighter, seemingly are more cheerful, because it is the fatherland."

This was the third venture into their home state for Morgan's horse soldiers since their forced withdrawal following the surrender of Forts Henry and Donelson in February. In July they had raided into the Bluegrass, returned briefly to Tennessee, and then in September as part of General Bragg's invasion force they had captured the Union garrison in Morgan's hometown of Lexington. But after Bragg blundered into battle at Perryville, lost his nerve, and ordered a general retreat, Morgan's men had to leave Kentucky again. "Our best and last chance to win the war was thrown away," Basil Duke afterward commented bitterly.

But now they were back again, and to celebrate the Christmas Eve march from Tompkinsville to Glasgow, several of the boys foraged some "swell head brandy," and a few overdid their holiday imbibing, growing "too heavy for their saddles," and had to be strapped on by their more sober comrades. During the afternoon, the 2nd Regiment overtook an enormous wagon drawn by twenty Percheron horses, "perhaps the largest wagon ever seen in the State of Kentucky." The driver was a Union sutler bound for Glasgow with Christmas delicacies for the federal camps there; Morgan's men captured it immediately. According to Tom Berry, one of Quirk's scouts, the wagon contained "a fabulous variety and quantity of good things to eat," and that night every mess in the brigade had something to brighten their otherwise drab Christmas suppers.

The regiments bivouacked that night five miles below Glasgow, the scouts having brought reports of strong Union cavalry movements in the area to the north. "Tis Christmas Eve," wrote James McCreary. "I am sitting with many friends—around a glorious campfire. Shouting, singing and speechifying make the welkin ring, for the boys have a superabundance of whisky and are celebrating Christmas Eve very merrily. We have not seen an enemy yet."

While the main body of the expedition was making camp south of Glasgow, Tom Quirk and his scouts approached the town. Having a mighty Irish thirst, Quirk took a few of his men into a Glasgow saloon. As they were dismounting, a patrol of the 2nd Michigan Union Cavalry came cantering down the street with the same objective in view—a glass of Christmas cheer. Scout Kelion Peddicord laconically described the unexpected meeting: "A collision was the result, then a skirmish, then—a stampede of all parties!"

With Quirk's company of scouts on this raid was seventeen-year-old Johnny Wyeth (later to serve with General Forrest and become his biographer). Quirk had refused to enlist Wyeth because of his youth, but allowed him to ride along as a sort of "independent" member of the company. Wyeth afterward recorded the events of Christmas Day, of how the scouts marched early through Glasgow and then swiftly up the road toward Munfordville. "About two o'clock in the afternoon, at Bear Wallow, our company was well in front when the vidette came back with information that the road was full of Yankees just ahead. With his usual reckless dash, Quirk drew his six-shooter and, yelling to his company to draw theirs, he dashed down the road toward the enemy. War was a new experience to me, and it was very exciting as we swept down the road at full tilt. Right ahead of us, as we swung around a turn, stretched across the turnpike, and field to one side of the road, was a formidable line of Federal cavalry. . . . Our one chance was to climb over the fence on the other side of the lane which we speedily did. Quirk and I went over the same panel, with the Federals shooting at us from the fence across the road, no more than thirty or forty feet distant."

Quirk received a head wound and when Morgan arrived on the scene and found his captain of scouts with a bloody handkerchief around his forehead, he ordered the Irishman to see a surgeon. But Quirk only grinned and declared he had a head built in County Kerry, so roughed by shillelaghs that a couple of bullet wounds were mere trifles. He assembled his scouts and resumed march in the advance. One of Duke's regiments had surrounded the Yankee patrol, capturing every man.

Rain began falling before dark, and the raiders crossed Green River in a downpour. That night they camped under beating rain only seven miles from the enemy's dry and cozy stockades along the L. & N. Railroad. At reveille there was sleet mixed in the rain; the men fumbled for saddles in the winter dark, trying vainly to dry their weapons.

Before resuming march toward their main objective—Muldraugh's Hill trestles—Morgan and his staff decided to take advantage of the proximity of the Bacon Creek bridge and strike a damaging blow there. Morgan gave the attack assignment to his 2nd Regiment, and the artillerymen moved up one of the two Parrott guns which they had captured early in December from the 12th Indiana Battery at Hartsville, Tennessee.

After a heavy pounding of the bridge's stockade, a truce party was sent in to inform the defenders that they were surrounded by Morgan's men. The bridge guards immediately surrendered. Dismounted cavalrymen came up to set the bridge ablaze. They also ripped rails from both approaches and cut down a few telegraph poles. For a few days at least, Rosecran's Nashville base was cut off from Louisville, and now nothing lay between Morgan's men and the

This railroad trestle at Whiteside, Tennessee, resembled the trestles at Muldraugh's Hill, which were the target of Brigadier General John Hunt Morgan's Christmas Raid, December 22, 1862–January 3, 1863. Courtesy of National Archives [Brady Collection], III-B-482.

Muldraugh's Hill trestles but thirty miles and well-defended Elizabethtown.

On the morning of December 27 the advance regiments were within six miles of Elizabethtown, and a quick sweep around would have brought them to the trestles by late afternoon. Morgan, however, decided that it would be wiser to capture the town's garrison rather than risk being caught between the forces there and those at the trestles. During the night the skies had cleared, and it was "a lovely sunny day, all nature seemed to be sparkling and smiling."

As the forward scouts approached the outskirts of Elizabethtown, they saw a Union corporal coming down the muddy road; he was waving a truce flag. The scouts held their horses warily until the corporal came up and asked in a thick German accent for their commander. They hustled him back to Morgan. The corporal saluted stiffly and handed over a message scrawled on the back of an envelope:

Elizabethtown, Ky., Dec. 27, 1862.

TO THE COMMANDER OF THE CONFEDERATE FORCES:
Sir; I demand an unconditional surrender of all your forces. I have you surrounded, and will compel you to surrender. I am, sir, your obedient servant,

H. S. Smith
Commanding U.S. Forces

Morgan could barely conceal his amusement, but he was in no mood for joking and quickly sent a reply back to Lieutenant Colonel Smith, informing him that it was his forces which were surrounded, not the Confederates, and that the Federal garrison should surrender. In a second message Smith refused to capitulate, and Morgan replied briefly that he would give the defenders time to remove women and children, and then would attack.

Colonel Leroy Cluke's 8th Kentucky Cavalry, which was up front that morning, was ordered to dismount, and then Morgan sent a battery up on a hill to the left of the road from where the gunners could fire down into the town. Lieutenant Colonel Smith's 600 Union soldiers were concentrated in brick residences and in two or three large warehouses facing the south, and it was into these that the Parrott guns and howitzers began to drop their shells while the dismounted men of Cluke's regiment moved in.

The fighting was brisk and noisy for a few minutes, but the outnumbered Federals soon had enough of grape and canister. Even before Lieutenant Colonel Smith finally complied with Morgan's surrender order, his men began waving white flags from windows. As the work of rounding up scattered Federals—and disarming and paroling them—delayed the raids until late in the afternoon, Morgan decided to make a temporary fortress of Elizabethtown and wait out the night. His men now had 600 Federal rifles at their disposal, as well as an abundance of captured ammunition.

Next morning bugles roused them early, Quirk's scouts and the 2nd Regiment in advance again, and before noon both sections of the brigade were in position around the two long wooden trestleworks at Muldraugh's Hill—the principal objective of the Christmas raid. Morgan sent truce parties in to both stockades, offering the defenders a chance to surrender, but again as at Elizabethtown the Federals were determined to make a fight of it.

The attacks began simultaneously, Duke's regiments against the upper trestle, Breckinridge's against the lower. After two or three hours' shelling, the 71st Indiana Infantry ran up white flags on both stockades, and 650 prisoners marched out to surrender. Under the parole system, the captives were required to sign oaths promising not to bear arms against the Confederacy until exchanged, and their names had to be entered on rolls to be forwarded to army headquarters where arrangements would eventually be made to exchange them for captured Confederates. As soon as they had signed their oaths, they were free to return home, in this case nearby Indiana.

Among Morgan's men at Muldraugh's Hill that day was an Indianian with Kentucky ties who had crossed the Ohio River to join the Confederate cavalry. He was Sergeant Henry L. Stone, and among the prisoners being paroled he recognized two men from his hometown of Greencastle, Indiana. He seized upon the opportunity to write a letter home:

Dear Mother, At the railroad trestleworks we captured the 71st Indiana,
including Billy Brown and Court Mattson. Lt. Col. Brown appeared
very glad to see me indeed. I was surprised to see him. . . . I happened
to go up to the house in which Gen. Morgan had his headquarters and
I hadn't more than seated myself by the fire when I looked around and
recognized Brown sitting by the same fire. I says, "Hello! Brown, what
are you doing here?" He looked for some time and recognized me at last
and shook my hand heartily. After talking a little I took my canteen and
called him aside to take a heavy horn of good old Cogniac brandy. I think
he took about three drinks. Next morning I wrote a letter and he said
he would take it home to you for me, and I think he will.

A few minutes after the Indianians surrendered, both trestles
were afire, flames licking high, black smoke spiraling into a light
blue December sky. For the raiders, December 28 was a day of high
accomplishment. After a week of hard marching, hard fighting, and
some bad cavalry weather, they felt that their lost Christmas had been
well sacrificed. Morgan summed it up for them in his official report:
"I had the satisfaction of knowing that the object of the expedition
was attained, and the railroad was rendered impassable for at least two
months. The two trestles were the largest and finest on the whole
road." (Morgan's estimate of a delay of two months was conservative.
It was mid-March 1863 before the Federals could rebuild the bridges
and restore service on the L. & N.)

Now that his mission was accomplished, Morgan faced an even
greater problem—that of marching back into Tennessee through all
the swarms of Union troops bent upon intercepting him. As soon as
he was satisfied that the trestles were destroyed, he formed columns
and turned eastward. At the mouth of Beech Fork on Rolling Fork
River the regiments bivouacked for the night, Quirk taking his scouts
across the stream for outpost duty.

During the night Colonel John M. Harlan, commanding a brigade
of five Union infantry and cavalry regiments, fell upon the raiders'
trail. Shortly after daybreak of the twenty-ninth, while crossing the
Rolling Fork, Harlan's pursuit force was close enough to begin shelling
the rear regiment.

Basil Duke, still on the southwest bank attempting to hold Harlan in check while the last companies forded the stream, was struck suddenly by a shell fragment. He fell unconscious from his horse, blood flowing from the side of his head. Shouts and cries of dismay ran through the line of men holding the last defensive position. Duke lay where he had fallen, motionless, shells bursting all around, and his men feared their twenty-four-year-old colonel was dead.

Captain Tom Quirk, who had been assisting Duke, ran forward and lifted the apparently lifeless colonel upon his horse, then mounted behind and splashed across the Rolling Fork. At the first farmhouse Quirk impressed a carriage, filled it with feather mattresses and blankets, eased the yet-unconscious Duke into the soft bedding, and set out at a fast pace for Bardstown and medical aid. The arrival in Bardstown was chronicled by a circuit-riding preacher, J. W. Cunningham: "About dark Morgan's men began to throng the streets. Among the arrivals was Basil Duke. . . . He had been wounded. It was necessary for him to be helped by others into the hall of Dr. Cox's two-story brick house and up the stairway to the north end room where he was laid on a thick pallet on the floor . . . I was invited to examine a cannon's work . . . a piece of skin and bone behind the ear was gone." As the Reverend Cunningham bent down, Duke opened his eyes and said cheerfully: "That was a pretty close call."

Having beaten off Harlan's understrength pursuit force, Morgan's men marched out of Bardstown next morning on the Springfield road. According to the Reverend Cunningham, Morgan was at the head of the column, dressed in a close-fitting round-about and pants of green woolen. "On his head was a black low-crowned soft hat with a broad brim . . . a splendid-looking man." Duke rode far back down the column in the feather-bedded buggy, one of Quirk's scouts handling the reins like a proud coachman.

One of the axioms of cavalry raiding is that it is always easier to get in than to get out, and it was never truer than on that bleak December evening. According to Bennett Young, Morgan saw that "the best way of escape was the longest way; that he could not whip the eight thousand Federals at Lebanon and he must manage to get around them. He determined to make a detour to the right of Lebanon, swing back on the road to Campbellsville, and rush to Campbellsville with all possible speed." Consequently a forced march was ordered at eleven P.M.

Every Morgan man who afterward recalled this march around Lebanon described the weather as the worst experienced during the entire war. The darkness was intense; the freezing rain turned to sleet and cut into their faces. Although most of them wrapped blankets around their bodies and covered their feet with strips of cloth, this was but slight protection against the sharp, penetrating winds whistling and rattling through the naked trees. Boot soles froze to stirrups; fingers and toes turned blue with cold. Even the wounded Basil Duke in his insulated buggy suffered from the bitterness of the frigid air.

When daylight came the column looked like a ghostly army, men sheeted in ice, horses steaming from exertion as they moved silently through the woods. It was the last day of the year, December 31, 1862. They spent New Year's Eve in Campbellsville, where they found an "abundance of corn, hay, molasses, crackers, and ham, and all are doing well."

The men celebrated the New Year by rising to early reveille bugles and beginning a rapid march toward Columbia. As the column wound down a high hill that afternoon they heard a rumble of faraway cannon—a trick of sound waves against leaden winter skies—carried and deflected from a bloody artillery duel at Stone's River many miles to the south. While Morgan's raiders were cutting the Union supply line, Rosecrans had marched out of Nashville to challenge Bragg. The continuous rumbling was haunting and foreboding, like some inexorable burden of the future. In Washington that day, Abraham Lincoln was signing the Emancipation Proclamation.

On January 3 they crossed the Tennessee line. "Here we are with oil cloths up and rain falling in a perfect deluge. The raid may be considered ended for we are again on Tennessee soil . . . railroad, telegraphs, Yankees and commissary stores have received a blow they will long remember."

Even before Morgan's men rode into Smithville, Tennessee, on January 5, Major General Horatio G. Wright, commanding at Cincinnati, was desperately attempting to deliver one million overdue rations to Rosecrans' army. Wright shipped the rations down the Ohio River to the Cumberland, but the Cumberland was at low water stage and there was only one light-draft boat available for transport to Nashville. "We must open the railroad soon," Wright telegraphed Brigadier General Jeremiah Boyle at Louisville, "or Rosecrans will starve."

The Christmas raid had come too late, however, to hinder Rosecrans' assault on Bragg's army. By the time the raiders reached Smithville, the Stones River Campaign was ended, both armies withdrawing from the field badly bloodied. Each side claimed victory, but Lieutenant McCreary noted on January 6: "Received dispatch of 'victory' of Bragg's army. Bragg deemed it expedient to fall back towards Tullahoma. I don't believe in such victories. Bragg's talent seems to be all on the retreat."

Weary as they were, Morgan's men found no prospect of rest at Smithville. Bragg ordered them to immediate duty covering the left of his retreating army. For the Kentucky horse soldiers, it looked like another long, hard winter in Tennessee.

Major General William Tecumseh Sherman led the early but ill-fated operation against Vicksburg through Chickasaw Bayou. From Frank Leslie's Illustrated History of the Civil War, 1861–65, *page 39.*

5

━━━⫷⫸━━━

Battle at Chickasaw Bluffs*

"While Grant was stymied at Holly Springs, Sherman launched a disastrous assault against entrenched Confederates in the first great attempt upon Vicksburg."

N ear midnight of Christmas Eve, 1862, a Confederate telegraph operator at DeSoto, Louisiana, just across the Mississippi River from Vicksburg, received an urgent message from a lookout at Lake Providence, sixty-five miles upstream. Seven gunboats and about sixty transport vessels loaded with Union soldiers were steaming downriver toward Vicksburg. As quickly as possible, the telegrapher crossed the Mississippi to deliver the message to Major General Martin L. Smith, commanding the garrison of 6,000 at Vicksburg.

General Smith and most of his officers were attending a grand ball, but the telegrapher in his muddy boots strode through the dancers to the commander. "Well, sir, what do you want?" Smith demanded. The telegrapher gave him the bad news, and the general signaled

---

[*For more than 100 years, many historians and writers have referred to the Battle of Chickasaw Bayou as the Battle of Chickasaw Bluffs. This is incorrect, but it is easy to understand why this misconception would exist. The line of bluffs towering above Chickasaw Bayou caused soldiers to refer to that engagement as the Battle of Chickasaw Bluffs. However, Chickasaw Bluffs is a specific geographic area located north of Memphis, Tennessee. The bluffs north of Vicksburg overlooking Chickasaw Bayou are known as the Walnut Hills. In fact, some accounts refer to this engagement as the Battle of Walnut Hills. The official name of the engagement as established by the U.S. War Department is the Battle of Chickasaw Bayou.]

the orchestra to cease playing. "This ball is at an end," he announced. "The enemy are coming down the river!"

The Union force approaching Vicksburg consisted of four divisions, about 30,000 men under command of Major General William T. Sherman. The flotilla left Memphis on December 20 as the right wing of a coordinated land and water assault upon Vicksburg launched by Major General Ulysses Grant who, with a similar force, was to march against the Confederate interior armies below Oxford, Mississippi, reaching Vicksburg at about the same time as Sherman.

Unknown to Sherman, two Confederate cavalry leaders, Generals Earl Van Dorn and Nathan B. Forrest, had already captured Grant's supply base at Holly Springs and wrecked the railroads above it, forcing Grant to fall back toward Memphis. If Vicksburg was to be taken in this operation, Sherman would have to do it alone.

Both the Union and the Confederacy stood keenly aware of the strategic value of Vicksburg. From the heights of the city, artillery commanded the Mississippi River, and as long as the Confederates held Vicksburg, that vital artery of transport was blocked. If the Union army could capture the citadel, it would control the river all the way to the seaport of New Orleans; the South would be split in two, and supplies and troops from the western states could no longer flow freely to the eastern Confederacy.

On Christmas Day, Sherman rendezvoused with Acting Rear Admiral David D. Porter's naval squadron at the mouth of the Yazoo; then the mighty armada steamed twelve miles up to previously selected debarkation points along the front of Johnson's Plantation. The ground upon which the army landed was actually an island about six miles square, the Yazoo on the north, an old bed of the Mississippi on the west, a long narrow lake or slough on the south, and Chickasaw Bayou on the east. The outskirts of Vicksburg lay only eight miles south, but a high ridge running somewhat parallel with the course of the Yazoo protected the city. From this descending height, with its occasional sharp bluffs, artillery commanded the approaches to Vicksburg.

"On the day after Christmas," a soldier of the 13th Illinois Infantry recorded, "having passed the night on board the steamer *John Warner*,

Acting Rear Admiral David Dixon Porter commanded the Mississippi River Squadron during operations against Vicksburg. From Frank Leslie's Illustrated History of the Civil War, 1861–65, *page 129.*

we debarked, formed in line, and stacked arms." The 13th Illinois was among the first to land, being a unit of Major General Frank Blair's brigade of Major General Frederick Steele's 4th Division. Behind the 4th Division came Brigadier Generals George W. Morgan's 3rd, Morgan Smith's 2nd, and Andrew J. Smith's 1st.

Debarkation operations continued for about twenty-four hours while General Blair's brigade of the 4th and Colonel John F. De-Courcy's brigade of the 3rd moved out to begin minor skirmishing with Confederate outposts. Late in the day a heavy rain began falling, adding to the difficulties of getting supplies, wagons, and artillery ashore.

"During the night the ground was reconnoitered as well as possible," Sherman reported, "and it was found to be as difficult as it could possibly be from nature and art." By "art" he was referring to the well-placed rifle pits and tangles of trees felled by the Confederates for defense. Just before daylight a rocket streaked across the sky to the east, and the troops broke into cheers. They believed it was a signal from Grant's army, supposed to be approaching in the Confederate rear. They still did not know that they could expect no support from Grant. By dawn of the twenty-seventh, the whole of Sherman's army stood ready to move out in four columns. A cold rain still dripped from dark, lowering skies. "All the heads of columns met the enemy's pickets and drove them toward Vicksburg."

Most of the preliminary skirmishing occurred on Mrs. Lake's plantation in front of Chickasaw Bayou. The main bayou ran in nearly a direct line between the Yazoo and Chickasaw Bluffs.* Before reaching the bluffs the bayou divided into two arms which the New York *Times* reporter described as "something shaped not unlike the letter Y." Each arm of the bayou ran along in front of the bluffs. On the crest of this high ground a county road ran northeastward from Vicksburg.

To reach Vicksburg, the Union force had to cross the two-forked bayou and storm Confederate fortifications which Sherman described as "a series of rifle-pits and batteries, and behind that a high, abrupt range of hills, whose scarred sides were marked all the way up with

[*This geographic area should be identified as the Walnut Hills.]

rifle-trenches, and the crowns of the principal hills presented heavy batteries."

Behind these defenses the Confederates brought up reinforcements as rapidly as possible. On Christmas Day, General Martin L. Smith assigned six regiments of Louisiana and Mississippi troops to Brigadier General Stephen D. Lee and made him responsible for operations along the Yazoo. Lee placed one regiment on the left of the line, one on the right, and concentrated his remaining four at Chickasaw Bayou. During the skirmishing of the twenty-sixth, Lieutenant General John C. Pemberton, commanding the Department of Mississippi and East Louisiana, arrived to assume overall command. By the following day, as Sherman's army began putting pressure on Lee's thin defense line, two brigades of Confederate reinforcements arrived, and four Georgia regiments (Brigadier General Seth M. Barton's brigade) settled in the center along Chickasaw Bluffs.

In the skirmishing of the twenty-seventh on Mrs. Lake's plantation, the 17th and 26th Louisiana and the 46th Mississippi did most of the fighting, capturing several men from the 22nd Kentucky and 16th and 42nd Ohio regiments (DeCourcy's brigade). During that night a light wind blew away the heavy clouds, and before morning stars glittered in the sky. At daylight the soldiers could see frost on open patches of grass in the plantation fields and a thin film of ice along the edges of the bayou.

With a few tentative bursts of artillery from their batteries along the bluffs, the Confederates broke the quietness of Sunday morning, December 28. Sherman ordered his divisions forward to test the Confederate lines. Any breakthrough would of course be exploited, but he was still waiting for some sign of Grant's approach before launching his main assault.

On the Union right, General A. J. Smith's 1st Division advanced until blocked by a tangled abatis which fronted Brigadier General John C. Vaughn's brigade of Confederate Tennesseans. At right center, General Morgan Smith led the 2nd Division to a sandy bog and was there pinned down by Confederate fire. When Smith rode forward to examine the situation, he was caught in a burst of fire from sharpshooters concealed in a canebrake. Turning to his adjutant, Captain Charles McDonald, the General remarked coolly: "Charley, I've got one of them." He had been shot in the hip. He tried to remain in his saddle, but fainted from loss of blood and had to be taken to the rear in an ambulance.

While this occurred, General George W. Morgan's 3rd Division at left center ran into heavy Confederate artillery fire. As on the previous day, DeCourcy's brigade (16th and 42nd Ohio, 54th Indiana, and 22nd Kentucky regiments) bore the brunt of the fighting. A soldier with the 42nd Ohio said the sun appeared "red and ominous through the mists" and that the firing on both sides was fierce and incessant until midmorning. Taking a considerable number of casualties, the brigade moved up to the right-angle bend of Chickasaw Bayou, forcing the 28th Louisiana to retreat from Mrs. Lake's plantation across the bayou to the Confederate entrenchments on the bluffs. Colonel Winchester Hall's 26th Louisiana provided covering fire for the 28th Regiment's withdrawal, which left the 26th in a vulnerable forward position. Before the day ended, forty bullets from sharpshooter's rifles perforated the 26th Louisiana's battle flag.

During this operation, Sherman ordered Blair's brigade of Steele's 4th Division out of its reserve position in order to give support to De-Courcy's brigade. Thus, more than three-fourths of Sherman's army was now operating on the west side of Chickasaw Bayou. Throughout the morning Steele's other two brigades on the east side of the bayou floundered through a morass of sloughs and lagoons. Late in the day, after Blair's regiments engaged in several sharp skirmishes with Louisiana troops, Sherman ordered the brigade to cross the bayou and link up with its division.

A wintry dusk was falling before all of Blair's troops (the 13th Illinois, 29th and 31st Missouri, and 58th Ohio regiments) could cross the muddy bayou. They were unable to reach their division, but took battle positions in a strip of heavy timber, where Blair's last orders of the day were to double pickets and to light no fires. Directly across the bayou from Blair's position, DeCourcy's men bivouacked in the fields of Mrs. Lake's plantation. Each brigade faced an opposite wing

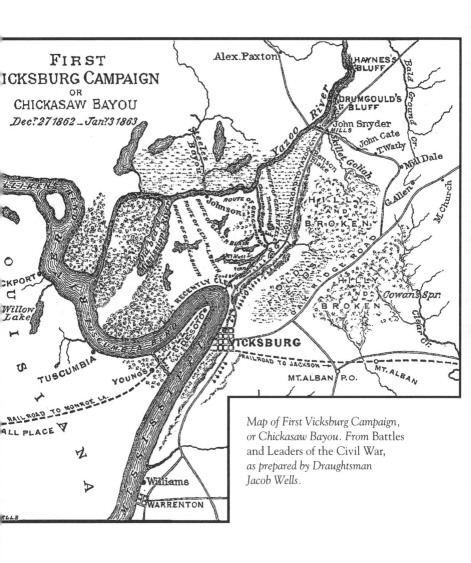

Map of First Vicksburg Campaign, or Chickasaw Bayou. From Battles and Leaders of the Civil War, *as prepared by Draughtsman Jacob Wells.*

of the Y-shaped body of water where two branches joined to form the wider bayou.

Terrain, more than planning, brought these two brigades into assault positions for the Battle of Chickasaw Bluffs. "All other approaches to the bluff were obstructed," the New York *Times* reporter noted, "while this was left open, and for fear that we should not see it, they stationed sharpshooters to attract our attention. Forces landed to drive them back found broad, excellent roads leading across the swamp directly toward the bluffs. This was a combination which would deceive a smarter man than Sherman. He fell into the trap at once, and thus it was that our attack was made at the point where it was."

On that evening (December 28) Sherman made his decision. "Not one word could I hear from General Grant who was supposed to be pushing south. Time being everything to us, I determined to assault the hills in front of Morgan on the morning of the 29th— Morgan's division to carry the position to the summit of the hill, Steele's division to support him and hold the county road. I had placed General A. J. Smith in command of his own division (First) and that of Morgan Smith (Second) with orders to cross on the sand-spit, undermine the steep bank of the bayou on the farther side and carry at all events to the levee parapet and first line of rifle-pits, to prevent a concentration on Morgan."

As Sherman laid his plans for the attack, the Confederates prepared to meet it. "On the conclusion of this day's fighting (December 28) it seemed highly probable," Pemberton said, "that on the next the enemy would make the attempt to carry our position by assault. The dispositions were made accordingly." Parapets were strengthened, additional trenches were dug, and troops repositioned. "During the night," said Stephen D. Lee, who was responsible for the defenses facing the Yazoo, "my command was re-enforced by two regiments and my line of battle fixed." He withdrew Winchester Hall's 26th Louisiana from its forward position in the triangle of the Y, "leaving the road and dry crossing open, virtually inviting the enemy to attack." With their bayonets, the Louisianans dug new trenches 500 yards upslope in the rear of those they had abandoned.

Various units of the Federal army were also busy that night. As a corduroy road and rough log bridge about ten feet wide formed the only dry passage across the right arm of Chickasaw Bayou, Morgan decided to bring up a pontoon train to construct an additional bridge. In the darkness, the engineers bridged the wrong stream—a slough running parallel with the bayou, and when the first light of dawn revealed their error they had to begin all over again. This time the alert Confederate gunners of Lieutenant J. A. Tarleton's Battery D, 1st Mississippi Artillery, thwarted the bridge builders with a few well-directed shots. Their cannonading started a general artillery duel along the length of the three-mile front.

The weather that morning was raw with signs of rain, but through the mists and powder smoke the Union soldiers could see that the Confederates had erected a signal station far back on the bluffs over-looking all the battleground. The correspondent for the St. Louis *Missouri Democrat* reported that "every movement of our troops could be signaled to the Confederate commanders. Many spectators were also posted there with glasses, among whom were a number of women."

About nine o'clock General Morgan abandoned hopes for completion of the temporary bridge and went forward to reconnoiter the bayou. The morass of mud and water was twenty-five yards across and would make a rushing attack impossible; the only alternative was to funnel soldiers over the narrow log bridge. Morgan did not like either prospect; he sent his adjutant back to Sherman's headquarters, respectfully asking him to come to the front.

When Sherman arrived on horseback, he informed Morgan that two of General Steele's brigades were being transferred back to the west side of Chickasaw Bayou, leaving only Blair's brigade on the east side, directly opposite Morgan's 3rd brigade under DeCourcy. For command purposes, Morgan would direct Blair's attack in conjunction with DeCourcy's, while Steele brought up the remainder of his division in support of Morgan.

Morgan called Sherman's attention to the difficult terrain in front of DeCourcy's position—the marshy bayou and the narrow corduroy bridge, both within easy range of Confederate artillery on the bluffs beyond.

"For a time," Morgan said afterward, "General Sherman made no reply. At length, pointing toward the bluffs, he said: 'That is the route to take.' And without another word having been exchanged he rode away to his headquarters behind the forest."

In a hasty conference with Steele, Morgan learned that Brigadier John Thayer's brigade was in position behind DeCourcy but that Brigadier General Charles Hovey's brigade was still unloading from boats at Johnson's Plantation. A few minutes later, Sherman's adjutant arrived with a verbal message: "Tell Morgan to give the signal for the assault; that we will lose 5,000 men before we take Vicksburg, and may as well lose them here as anywhere else."

"Tell General Sherman," Morgan replied, "that I will order the assault; that we may lose 5,000 men, but that his entire army could not carry the enemy's position in my front, that the larger the force sent to the assault, the greater will be the number slaughtered."

With no hope now of changing Sherman's battle plan, Morgan sent orders to Blair and DeCourcy to form their brigades for a coordinated attack across the two arms of the bayou. DeCourcy came hurrying back. "General, do I understand that you are about to order an assault?" he asked.

"Yes, form your brigade!" Morgan responded.

"My poor brigade!" DeCourcy cried, and then saluted. "Your order will be obeyed, General."

Shortly before noon, Morgan ordered his artillery to open fire. To his right, the batteries of A. J. Smith's 1st Division also laid down a barrage for a diversionary attack. "This attack," Sherman later said, "had to be made across a narrow sand bar and up a narrow path, as a diversion in favor of Morgan." The regiment chosen for this dangerous feint was the 6th Missouri, which took heavy casualties before reaching the foot of Chickasaw Bluffs directly under the Confederate rifle pits. There for the remainder of the battle, the Missourians were compelled to hover close against the steep bank, yet they drew a full Confederate regiment away from the main attack point.

Blair and DeCourcy meanwhile sent their brigades into battle. "The regiments under my command were drawn up in two lines of battle about 150 feet apart," Blair said, "the 13th Illinois holding the right front and the 58th Ohio in the rear. The 31st Missouri occupied the left front, with the 29th Missouri in rear."

"The orders were 'Guide Right, double-quick'," Albert Sibley of H Company, 13th Illinois later recalled. "I looked at the line just before we came to the water, which many could not jump across, and I remarked that though the wings traveled a little the fastest, and the line curved a little . . . the front was bold and magnificent."

From the bluffs General Stephen D. Lee watched the blue lines of his enemy "move gallantly up under our artillery fire." Lee had eight cannon cross-firing upon what he estimated to be 6,000 Union troops. Actually, fewer than 4,000 men of Sherman's mighty army were committed to the battle—about 1,800 in Blair's brigade, 1,500 in De-Courcy's, and a few hundred in Thayer's troops. Waiting for them were seven Confederate regiments dug in on the high ground—the 17th, 26th, and 28th Louisiana, the 42nd Georgia, and the 3rd, 30th, and 80th Tennessee.

General Blair's advance was first slowed by a tangle of young cotton-woods which the Confederates had cut down and entwined among the stumps. After passing through this obstacle, the Federal troops reached the "deep and miry" bayou. Blair was mounted, but the correspondent of the *Missouri Democrat* reported that "his horse got inextricably mired, and the general coolly slid down his head, and led his brigade the remainder of the way on foot." One of the Ohioans in DeCourcy's brigade just across the bayou was surprised to see Blair, with two pistols drawn, floundering through the mud and water with his men.

As soon as Blair's troops struggled out of the bayou they had to climb a ten-foot embankment covered with a strong abatis and crowned with rifle pits from which the Confederates had withdrawn in favor of entrenchments higher up the slope. DeCourcy's 16th Ohio poured into the abandoned pits just as Blair's 13th Illinois reached the same position. Clambering over the first line of pits, the Illinois troops drove on toward the Confederates' second line.

The "gallant charge" of the Union's 6th Missouri Infantry Regiment failed to break through the Confederate fortifications, trapping them against an embankment. Under cover of darkness later that evening, their commander, Lieutenant Colonel James H. Blood, led them out, with a loss earlier of fourteen killed and forty-three wounded. From Harper's Weekly, January 31, 1863.

General Pemberton, who observed the Union assault, reported that the soldiers in blue "moved gallantly forward under a heavy fire of our artillery." He said they advanced to within 150 yards of the Confederate main defense line "when they broke and retreated, but soon rallied, and dividing their forces sent a portion to their right, which was gallantly driven back by the 28th Louisiana and 42nd Georgia Regiments with heavy loss."

DeCourcy's brigade, which attacked simultaneously with Blair's, had to advance by columns in order to make use of the narrow bridge. Although the 22nd Kentucky and 42nd Ohio moved quickly across, they became entangled in an almost impassable abatis and their rear units blocked the crossing. DeCourcy ordered the 16th Ohio and 54th Indiana into a flanking movement, and to his and Morgan's surprise they crossed the bayou without a bridge. These troops struggled out of the muddy water and deployed on the open slope. As they began charging toward the first line of abandoned rifle pits, DeCourcy said that a "fearfully destructive fire poured in from front, left, right, and even rear, for as soon as these regiments had advanced a few hundred yards toward the works the enemy opened with a battery in rear of the left of their advance." In other words, DeCourcy was forced to advance against a concave line of battle.

"All formations were broken," Morgan said. "The assaulting forces were jammed together and, with a yell of desperate determination, they rushed to the assault and were mowed down by a storm of shells, grape, and canister, and minie-balls which swept our front like a hurricane of fire." In a matter of minutes, twelve officers of the 16th Ohio, including the commander, were casualties. The commander of the 58th Ohio and three officers of the 22nd Kentucky were killed.

Thayer's brigade of five Iowa regiments meanwhile had been brought up in column as support for DeCourcy. "About 2 P.M.," General Thayer said, "I received an order from General Steele to move my brigade forward. By advice of General Morgan I dismounted and directed all officers mounted to do the same, as we would be sure to draw the fire of the enemy's sharpshooters if mounted. The 4th

Iowa, Colonel J. A. Williamson, was on the right. I took my place at the head of the column and moved forward by the right flank."

By this time the bridge over the bayou was cleared, and the 7th and 4th Iowa pushed rapidly across. "As the head of the column merged from the crossing," Colonel Williamson later reported, "it became exposed to a terrific fire of musketry from the intrench-ments in front and also to a fire from the enemy's batteries on the right and left flanks." After effecting the crossing, General Thayer ordered Williamson to file sharply to the right. It was Thayer's under-standing that his brigade was to form an assault force on the right of DeCourcy. To move into this position his men had to dismantle a rail fence. While this operation was under way, Thayer told Colonel Williamson to form the regiment into line while he went back to bring his other four regiments into parallel lines for an assault on the heights.

"When I turned back," Thayer said afterward, "to my dismay and horror, I found only the 4th Iowa Infantry had followed me. No other regiment was to be seen. It was awful—a repetition of Balaklava, although mine was infantry and Earl Cardigan's force was cavalry."

What had occurred was the result of a misunderstanding of orders. A few minutes after Thayer led the 4th Iowa across the log bridge, Morgan encountered Steele and hurriedly advised him to make certain that Thayer's brigade kept turning to the right of DeCourcy's troops. Believing that Morgan meant that the other Iowa regiments were to move to the right of the bridge crossing, Steele consequently turned them too far to the right, and they were blocked by an impas-sable tangle of trees which had been felled on both sides of the bayou.

(For years this misunderstanding was to be a point of contention between Thayer and his superior officers. In 1891, after he became governor of Nebraska, Thayer wrote: "My regret always has been that I did not prefer charges against Morgan and Steele, for between them they were responsible for one of the most terrible blunders which has ever occurred in military affairs.")

Thayer was in turn criticized for ordering the 4th Iowa to with-draw. "It was nothing but slaughter for it to remain," he declared.

During the thirty minutes the regiment was under fire, 112 of its 480 officers and men became casualties.

By this time Blair was dismayed by the rapidly thinning ranks of his brigade. "Some reached the foot of these formidable works only to pour out their lives at the base," he said. The *Missouri Democrat* correspondent who was with him wrote that "the ground was covered with the dead and dying. The brigade went into action with less than 1900 men, and of this number 645 were lost in killed, wounded, and taken prisoners."

DeCourcy's 16th Ohio, 22nd Kentucky, and 54th Indiana were shattered. "I resolved not to expose the 42nd Ohio to useless destruction," he said. "I therefore halted this regiment and deployed it to cover the retreat of the repulsed regiments." Except for artillery strikes, the Union soldiers did little damage to the Confederates. As one of DeCourcy's officers said, "Hardly a shot had been fired by our advancing column. The fire which it faced had been so terrible that it could not stop to fight at such hopeless odds."

Colonel Winchester Hall of the 26th Louisiana was amazed that the union infantrymen were able to come within fifty yards of his entrenchments under such a terrific storm of shot and shell. General Stephen D. Lee, after complimenting his Tennessee riflemen for their coolness and steady fire, expressed admiration for the attacking Union forces. "No troops could have behaved better than the troops which reached the plateau. They were met by a withering fire of eight guns and several regiments from the front and two regiments on the right flank, and the column rapidly melted away. . . . As soon as they began to get close to our line they were literally mowed down. . . ."

Lee said nothing about a rout or panic among the Union soldiers, but other Confederate officers reported that they retreated in "wild confusion" or "like a frightened flock of sheep." General Morgan admitted that his attacking force was terribly repulsed but was not beaten. "Our troops fell back slowly and angrily to our own line, halted, re-formed, and, if ordered, would again have rushed to the assault."

Late on that cloud-darkened afternoon the 6th Missouri Infantry, which had attempted a diversionary attack a few hundred yards to the Union right, still lay trapped below an overhang of Chickasaw Bluffs. In trenches directly above them sat riflemen of Colonel C. H. Morrison's 31st Louisiana. Two companies of the Missourians had brought along picks and spades in hopes of breaching the Confederate fortifications from below, but a flanking movement by Colonel C. D. Phillips's 52nd Georgia forced the Missourians to cling to cover under the embankment. "No more desperate enterprise was ever undertaken," commented the correspondent for the *Missouri Democrat*. Conversations between opponents were carried on throughout the afternoon. "What regiment is below?" asked one of the Louisianans. "Sixth Missouri," came the proud reply. The Louisianan countered with: "You're too brave a regiment to be on the wrong side." Later in the day a Missourian called out: "Have you got anything to eat up there? I'm hungry." The Louisianans, being served hot bread from Vicksburg kitchens, immediately dropped down a large loaf, and the Missourians cheered loudly. Not until after nightfall, however, was Lieutenant Colonel James Blood able to extricate the Missourians from their precarious position. "Under cover of the rain and darkness he brought his regiment, a company at a time, until all were over."

On the main battlefield, as the Union regiments retreated, Confederate soldiers from the 17th and 26th Louisiana moved out about 100 yards to capture 21 officers and 311 enlisted men. Most of them were wounded or suffering from battle fatigue, the majority being from DeCourcy's luckless 16th Ohio and 54th Indiana.

According to General Morgan, Sherman refused to let him send out a truce party to recover dead and wounded until dusk had fallen. "It had become so dark that the flag could not be seen, and the escort was fired upon and driven back. The next morning, December 30th, I sent another flag. . . . a truce was promptly granted and all of our wounded that had not been carried into the Confederate lines as prisoners, and our dead, were at once brought within our lines. It has been charged that the enemy on the field of Chickasaw stripped our dead of their clothing. That charge is unjust and should not go into history. I saw our dead as they were brought in; all were in their uniforms." Newspaper correspondents reported that many Confederate soldiers came down to the flag of truce "and in some instances assisted in burying the dead."

When the losses were totaled for the four days of fighting, the ratio was ten to one—almost 2,000 Union casualties against fewer than 200 for the Confederates. Despite this serious reversal, Sherman was not yet ready to abandon his efforts to take Vicksburg. He still held hopes that Grant's army would suddenly appear in the Confederate's rear. For forty-eight hours following the repulse at Chickasaw Bluffs, he busily planned a new attack. Admiral Porter would transport 10,000 men up the Yazoo to Snyder's Mill; there the troops would storm ashore and attempt to turn the Confederate right flank. Weather foiled all his plans. A dense fog made it impossible for the boats to move, and then torrential rains turned the army's base into a quagmire. Fearing a flood which might drown his entire command, Sherman on New Year's Day ordered a general withdrawal.

On January 2 the flotilla steamed out of the Yazoo and up the Mississippi to Milliken's Bend. There Sherman met Major General John McClernand, who carried orders in his pocket placing him in command of the river expedition and reducing Sherman to a corps commander. McClernand also brought news of Grant's retreat in Mississippi.

On that January day in 1863, Vicksburg seemed secure to the Confederacy; Pemberton showed evidences of a brilliant career; McClernand appeared to be a rising star among the Union commanders; and Sherman's future looked very dark indeed. But another six months of siege and battle lay ahead for Vicksburg, the key to the western Confederacy. When that grueling campaign was ended in July not one of these foretokens of January would prove to be true.

Brigadier General Stephen D. Lee, as commander of Provisional Division, 2nd Military District, Department of Mississippi and East Louisiana, played a major role in repelling Sherman's attack at Chickasaw Bayou. From Battles and Leaders of the Civil War.

BELOW: *The location of cannon in this war-time sketch depicts the forward advance of the Union's Second Division under Brigadier General Morgan L. Smith, who was able to look across Chickasaw Bayou and see the bluffs immediately north of Vicksburg, but could not mount an effective attack without suffering heavy casualties. From* Battles and Leaders of the Civil War.

Colonel Benjamin H. Grierson led approximately 1,700 cavalrymen in a sixteen-day, 800-mile ride through the heart of Mississippi to distract Confederate forces from Major General Ulysses S. Grant's campaign against Vicksburg. From Frank Leslie's Illustrated History of the Civil War, 1861–65, page 416.

6

'the most brilliant expedition of the war'

Grierson's Raid

"In a 17-day march across Mississippi and Louisiana, these 1,700 troopers tied up thousands of Confederate soldiers and diverted attention from Grant's advance on Vicksburg."

*U*nlike many cavalry expeditions of the Civil War, Grierson's Raid, which began on April 17, 1863, at La Grange, Tennessee, and ended seventeen days later at Baton Rouge, Louisiana, was a real contribution to an important military victory—the capture of Vicksburg. It was a classic example of continuous military deception, a journey in suspense with success or failure in doubt until the last day.

"A cavalry raid at its best," said Sergeant Stephen Forbes, one of Grierson's cavalrymen, "is essentially a *game* of strategy and speed, with personal violence as an incidental complication. It is played according to more or less definite rules, not inconsistent, indeed, with the players' killing each other if the game cannot be won in any other way; but it is commonly a strenuous game, rather than a bloody one, intensely exciting, but not necessarily very dangerous."

To understand the purpose of the raid, one must review the progress of the Union army from the Battle of Shiloh in April 1862 through the sluggish operations around Corinth and Iuka in the summer of that year, General Grant's failure to move down through Mississippi, and General Sherman's repulse at Chickasaw Bluffs in December. During the winter of 1862–63, Grant amassed a huge army

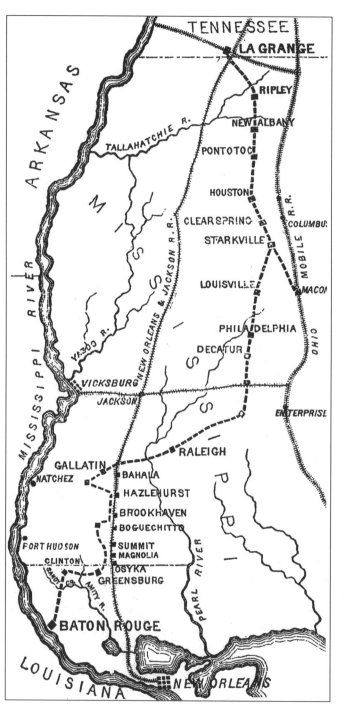

Map of Grierson's Raid (broken line) from La Grange, Tennessee, to Baton Rouge, Louisiana. From Harper's New Monthly Magazine, February 1865.

across the Mississippi River from the impregnable heights of Vicksburg. By springtime he was preparing to make his eighth attempt to capture that stronghold, which President Lincoln considered the key to victory in the West. "The war can never be brought to a close until that key is in our pocket," Lincoln said.

Grant was determined that this assault must succeed, and as a part of his operations he planned a cavalry strike straight down through the heart of Mississippi. The raid would have two purposes: (1) to sever the railroad which brought Confederate munitions and supplies to Vicksburg from the east; (2) to distract the Confederate high command's attention from the Union Army as it prepared to move across the river. The raiders must be seasoned cavalrymen; the timing of the raid must be coordinated with Grant's attack.

To lead the raid, Grant chose Colonel Benjamin Henry Grierson, assigning him three cavalry regiments, the 6th and 7th Illinois and the 2nd Iowa, with a supporting detachment of six two-pounder guns from Battery K, 1st Illinois Artillery. Most of these men had eighteen months of training and combat experience behind them.

Benjamin Grierson was thirty-seven, a wiry, gangling man, his swarthy, scar-marked face surrounded by rich black hair and a beard worn in the down-spreading spade shape of the times. He was a musician with a profound distrust of horses, and he would have much preferred leading an orchestra than a brigade of wild-riding cavalrymen.

Grierson's distrust of horses dated from an accident when he was eight. A supposedly friendly pony had kicked him in the face, splitting his forehead and mangling one cheek. For two months he was blinded, and he carried the scars to his grave. At thirteen, when his family lived in Youngstown, Ohio, after moving there from Pittsburgh where he was born, he had organized his first concert band. Before he left Ohio for Illinois in 1851, he was composing and arranging music for bands and orchestras.

In Illinois, Grierson set himself up as a music teacher in the pleasant little village of Jacksonville and began organizing amateur bands there and in neighboring towns. By 1858, he was an active partisan for Abraham Lincoln, composing several songs for his political campaigns. When the war came in 1861 and Lincoln issued the first call for volunteers, Grierson joined an infantry company and went to Cairo, Illinois. While there he was offered a major's rank in the only service he wished to avoid—the cavalry.

Considering his early misfortune with the pony, it is not surprising that he tried to avoid going into the war burdened with cavalrymen and their skittish mounts. He countered the Army's offer with a request to be transferred—anywhere to avoid cavalry service. But the commanding general of the Western Department, Henry W. Halleck, flatly refused. "General Halleck," Grierson later said, "jocularly remarked that I looked active and wiry enough to make a good cavalryman."

And so in December 1861, Major Benjamin Grierson reported for duty with the 6th Illinois Cavalry Regiment, at Shawneetown, Illinois. A few months later he became a colonel of the regiment. During most of 1862, Grierson's 6th Illinois was engaged in hard riding and fighting in Tennessee and northern Mississippi with General Sherman's army.

Early in April 1863, Grierson received orders to start a raid from La Grange, Tennessee, on the seventeenth, to coincide with Grant's movements against Vicksburg. At dawn of that day, he led his 1,700 cavalrymen southward, the columns of twos coiling down into the shortleaf pine forest, across Wolf River, and through the blue hills into Mississippi. They moved at the standard rate of three miles per hour, with ten-minute rest stops. Near Ripley, after a brief skirmish with a small Confederate scouting party, the brigade went into camp a few miles east of Colonel William C. Falkner's plantation. (Colonel Falkner was the great-grandfather of novelist William Faulkner, who added a "u" to the family name.)

For the next three days they marched steadily southward, meeting no opposition; but by April 19, Confederate commanders in eastern Mississippi were beginning to suspect that this Union cavalry expedition was more than a mere reconnaissance. On the evening of the nineteenth, a Confederate courier rode into headquarters of the 2nd Tennessee Confederate Regiment near Verona with news that a heavy Union cavalry force was at Pontotoc. Suspecting that the Yankees' objectives were Confederate supply bases, the commander of the 2nd Tennessee, Colonel Clark Barteau, ordered all available mounted men to prepare for a night march against the enemy.

At midnight, Colonel Barteau started his troops westward. Ironically, Barteau was not a native Southerner; he was an Ohioan, born less than 100 miles from Grierson's home in Youngstown. He had moved to Tennessee to become a teacher and newspaper editor; by the time the Civil War began, he was a fully committed Southerner, eager to join the Confederate Army.

Before dawn on April 20, the fourth day of the raid, Grierson played his first trick against the Confederates. All ailing men and failing horses were ordered out of company ranks, organized into a "Quinine Brigade," and placed under command of Major Hiram Love of the 2nd Iowa for return to La Grange.

A dismal drizzle was falling when Major Love and his detachment of 175 men filed out of the encampment. One of the two-pounder cannon, with its complement of corporal and five men, rolled down to join the procession. Above the rattle of coffee tins and harness chains the commands came hoarsely through the dripping trees: "Fours right! March! Halt! Forward, march!" The Quinine Brigade swung away beyond the wooded camp in columns of fours to leave behind them imprinted on the road the apparent evidence that a regiment had turned back here.

A few hours later Colonel Barteau's Confederate column rode into Pontotoc, discovered the reversed track, and lost valuable time before learning that the main column was still headed south down the road to Houston. On that same day, Lieutenant General John C. Pemberton, directing the Confederate defense of Mississippi, took first notice of Grierson's expedition by dispatching a message to Brigadier General Daniel Ruggles at Columbus: "This is a mere raid, but should not be unmolested by you."

Next morning Grierson was below Houston, preparing a new deception for the Confederates. This time he chose Colonel Edward Hatch's 2nd Iowa as a decoy party; Hatch's mission was to disengage the main column from the enemy now pressing behind it, leaving Grierson free to continue rapidly southward.

Before the day ended, Hatch's Iowans and Barteau's Tennesseans came together near Palo Alto in a sharp running fight. The two-pounder gun assigned to Hatch's regiment proved the decisive factor, and the Iowans shook themselves loose from their pursuers and made their way back toward La Grange.

Meanwhile Grierson's main column had moved below Starkville. On the morning of April 22 he detached another decoy group, this time a single company of thirty-four men, Company B of the 7th Illinois. The commander of Company B was Captain Henry C. Forbes, a sensitive, well-read farmer from northern Illinois who usually carried a copy of Emerson's *The Conduct of Life* in his saddlebag. He disliked military life intensely, but had a high sense of duty and felt a personal responsibility for the safety of his men, one of whom was his younger brother, Stephen Forbes.

Captain Forbes's mission was to turn east, approach Macon, and create enough disturbance to convince the enemy that his company was the main body of raiders. Afterwards, he could attempt a return to La Grange or rejoin the main column. Either alternative would be perilous. Company B was too small a force to offer much resistance to attack, and unless luck was with them, capture was almost inevitable.

As soon as Company B moved out, Grierson turned the main column westward, seeking a route around flooded bottomlands. The march was slow and difficult, through gloomy cypress swamps, and by day's end they were only ten miles below Louisville. They found dry ground on Estes Plantation and camped until daylight.

During the first week of the raid, Grierson had encouraged the organization of a scouting group known as "the Butternut Guerrillas," placing them under command of Lieutenant Colonel William Blackburn. Had Blackburn lived longer than the twenty-six more days which fate allotted to him, he might have become the "Jeb" Stuart of the Union Army, for there was an insouciant, extravagant quality in his character matching that of the brilliant Virginian. Blackburn loved hard rides and dashing charges, and if any member of Grierson's raiders deserved to wear a plume in his hat, he was the man.

Early in the war, Blackburn had been attracted to a kindred spirit in his ranks, Sergeant Richard Surby, a Canadian who had moved to Illinois and answered the first call for volunteers in 1861. Surby was, in his own words, "possessed of a venturesome disposition," and it is probable that a conversation he had with Blackburn led to the organization of the Butternut Guerrillas. "I received orders," Surby later wrote, "to take six or eight men, proceed at once on the advance and procure citizens' dress, saddles, shot guns, and everything necessary for our disguise."

On April 23, the seventh day of the raid, the Butternut Guerrillas proved their worth at Pearl River. As the column approached the flooded stream, Grierson grew concerned over the safety of the single bridge crossing. He knew that if news of the raid had swept ahead of them, the bridge certainly would be heavily guarded, might already have been destroyed. And should the crossing be blocked, the delay would give the Confederates time to assemble troops along the now obvious objective of the raid, the Vicksburg railroad.

He ordered Lieutenant Colonel Blackburn to send his scouts forward on the double with instructions to use extra caution in approaching the bridge. If the bridge was unguarded they were to secure it immediately, but if heavily guarded, that information should be brought back at once to the main column.

The Butternut Guerrillas, in their civilian dress, galloped away over a narrow road running through thinly settled country. About two miles before reaching the bridge, Sergeant Surby took a short lead over his seven scouts. A few moments later he saw an old man approaching on a mule. "We entered into conversation," Surby wrote afterwards. "The old man informed me that guards were stationed at the bridge, numbering five in all, his son being one of the party. They had torn up several planks from the center of the bridge, and had placed combustibles on it ready to ignite at our approach."

Surby then asked the old man his name and place of residence, and when they were given, he took pencil and paper from inside his

A combination of trickery and courage enabled Sergeant Richard Surby and seven Butternut Guerrillas on April 23 to save this bridge over the Pearl River, thus enabling the main body of Grierson's three regiments to cross shortly thereafter. The artist exaggerates the size of the bridge and the number of men defending it. From Harper's New Monthly Magazine, *February 1865.*

shirt and wrote down the information. This frightened the old man and he began to babble: "Gentlemen, gentlemen, you are not what you seem to be, you certainly are Yankees!"

Resolved to frighten the man into unconditional surrender of the bridge, Surby replied quickly: "It lies in your power to save your buildings from the torch, to save your own life, and probably that of your son, by saving the bridge."

Trembling with fear, the old man said that he was confident of saving the bridge. Surby ordered him to return and advise the guards to surrender and accept paroles; if they damaged the bridge the old man's house and barns would be destroyed.

"I impatiently followed the figure of the old man with my eye," Surby later wrote. "When within a dozen yards of the bridge, he halted, and commenced telling his errand; but ere he was hardly half through, I could perceive some signs of uneasiness on the side of his listeners; they all at once jumped upon their horses and away they went. We then advanced to the bridge and replaced the planks." Thus through sheer audacity and trickery, the bridge was captured.

Again, in the early morning of April 24, the Butternut Guerrillas outfoxed the Confederates by moving leisurely into Newton Station and obtaining information concerning military strength in the town and the expected arrival times of trains on the railroad. Newton was Grierson's main objective, a small station on the Vicksburg railroad. The scouts reported back to Blackburn, and blue-uniformed cavalrymen were soon galloping into the startled town.

Less than a mile to the east, above a pine forest, a black streamer of smoke marked the slow approach of a freight train. Blackburn immediately sent pickets scattering through the town to block roads and approaches. He ordered his troops to conceal themselves from view of the oncoming train; the men dismounted and horse-holders led the mounts behind buildings.

A few moments later the oversized cowcatcher of the squat little freight engine emerged from the pines. It was a noisy train, with wheels pounding, cars rattling, locomotive puffing and blowing with its weight of twenty-five loaded cars. Blackburn stood beside the station, inconspicuous in the shade, watching its slow approach. A brakeman dropped off a sidestep, hurried to the switch, turned and locked it in place. The train crept slowly onto the siding.

If the engineer glanced at the railroad station, he saw only Colonel Blackburn, whose blue uniform was concealed by dust and a caking of mud, and three Butternut Guerrillas in civilian dress. The town itself seemed deserted. Unseen horses nickered, answered by others. The engine began to slow, its wheel flanges clanking. Steam and smoke swirled across the front of the little station.

Then, on a signal from Blackburn, the cavalrymen in a sweeping charge swarmed out on foot from behind buildings. Within a few seconds they had captured their first train. It was loaded with railroad ties, bridge planking, and ordnance and commissary supplies for Vicksburg, all precious to the Confederacy, necessary for the continuing defense of Vicksburg.

A few minutes later they captured a passenger train headed in the opposite direction, and soon afterwards Grierson led the main column into Newton Station to find the town swirling with dust, smoke, steam, and confusion.

By early afternoon the raiders had wrecked a long section of track and destroyed telegraph wires. They had dealt a severe blow not only to the railroad but to Vicksburg defenses. On that same day, Grant was making his last reconnaissance before ordering his army across the Mississippi to cut off Vicksburg.

After the raid on Newton Station, Grierson's troopers knew that only cunning and swift movement could save them from disaster. The enemy was at every compass point and would surely pursue them with renewed fury. Would Grierson order them back north into a countryside filled with aroused citizens and Confederate soldiers? It seemed unlikely, and few were surprised when their commander ordered the column southward into the unknown heartland of the enemy.

Meanwhile, the thirty-four men of Captain Forbes's Company B who had been detached forty-eight hours earlier had more than fulfilled their mission by creating diversions at Macon and Enterprise. At Enterprise, they deceived Confederate forces there into believing they were more than 1,000 strong, and by dawn of April 25 they were galloping down the road into Newton Station, where fires kindled by Grierson's men the previous day still drifted smoke over the desolate town.

Since three men could move faster than thirty-four, Captain Forbes asked for volunteers to ride on and overtake the column. One of the volunteers was his younger brother, Sergeant Stephen Forbes, who left a vivid account of that swift gallop: "Black night now fell, with drizzling rain, and we dismounted now and then to make sure, by feeling the road, that we were still on the track of the regiments." Once or twice Stephen thought he heard voices and hoofbeats ahead, but when he dashed forward in the solid blackness, he found nothing but the bitter frustration of one who pursues a mirage. At last he sighted a lantern flickering like a yellow firefly far down in the trees, and then out of a canebrake came a call to halt.

The destruction of railroad tracks by Federal troops was an ongoing objective of most raiding parties and was eagerly carried out by Grierson's horse soldiers. From Frank Leslie's Illustrated History of the Civil War, 1861–65, *page 270.*

"Company B!" he shouted. The pickets responded with a cheer: "Company B has come back!"

Stephen and his two companions reached Grierson just as the colonel was turning his horse onto a bridge across Strong River. The young sergeant halted beside Grierson: "Captain Forbes presents his compliments, and begs to be allowed to burn his bridges for himself!"

Grierson assured Sergeant Forbes that the bridge-burning detail would be augmented into a guard detachment to await the arrival of Company B. A few hours later, Captain Forbes's company crossed the bridge safely, and left it in flames behind them.

Proof that Company B's diversionary movement had completely deceived the Confederates exists in a message which General Pemberton sent to Brigadier General J. R. Chalmers that same day: "Move with your cavalry and light artillery via Oxford, to Okolona, to intercept force of enemy." At that very hour, Grierson's raiders were 200 miles south of Okolona!

During the next two days, April 27–28, the raiders captured a ferry and crossed a river to Hazlehurst, dispatched a false telegram to

General Pemberton's Confederate headquarters in Jackson advising him that the Union raiders were moving in a northerly direction, and then in actuality galloped straight westward toward the Mississippi River. Aware of Grant's plan for crossing the river and attacking Vicksburg from the landward side, Grierson now had high hopes of joining forces with that besieging army.

By this time, General Pemberton had learned the bitter truth—that at least two regiments of Union cavalry had cut his Vicksburg railroad, and were now south of his headquarters. He became so concerned over the presence of enemy forces driving through the heart of Mississippi that he fell into Grant's trap: he ordered Colonel Wirt Adams' Confederate cavalry withdrawn from defensive positions along the Mississippi River, leaving the eastern bank around Grand Gulf open for an unopposed landing by Union troops. Grierson's raid had now fulfilled both its missions.

Pemberton's orders, however, made it impossible for Grierson to connect his cavalry with Grant's invading army. Near Union Church on the afternoon of April 28, the raiders' pickets were fired upon by Confederate riflemen. For the first time since leaving La Grange, after eleven days of marching through Confederate territory, the 6th and 7th Illinois Cavalry were now challenged by a sizeable enemy force. In a sharp skirmish, one raider was wounded. At dusk, when fighting ended, Grierson still held Union Church, but he shrewdly decided that he must turn southward for Union-held Baton Rouge.

If he had had any inkling of the numerous Confederate units that were racing to trap his column, he might have been more hesitant about turning east toward Brookhaven. In addition to Wirt Adams' cavalry waiting in ambush west of Union Church, three companies of mounted infantry were hurrying down from Jackson. From the south, 2,000 infantrymen, 300 cavalrymen, and a battery of artillery were moving to close the roads to Baton Rouge.

After burning trestles along the New Orleans & Jackson Railroad, the raiders moved southward along the tracks to Summit, destroying military supplies and "capturing" thirty barrels of rum, which Grierson prudently ordered destroyed to avoid a premature celebration by his thirsty troopers. That night, when the raiders went into camp on an isolated plantation, their fantastic luck still held. Two large Confederate forces, desperately searching for them, also went into camp, one only four miles west of Grierson's men, the other fifteen miles to the east. None of the three was aware of the presence of the others.

At dawn on May 1, the fifteenth day of the raid, there was nothing to indicate that Grierson's luck might change. The column moved rapidly along the thickly forested watershed between the Amite and Tickfaw Rivers, encountering only a few civilians during the morning. Around ten o'clock the scouts discovered the tracks of an enemy force which was traveling in the same direction the column would have to follow in order to cross the Tickfaw at Wall's Bridge. Grierson immediately ordered Blackburn to take Sergeant Surby's Butternut Guerrillas forward and scout the bridge.

After a comic opera encounter with two Confederate officers, Surby easily captured them, but as he and Blackburn started across the bridge they found themselves suddenly ambushed. Rifle fire exploded out of the forest; both Blackburn and Surby were severely wounded. The scouts fell back in disorder until the main body of raiders came galloping down the sandy road. Grierson dismounted his men, ordered the two-pounder guns into action, sent two battalions of the 6th Regiment to right and left in flanking movements, and then charged the bridge with a third.

Outmanned and outgunned, the Confederate ambush collapsed and became a rapid retreat. While the 6th Illinois was still in pursuit, the 7th went forward to gather up the casualties. Five men had been wounded, five had been captured and taken away by the fleeing Confederates. As soon as beds could be found in a plantation house for the wounded, Grierson ordered the march resumed. (Two of the wounded men later died, one of them being Lieutenant Colonel Blackburn.)

From the time they crossed the Amite River at midnight, through the twelve hours until noon of May 2, Grierson's 900 tired, hungry raiders dared not risk their luck again by halting to eat or rest. Baton Rouge, their goal and sanctuary, still lay thirty miles away, and even

Colonel Benjamin H. Grierson (unidentified) and officers gather under a brush arbor after arriving in Baton Rouge, Louisiana. Courtesy of Andrew D. Lytle Collections, MS 1254, Louisiana and Lower Mississippi Valley Collections, Louisiana State University Libraries, Baton Rouge, Louisiana.

a short delaying fight now might give the enemy time to bring up forces too formidable to outrun or defeat, might undo all their clever feints and long, hard rides. And so they moved on through the night under the ghostly moss-hung trees, past shadows of plantation houses and sugar mills. Sleep was now the enemy. Fifteen days and nights of riding—with nerves and muscles always taut, with rest measured out by minutes—began to take their toll now.

Three miles west of the Comite River, they halted near a large plantation house. The regiments were ordered to fall out, feed, and rest. "So tired they were," Grierson later wrote, " they scarcely waited for food, before every man save two or three was in a profound slumber." To keep himself awake Grierson entered the plantation house, wandered into the parlor and began playing upon a piano which he found there. "I astonished the occupants by sitting down and playing . . . and in that manner I managed to keep awake, while my soldiers were enjoying themselves by relaxation, sleep, and quiet rest."

Grierson did not record what music he played at his moment of triumph, but he did tell of his thoughts: "Only six miles then to Baton Rouge and four miles would bring us inside the lines guarded by the soldiers of the Union. Think of the great relief to the over-taxed mind and nerves. I felt that we had nobly accomplished the work assigned to us and no wonder that I felt musical; who would not under like circumstances?"

A short time later, a Union cavalry patrol out of Baton Rouge approached the plantation where the raiders were resting. As the Baton Rouge command had heard nothing of Grierson's raid, the patrol suspected the dusty horses and men were Confederates and prepared for a fight.

Colonel Grierson described the encounter: "I rode out to meet them, and found it difficult to approach, so cautious were they, with their skirmishers creeping along behind the fences. By this time the captain in charge of the patrol had dismounted his men." Grierson also dismounted and walked forward, waving his handkerchief and shouting out his name. "The captain then climbed on the fence while I kept on towards him, and soon thereafter he jumped off to the ground and when we met and shook hands, his soldiers sprang up and clambered onto the fence and gave a shout."

That afternoon the raiders entered Baton Rouge on parade. It was probably the most tatterdemalion procession ever officially sponsored by the United States Army, moving into the streets of Baton Rouge about three o'clock in the afternoon of May 2, 1863. A number of the raiders had exchanged their woolen blouses for captured linen dusters; many were hatless, trousers were ripped and torn, boots were cracked and crusted with mud.

"For half a mile before entering the city," wrote Grierson, "the road was lined with wondering spectators, old and young, male and female, rich and poor, white and black, citizens and soldiers. Amidst shouts and cheers, and waving of banners, heralded by music, the tired troops marched through the city, around the public square, down to the river to water their horses, and then to Magnolia Grove, two miles south of the city."

Thus was ended Grierson's Raid. "The most brilliant expedition of the war," said General Sherman when he learned of it. And General Grant, who was now approaching Vicksburg and ultimate victory, saluted the raid's importance with one of his terse comments: "It will be handed down in history as an example to be imitated . . . Grierson attracted the attention of the enemy from the main movement against Vicksburg."

Brigadier General John Hunt Morgan, an outstanding cavalryman and raider who found it difficult to operate within the constraints often imposed by his superiors, violated General Braxton Bragg's instructions that prohibited crossing the Ohio River. From Frank Leslie's Illustrated History of the Civil War, 1861–65, page 406.

7

The Great Raid Begins

(Morgan's Raid In Indiana and Ohio)

1

Although General (John Hunt) Morgan was confident in early June of 1863 that he would receive authorization for a raid across the Ohio River, (General) Braxton Bragg never issued such an order. Bragg only wanted Morgan to enter Kentucky and make a threat against Louisville—a mere diversionary raid to take pressure off the Army of Tennessee for a few days.

Bragg's forces had been seriously weakened by the sudden removal of several divisions under General Joseph E. Johnston, rushed to Mississippi in hopes of relieving besieged Vicksburg. Fearing for the safety of his army after Johnston's departure, Bragg decided to withdraw to more easily defended positions below the Tennessee River. To accomplish this maneuver without inviting attack, he needed action elsewhere to distract the enemy's attention. A raid by Morgan, he thought, would be sufficient distraction, and it was for this reason in the main that Bragg granted Morgan permission to march north.

When final orders reached Morgan's headquarters at Alexandria, instructing him to move into Kentucky—but not to cross the Ohio River—Morgan decided forthwith that he had had enough of Bragg's timidity. He was determined to strike for Indiana as planned. He revealed his decision to disobey Bragg to only one officer, his brother-in-law, Basil Duke. In recording the incident afterward, Duke made no apologies for his commander, stating simply: "So positively were Morgan's convictions that in order to be of any benefit in so grave a crisis, his raid should be extended to Northern territory, he deliberately resolved to disobey the order restricting his operations in Kentucky."

On June 11, Morgan started his regiments north to the Cumberland, where he planned to capture the Federal garrison at Carthage and clear the river crossings before beginning a lightning dash across Kentucky. Late in the day, however, a courier arrived from Bragg's headquarters with a message which delayed all his well-laid plans. A heavy Union raiding party was reported pushing into eastern Tennessee, threatening General Buckner's small defending army, and Bragg ordered Morgan's cavalry to intercept.

As a result of this order, the following three weeks were utterly wasted in hard marches over rugged country and bad roads, the division moving east through Gainesboro and Livingston, and then north across the Kentucky line to Albany, only to discover that the Federal force—if it ever existed—had completely vanished.

This wild-goose chase not only delayed Morgan's raid for three weeks, it wore down horses and used up carefully hoarded rations. Under pouring rains that flooded roads and creeks, the regiments swung back westward through the hills to the Cumberland approaches near Burkesville, camping long enough to commandeer grist mills for grinding corn and blacksmith shops for shoeing horses.

By July 2 the rains had stopped. Morgan held a final conference with his regimental commanders, informing them definitely that they were going across the Ohio. He traced the route on a map, indicating four main danger points—the crossing of the flooded Cumberland just ahead of them, the crossing of the Ohio west of Louisville, the long march north around Cincinnati, and the recrossing of the Ohio east of Cincinnati. Later he told Duke privately that they might not have to recross the Ohio River; he had learned that General Lee was invading Pennsylvania, and if all went well Morgan's men might keep marching eastward and join Lee.

Union troops and local militias were often instrumental in hastily constructing impromptu barricades by felling trees and digging entrenchments to repel Brigadier General John Hunt Morgan and his cavalrymen during their raids on Kentucky, Indiana, and Ohio towns, June 27–July 26, 1863. From Harper's New Monthly Magazine, *August 1865.*

All were cautioned to secrecy concerning the invasion of Indiana and Ohio, and the colonels evidently kept tight security. None of the men suspected that they were going beyond Kentucky, although at least one was hopeful of it. Sergeant Henry L. Stone, whose family lived in Greencastle, Indiana, writing from the "South Bank of the Cumberland, five miles from Burkesville" mentioned that he had heard "Captain Hines with 90 men is in Indiana. . . . I wish I was with him. . . . I wish our whole command could go into Hoosier."

Below Burkesville that day, Morgan had ten regiments assembled, all far under strength, one of them the hastily organized 14th Kentucky Cavalry, scarcely larger than a company, commanded by the General's brother, Colonel Richard C. Morgan. The 2nd Kentucky was led by its acting commander, the fiery Major Thomas B. Webber, Colonel Bowles being unable to make the journey. Four three-inch Parrott guns and a section of twelve-pounder howitzers comprised the division's artillery support under Captain Ed Byrne. Total present for duty was 2,460 men, about 1,500 of them in Duke's 1st Brigade, the others in Colonel Adam Johnson's 2nd Brigade.

"In high feather and full song," reported George Mosgrove, "Morgan's gallant young cavalrymen formed in columns, looking toward Kentucky." When General Morgan, smartly uniformed and mounted on his favorite, Glencoe, rode along the column to the front, the men cheered and sang:

> *"Here's the health to Duke and Morgan*
> > *Drink it down;*
> *Here's the health to Duke and Morgan*
> > *Drink it down;*
> *Here's the health to Duke and Morgan,*
> > *Down, boys, down, drink it down!"*

Morgan rode on, smiling and waving. Behind him came Duke, a flowing plume in his hat, and they all marched out for the Cumberland singing "My Old Kentucky Home."

The river was rain-swollen, more than half a mile wide, running out of its banks and filled with driftwood tumbling and rocketing through the foam. The 2nd Kentucky moved above Burkesville, the men out searching for boats, finding nothing but a few frail canoes. They lashed these together and made crude floorings of fence rails.

"We turned the horses in," Sergeant Stone wrote a few days later, "and the men came over in the canoes with their saddles—the wagons were put on canoes, piece at a time and brought over." At some places driftwood covered almost the entire surface, and to secure their animals the men had to enter the water holding to a canoe-raft with one hand and to their horse's mane or tail with the other.

As bad as was the flooded stream, it had one beneficial effect; there was no organized resistance to the crossing. The Federals were confident the river would stop Morgan, and only a few scattered patrols were on the north bank.

Bennett Young, crossing with Quirk's scouts, described one of the few encounters with the Yankees: "Those who had clothing on rushed ashore and into line, those who swam with horses, unwilling to be laggard, not halting to dress, seized their cartridge boxes and guns and dashed upon the enemy. The strange sight of naked men engaging in combat amazed the enemy. They had never seen soldiers before clad only in nature's garb."

The Union soldiers opposing the dangerous Cumberland crossing were of Frank Wolford's Kentucky regiment, and Morgan's men were thankful there were so few of them. With Tom Quirk's scouts in the lead and the 2nd Regiment close behind, the columns of dripping horses and men moved on toward Marrowbone Creek. Here, about midafternoon, the scouts charged a Union encampment, and the dauntless Irishman took a bad bullet wound in the arm. "Only one man received a wound," Kelion Peddicord noted laconically, "Captain Tom, whose rein arm was broken."

But the scouts regarded Quirk's misfortune as an ill omen; they had come to consider their bold leader as indestructible. Over his profane protests, Quirk was ordered back to Burkesville to convalesce, and for the first time the 2nd moved into Kentucky without Tom Quirk up front to serve as eyes and ears for the regiment. By night-fall of the following day the regiment was seven miles beyond

Columbia, with other units of the division strung out far behind. It was three o'clock the morning of July 4 before the rear regiment entered Columbia, bivouacking in the streets. Duke in the meantime had sent Captain Franks and the scouts forward to reconnoiter the Tebb's Bend bridge at Green River. Franks reported back before dawn that the Yankees at the bridge appeared to be expecting an attack. They were as busy as beavers, he said. All through the night the scouts had heard the ringing of axes and the crash of falling timbers.

At daybreak of July 4, the meaning of all this night activity was revealed to Franks and his men. Across the narrow peninsula entering Tebb's Bend, a 100-yard breastwork blocked the neck of land, facing south and barring access to the bridge. It was a sturdy abatis of logs and tangled brush, with rifle pits protected by fence rails, wire and sharpened pieces of wood.

Morgan was up front before the sun rose, ordering Captain Byrne to open with his battery. After one round was fired into the barricade, Lieutenant Joe Tucker was sent forward under a truce flag with a message to the Union commander, demanding unconditional surrender. Tucker found the commander to be Colonel Orlando H. Moore of the 25th Michigan Infantry, with about 200 men dug in shoulder to shoulder. Moore read Morgan's message, smiled, and said to Tucker: "Lieutenant, if it was any other day I might surrender, but on the Fourth of July I must have a little brush first." He then wrote a brief note to Morgan: "It is a bad day for surrender, and I would rather not."

The 2nd Regiment took no part in the fight at Tebb's Bend bridge, the 2nd Brigade having passed through Duke's regiments during the early morning march up from Columbia. Colonel D. W. Chenault's 11th Kentucky, being in advance, led the assault dismounted, a straight frontal attack across open ground with bugles blaring. As the first wave ran into fallen timbers and brush, it collapsed under the close fire of Moore's determined Michigan infantrymen. Chenault was killed as he climbed the barricade, falling back into the debris. Two succeeding attacks also failed.

"Many of our best men were killed or wounded," Major McCreary noted in his journal that night. "It was a sad, sorrowful day, and more tears of grief rolled over my weatherbeaten cheeks on this mournful occasion than have before for years. The commencement of this raid is ominous. Total loss in killed and wounded—71." Among the dead was Alexander Tribble, Lieutenant Eastin's companion in the celebrated duel with Colonel Halisey. Tribble had only recently been promoted to captain and transferred to Chenault's regiment from the 2nd Kentucky.

After three hours, with the morning still young, Morgan called the useless fighting to an end. Under another flag of truce he sent a second message to Colonel Moore, requesting permission to bury his dead. Moore gave consent, delivering the bodies to the front of his line.

After burying their dead and bypassing Tebb's Bend, the regiments moved north through Campbellsville and out on the road toward Lebanon. They knew it had been a bad Fourth of July for Morgan's raiders, but they did not know how terrible a day it had been for the Confederacy. In Pennsylvania, Lee's army was beginning its retreat after disaster at Gettysburg; on the Mississippi, Vicksburg was surrendering to Grant. Morgan's raiders, instead of invading a country wavering and divided after two years of indecisive war, would find the people celebrating their first real victories, reunited in a determination to bring the war to a triumphant end.

Completely unaware of these portentous events, the raiders camped that Fourth of July night five miles west of Lebanon.

2

From reports of scouts, Morgan and Duke learned before six o'clock the morning of July 5 that Lebanon was defended by Lieutenant Colonel Charles Hanson's 20th Kentucky Infantry with detachments from three other Kentucky Union regiments, a total force of nearly 500 men. Hanson was a brother of Roger Hanson, the Confederate leader who had welcomed Morgan's Lexington Rifles when they first came down to Green River from the Bluegrass. The 20th Kentucky was also a Bluegrass regiment, containing former friends, near relatives, and even brothers of men in Morgan's command.

Hoping to take Lebanon without a clash between brothers and friends, Morgan decided on a bold show of force. Ordering his regiments to form a two-line front, he marched them up to the edge of town, the forward skirmish line spread out for two miles across open fields bordering the turnpike, Byrne's battery at center on the road. Hanson had thrown up a crude breastwork where the pike entered the town, and Morgan ordered Byrne to shell it. As soon as the breastwork's defenders scurried back into town, Morgan sent his adjutant and occasional editor of the *Vidette,* Lieutenant Colonel Robert Alston, forward under a truce flag to demand a surrender.

To Alston's discomfiture, he was fired upon as he approached Hanson's headquarters, and when his own men attempted to cover him with retaliating fire, negotiations almost came to a sudden end. After the tense situation finally quieted, Hanson informed Alston that he had no intention of surrendering. "Then notify the women and children to leave immediately," Alston replied. "The town will be shelled."

As soon as Alston departed, Hanson concentrated his men in a sturdy brick railroad depot, an excellent defensive position according to Sergeant Henry Stone: "Our artillery could not bear on it, only at the roof." Colonel Roy S. Cluke's 8th Kentucky opened with a vigorous assault, but this was to be no quick victory. Before Morgan's scouts had circled the town and cut telegraph wires to Louisville, Hanson had received orders to hold out on the assurance that reinforcements would arrive in a few hours.

July 5 was a torrid summer day, the temperature soaring into the nineties by midmorning, and the 8th Kentucky was pinned down around the depot in patches of high weeds that held the heat. Lying on their bellies, half-smothered and choking for want of water, carefully hoarding their diminishing supply of ammunition, Cluke's men could neither advance nor retreat.

Although Lebanon was completely surrounded now, Morgan

could neither take the town nor withdraw until Cluke's men were extricated from the weed patches around the depot. Basil Duke, watching the deadly duel, was reminded of the 2nd Regiment's fight in Augusta and realized that what was needed was a regiment experienced in street fighting. With Morgan's permission he ordered Major Webber to bring the 2nd Regiment into the siege. "The 2nd had tried that sort of work before," Duke said. "Major Webber skillfully aligned it and moved it forward."

Kelion Peddicord, who went in with the scouts in the 2nd's first attack wave, said they charged all the way up to the rear of the depot, with the boys of the 8th cheering them on. Some ran their rifles and pistols through windows, firing blindly inside, others stormed the doors and broke them down. "A street fight," commented Peddicord dryly, "is one of the most desperate modes of warfare known to a soldier. The advantage is strongly against the storming party."

Colonel Hanson surrendered, but the 2nd and 8th regiments paid a high price for the victory. Almost at the moment Major Webber gave the 2nd orders to charge, nineteen-year-old Lieutenant Tom Morgan, the General's favorite brother, was killed. "Poor Tommy Morgan," Robert Alston wrote in his diary that day, "ran forward and cheered the men with all the enthusiasm of his bright nature. At the first volley he fell, pierced through the breast." His brother Calvin caught him as he fell, and he died in Calvin's arms; his only words were: "Brother Cally, they have killed me."

By three o'clock on that hot afternoon, Adjutant Robert Alston and Captain William Davis had the prisoners lined up and were issuing paroles. In the midst of these activities, scouts brought warnings of approaching Union cavalry in strength—Hanson's promised reinforcements arriving too late to save him. To avoid another costly fight, Morgan ordered regiments formed and started columns moving rapidly north toward Springfield. Alston and Davis herded their unparoled captives together, marching them on the double-quick along the same route.

About halfway along this dusty eight-mile stretch of road, a raging rainstorm overtook the prisoners and their guards. "Hardest rain I ever experienced," Alston commented. The water-soaked, bedraggled column did not reach Springfield until after dark.

While Morgan's raiders moved on through the night toward Bardstown, Alston and Davis established paroling headquarters in a comfortable Springfield house, the owner's lovely daughters, Frances and Belle Cunningham, watching the proceedings with fascination. For William Davis and Frances Cunningham it was love at first sight, and when the last prisoner was released, Captain Davis reluctantly obeyed Alston's order that he move out and rejoin his command.*

But Alston himself delayed departure. "Wet and chilly, worn out, tired and hungry," he fell asleep, was aroused by his orderly just before dawn, and started hurriedly for Bardstown. When he reached a point on the road where he expected to find Morgan's rear guard, a party of cavalrymen appeared out of the gray morning fog. "Supposing them to be our pickets," he explained later, "I rode up promptly to correct them for standing in full view of anyone approaching, when to my mortification I found myself a prisoner. My God! how I hated it, no one can understand." Like a true cavalryman, Alston's first thought was for his fine mare, "Fannie Johnson, named after a pretty little cousin, of Richmond, Va. I said, 'Poor Fannie, who will treat you as kindly as I have?' I turned her over to a captain and begged him to take good care of her, which he promised to do."

One by one, Morgan was losing the officers he most depended upon, and he was not yet across the Ohio.

3

The 2nd Kentucky and other regiments of Duke's brigade were in Bardstown by daylight of the sixth, and enjoyed the benefit of a six-hour rest while Adam Johnson's 2nd Brigade marched on through town to take the advance. Most of Duke's boys lounged in the shade

---

[*The romantic wartime letters of William Davis to Frances Cunningham, which began as a result of this meeting and led to their marriage in 1866, were carefully preserved by the recipient, and are now in the Filson Club, Louisville, Kentucky.]

of a sycamore grove, but Lightning Ellsworth rode off with a detachment to Bardstown Junction on the L. & N. Railroad.

Ellsworth was amused to find the operator there wearing a uniform—recently issued to Union telegraphers—dark blue blouse, blue trousers with a silver cord on the seam, a natty buff vest, a forage cap with no ornaments or marks of ranks. "Hello, sonny," said Ellsworth as he showed his cocked revolver. "Move an inch except as I tell you, and you'll be buried in that fancy rig."

In a few minutes Ellsworth learned that strong Union cavalry forces were gathering in the rear, no more than twenty-four hours behind Morgan's main column. From every message he intercepted, it was evident the Yankees were certain that Morgan's raiders were bound for Louisville, and troops were being concentrated there for an expected attack.

John Morgan, meanwhile, was preparing the way for his river crossing into Indiana, the selected jump-off point being Brandenburg, Kentucky, on the Ohio River. He started Captains Sam Taylor and Clay Meriwether and their companies of the 10th Kentucky by forced march direct to Brandenburg. They were told they would probably find Captain Tom Hines, who had been scouting the area for several weeks, somewhere around that town. They were to join forces with Hines and capture Brandenburg, as well as any boats which might be lying at the landing.

At the same time Morgan ordered the love-smitten captain, William Davis, to take Company D of the 2nd Kentucky and Company A of the 8th Kentucky on a diversionary expedition east of Louisville. Davis's mission was to cut telegraph wires, burn railroad bridges, and create the impression that his two companies comprised Morgan's entire raiding force. They were to aim for Twelve Mile Island above Louisville, cross the Ohio River there, and attempt to rejoin Morgan's raiders at Salem, Indiana.

Lieutenant George Eastin of D Company was second in command. When he rode off with Captain Davis at the head of his company, Eastin was still proudly wearing his talisman, the sword of the Union colonel, Dennis Halisey.

In a letter to Frances Cunningham, Davis told of how he first learned of Morgan's plans to invade Indiana. "When within ten miles of Shepherdsville [on the afternoon of July 6] Gen'l Morgan explained to me his intention of crossing the Ohio at Brandenburg, and ordered my detachment to create a diversion by operating between Louisville and Frankfort. Rapidly pushing forward ahead of the column, I crossed Salt river at an almost impracticable ford three miles above Shepherdsville and directed my course toward the railroad some thirty miles above Louisville."

At the same time, the main column was turning northwestward, away from Louisville, still twenty-four hours ahead of the Union cavalry massing behind. Morgan was rather certain that no attack would be forthcoming from Louisville, where the enemy was gathering in fearful anticipation of the raiders' striking there.

4

Early on the morning of July 7, Sam Taylor and Clay Meriwether led their companies into Brandenburg. Being so far north, the town was not garrisoned. The people appeared to be either apathetic or Confederate in sympathy, and no fight was offered. The only vessel at the landing was a small wharf boat, but Taylor and Meriwether learned that a packet steamer running between Louisville and Henderson was due in early that afternoon. A faster mailboat usually passed about the same time, but made no scheduled stops.

Brandenburg was a small town built high on a hill. From the crest the winding river could be observed for several miles in either direction. After placing lookouts on the highest points and pickets along roads entering the town, the two captains permitted their men to laze away the morning on the river front. Shortly after noon, a boarding party was ordered on to the wharf boat. Around one o'clock lookouts signaled that a steamer was coming, and the men on the wharf boat were instructed to ready their weapons and keep under cover.

Promptly on schedule the steamboat *John T. McCombs* rounded the last bend, sounded its hoarse whistle, and slowed its chugging engines. With paddle wheels splashing silvery in the July sunshine, it turned in to the Brandenburg landing.

The instant the packet eased alongside the wharf boat, forty fully armed Confederate cavalrymen leaped aboard, much like the pirates of a certain seagoing Morgan. In a matter of seconds, the *John T. McCombs* was in Rebel hands. Captain Ballard, the crew and fifty passengers, caught by surprise, were without arms and offered no resistance.

A few minutes later a fast mailboat, the *Alice Dean*, came puffing upriver. From the pilothouse of the *McCombs*, Clay Meriwether watched until he was certain the *Alice Dean* did not intend to stop, then ordered Captain Ballard to steam out toward her.

Some accounts of the capture of the *Alice Dean* claimed the Confederates ran up distress signals to lure the second boat alongside. According to a report in the *Cincinnati Gazette*, however, which was based on witnesses' stories, "the *McCombs* was headed out just in time to touch her bows, when the Rebels who were concealed on the *Mc-Combs*, jumped on board the *Dean* and effected the capture of that boat also."

The Cincinnati newspaper also reported that passengers were assured their private property would be respected. Ten thousand dollars in the boats' safes were returned to the various owners, and all were liberated with instructions not to try to leave Brandenburg. Guards of course were placed on both vessels, officers and crews being held aboard.

About nine o'clock the next morning the 2nd Kentucky, with Morgan and Duke riding in the advance, came trotting into Brandenburg, the other regiments strung out in columns of fours under a long dust cloud in the rear. The town's main street sloped straight to the river, which was still covered by a streamer of early-morning fog concealing the Indiana shoreline. This was the first time the boys of the 2nd had looked upon the Ohio since their fight at Augusta in 1862, and from what they could see of it the dark greenish brown stream was running full.

Captains Taylor and Meriwether rode out to meet the column, giving Morgan the good news of the capture of the two passenger steamers. They also informed Morgan that Captain Tom Hines had brought in what was left of his command to Brandenburg.

The officers rode on down to the landing, where they found Hines "leaning against the side of the wharf boat, with sleepy, melancholy look—apparently the most listless, inoffensive youth that was ever imposed upon." Morgan dismounted and talked with Hines for several minutes. The young captain had much to report of conditions in Indiana, the roads, the towns, what help or resistance might be expected from the people. At the end of their conversation Morgan informed Hines that he was to take command of the scouts, the third officer to replace Tom Quirk within the week.

Establishing headquarters in a many-windowed house on the town's highest hill, Morgan began issuing orders for the river crossing. Captain Ballard of the *McCombs* and Captain Pepper of the *Alice Dean* were given instructions, a Parrott gun was placed aboard each steamer, and bales of hay were stacked along the bulwarks for defense.

The veteran 2nd Kentucky, with Hines leading the scouts, was chosen to make the first crossing on the *Alice Dean*. Colonel W. W. Ward's 9th Tennessee would follow on the *McCombs*. There would be no room for horses; they would come over on the second trip.

While the men were loading, the river mist thinned slightly, then suddenly burned away under the sun to reveal a line of enemy riflemen along the Indiana banks. A few moments later the Indianians opened fire, flashes spouting from 100 weapons, quickly followed by a long leaping flame and the sullen roar of a fieldpiece.

Across the 1,000 yards of rippling brown water the background was incongruously peaceful and pastoral, like a Currier and Ives color print—two or three neat farmhouses with tan haystacks in yellow fields, strips of trees and underbrush in two shades of green, fresh light green near the river, dark green on the farther ridge.

The enemy's big gun flashed again, the shell whistling across, a piece of it wounding one of the 1st Brigade's quartermaster officers. Through his field glass Basil Duke found the gun; it was an ancient cannon mounted on the chassis of a farm wagon, propelled by hand. The riflemen were dressed in a mixture of militia uniforms and rough farm clothing. They fired another volley, but their range was less than the river's width.

From the hilltop where Morgan had his headquarters, Captain Byrne opened up now with blasts from his Parrott guns, followed by repeated barks of the howitzers. As the Indiana defenders broke and ran for the ridge in their rear, the steamboats were signaled to move out. Paddle wheels churned on the *Alice Dean*; she shuddered briefly and slid away.

On board at the moment, Major Tom Webber was entering the pilothouse. He curtly instructed the pilot as to where he wanted the 2nd Regiment landed, warning the man that any attempt at delay or sabotage would be dealt with severely. The pilot tipped his cap respectfully, then as he turned to watch Webber leave, he saw a Kentucky giant looming in the doorway, a sun-scorched soldier with an axe slung over his shoulder, a long rifle in one arm, a big navy revolver in his belt. This was Tom Boss of C Company. "I'm here as guard to see you act right," Boss growled sternly. "I don't want no nonsense."

Boss found a seat in a corner, hitched his revolver into reach, and placed his rifle across his knees. As the *Alice Dean* chugged across the river the pilot attended strictly to business, easing the bow in for a perfect landing. As soon as the plank was pushed out and the first platoon of cavalrymen began hurrying ashore, the man breathed a sigh of relief. He turned to Boss and said: "My name is Smith. Would you object to telling me yours?"

"Oh, no," replied Boss affably, "I don't mind who I make acquaintance with. My name's Tom Boss."

To make conversation the pilot asked: "How long do you remain on your post when you're on guard duty?"

"Well," Boss answered, "we cavalry stand four hours on and eight off. The webfoot infantry stand two on and four off. But we generally do twice as much work as they do so we need twice as long rest." The big Kentuckian raised up to see how the boys were doing ashore. They were forming lines and keeping a close watch on the wooded ridge where the Indianians, had disappeared. Everything was quiet. "Mr. Smith," Boss drawled, "you got anything on this boat to drink stronger'n water? I'm beginning to feel powerful dry."

"Certainly," replied the pilot. "I'll get it for you." Mr. Smith excused himself, dropped down the ladder to the ship's bar and returned after a minute or so with two strong toddies. He intended to drink one of them himself, feeling an acute need for a restorative after the strain of crossing with that fierce-looking giant at his back.

But when the pilot came within reach of his guard, Boss thrust out both long arms, grasped a glass in each hand, and drained one after the other with scarcely a pause between drinks. Smacking his lips, he thanked the pilot, then added casually: "You needn't bring any more, Mr. Smith, until just before I'm relieved. I don't like to drink too much while I'm on duty."

Tom Boss's comrades, meanwhile, had established a bridgehead on the sloping riverbank, and the *Alice Dean* was reversing engines to make room for the *McCombs*, which was coming in with the 9th Tennessee.

The *Dean* had scarcely recrossed to the Brandenburg landing when an unexpected intruder appeared in the bend of the river, the gunboat *Elk*, a snub-nosed craft boarded up tightly with heavy oak planking, three howitzers thrust out of embrasures. "A bluish-white, funnel-shaped cloud spouted out from her lefthand bow and a shot flew at the town, and then changing front forward, she snapped a shell at the men on the other side."

Horse-holders of the 2nd Kentucky who were waiting at the Brandenburg landing to load the regiment's animals drew them hurriedly back out of view. Across the river the dismounted cavalrymen, feeling lost and helpless without their horses, took cover in the forested ridge.

From his headquarters vantage point, General Morgan had been watching the approach of the *Elk* for several minutes. He now ordered Captain Byrne to change the position of his biggest guns, and shortly thereafter solid shot was skipping all around the *Elk*, followed by bursting shells. After about an hour's dueling the *Elk* turned and headed back upriver toward Louisville to spread the alarm and summon reinforcements.

As soon as the gunboat was out of range, the 2nd's horses were led aboard the *Alice Dean*, and the work of crossing the regiments was resumed. About sundown, Duke's brigade was on the Indiana shore, and Adam Johnson's regiments began moving across.

By midnight the rear guard was landing on the Indiana bank. When the last man stepped ashore, Morgan issued orders to burn both boats, but Basil Duke intervened and saved the *John T. McCombs*, Captain Ballard being an old acquaintance. Ballard promised to take his boat upriver to Louisville so that it could not be used to ferry pursuing Union troops, who already were beginning to appear on the Brandenburg wharf.

As the flames of the *Alice Dean* lighted the river, a few of these advance enemy troops fired a futile round of rifle fire toward Indiana. The alligator horses in Morgan's rear guard only laughed, waved their hats, and rode off into the dark woods.

There is no record of how John Morgan felt as he watched the last of his men come ashore into Indiana, knowing that he had successfully invaded the enemy's country. But as he watched the *Alice Dean* burning brightly and the *McCombs* splashing away toward Louisville, he knew there was now no turning back. He was cut loose from Kentucky; he was acting against orders, but he had accomplished what other western commanders had only dreamed of doing, and there must have been elation with that realization.

Sergeant Henry Stone, the boy from Greencastle, Indiana, who was attached to Hines' scouts, recorded that he "experienced some peculiar sensations as I set foot on Indiana soil." Stone found time to write a letter to his father, beginning it "On the Ohio River 30 Miles Below Louisville, Wednesday 8th July 1863." After describing the crossing, he wrote: "Wake up old Hoosier now. We intend to live off the Yanks hereafter and let the North feel like the South has felt of some of the horrors of war—horses we expect to take whenever needed, forage and provisions also. In fact it is concluded that living is cheaper in Indiana and Ohio than Tennessee. . . . I hope I'll get close enough to pay you a visit. This will be the first opportunity of the Northern people seeing Morgan and they'll see enough. I just imagine now how the women will bug their eyes out at seeing a Rebel army."

Crossing with the 2nd Regiment, Stone helped establish the first bridgehead, then moved on into the deserted countryside—the morning's defenders on the riverbank having completely vanished. They burned a flour mill, marched inland six miles, and went into camp in a meadow, waiting for the other regiments to build up behind them. As twilight came on, the liquid July heat intensified, became heavy with the smell of horses and smoke from cooking fires. Fireflies blinked in the dark foliage; bugles rang in the summer night. Voices of many men mingled as they sought their proper outfits in this strange Yankee country.

"Some of the boys gave champagne parties that night," said Kelion Peddicord, "which doubtless was taken from the stores of one of the steamers, as also were a few other luxuries that had so mysteriously come into their possession. After satisfying their unnatural appetites, all took a sly snooze, dreaming of home and of the fair fields beyond the waters."

5

Before daylight of the ninth, bugles were blowing boots and saddles. Although Colonel Adam Johnson's 2nd Brigade led the order of march, out in front was that short-lived scouting regiment, the 14th Kentucky Cavalry, which contained a number of men and officers from the 2nd Regiment. General Morgan had formed the 14th as a special command for his brother, Dick Morgan, who had recently transferred from Virginia.

Operating with the 14th were the scouts, now under Tom Hines, along with other veterans from the 2nd Regiment's Company A. In addition there were twenty men from Billy Breckinridge's 9th Regiment, which had been serving as a delaying force far in the raiders' rear and failed to reach Brandenburg in time to make the crossing with Morgan. Several of these men were originally members of the 2nd Kentucky.

Among the scouts that morning who rode in the van singing "Here's to Duke and Morgan" were Kelion Peddicord, Henry Stone, Winder Monroe, Leeland Hathaway, Jack Messick, and the shifty John T. Shanks. Each of them was riding into strange adventures which would extend far beyond the few days of the great raid—into events involving espionage, dramatic prison escapes, gallantry, romance, dungeons, and betrayal.

This summer morning, however, they were chiefly concerned with discovering the presence of the enemy as they rode straight northward toward the town of Corydon, past alternating patches of woodland and cornfields, carefully scouting farmhouses from which the occupants had fled, seemingly vanished from the earth, leaving doors wide open in their precipitate haste.

About ten o'clock that morning they met their first resistance point, a party of home guards—the same force which had appeared on the shore opposite Brandenburg the previous morning—who were posted behind a heap of fence rails on the Corydon road. Bringing up his regular regiments, Colonel Johnson overran these inexperienced defenders, pursuing them all the way to the outskirts of Corydon.

Here, Johnson found a solid barricade of logs, rails, and underbrush piled high across the road. A cavalry charge was out of the question, and after the first dismounted company was repulsed with several casualties, he waited until the 2nd Kentucky and 9th Tennessee came up. "A flank movement to the right and left," Johnson reported, "gallantly led by the 2nd Kentucky on the right and Ward's on the left caused the enemy to disperse in confusion."

One of the Corydon defenders describing the action said "the enemy opened upon our forces with three pieces of artillery, making the shells sing the ugly kind of music over our heads. . . . In the meantime the enemy had completely flanked the town . . . the fighting was very sharp for the space of twenty minutes. . . . After the field was taken by the enemy they moved forward, and planted a battery on the hill south of town, and threw two shells into the town, both of them striking near the center of main street, one exploded but did no damage. Seeing the contest was hopeless . . . Col. Jordan wisely hoisted the white flag and surrendered."

According to the Corydon *Weekly Democrat,* the raiders lost eight killed and thirty-three wounded in the attack, and took their revenge by seizing "everything they wanted in the eating and wearing line and horses and buggies. The two stores were robbed of about $300 each and a contribution of $700 each was levied upon the two mills in town."

Morgan arrived in Corydon in time for lunch, and during a casual conversation with the hotelkeeper's daughter learned the startling news that General Lee had been defeated at Gettysburg and was in retreat. If this were true—and the newspapers he was shown corroborated the story—he knew he must now abandon plans to march into Pennsylvania.

As he rode northward out of Corydon he found small comfort in reports from some of his officers that a few houses along the way were displaying the lone-star flag of the Knights of the Golden Circle, and that his own picture had been seen in one or two windows. John Morgan had little use for Copperheads. If these so-called Northern friends of the South really wanted to help, he reasoned, they should join the Confederate Army and fight.

By nightfall his regiments were within sixteen miles of Salem. He ordered the men into camp, with pickets doubled. Lee may have been beaten at Gettysburg, but John Morgan was resolved to continue the raid as planned.

Using all his tricks of deception, he had already spun an intricate web of confusion as to his intentions. In Brandenburg he had permitted known Union sympathizers to overhear elaborate plans for marching to Indianapolis to burn the State Capitol and release Confederate prisoners at Camp Morton. He also spread a story that General Nathan B. Forrest, with 2,000 more Confederates, was close behind him. All day the telegrapher, George Ellsworth, had ridden beside Morgan, and at every telegraph line Ellsworth swung aloft with his portable set, tapping the wires and transmitting misleading reports as rapidly as Morgan could dictate them. Wires were always cut behind them, so that nowhere in southern Indiana could Union forces check the raiders' whereabouts or coordinate their own movements.

It was no wonder that as the day wore on terror rolled northward across Indiana, newspapers printing extra editions, every rumor increasing the size of the invading force. (Although Morgan crossed only 2,000 men at Brandenburg, no Northern paper during the raid ever used a figure of less than 4,000, and often it was increased to as many as 20,000.)

By nightfall every city and town in the Middle West was looking for Morgan's terrible raiders, and even 300 miles away on the Illinois prairies a village became panic-stricken when a charivari party serenaded a bride and groom with trumpets and tin pans. Residents not in on the affair were certain the noise heralded the advent of Morgan's bloodthirsty raiders, and ran helter-skelter in their night clothes to hide in the cornfields until daybreak.

6

Unaware of the widespread panic they were creating, Morgan's men awoke that same morning (July 10) in the peaceful dewy fields below Salem, Indiana, and resumed their steady march straight northward. In Indianapolis, Governor Oliver P. Morton had declared a state of emergency and was posting warnings throughout the city: "In order to provide against possible danger it is requested that all places of business in Indianapolis be closed this afternoon at three o'clock, and that all ablebodied white male citizens will form themselves into companies and arm themselves with such arms as they can procure, and endeavor to acquaint themselves with military tactics." At Brandenburg that morning, pursuing Union cavalry began crossing the river in strength, still twenty-four hours behind the raiders.

As there were two roads running north to Salem, one through Greenville, the other through Palmyra, Morgan separated his brigades.

Tom Hines' scouts led one column, the 2nd Kentucky the other, and the march turned into a race along parallel roads between these old regimental comrades. Occasionally during the morning they could see each other's dust trails across the green countryside, and rival flankers met each other as they sought provisions and fresh horses at farms off the main roads.

As Sergeant Henry Stone had written his father in Greencastle, they intended "to live off the Yanks hereafter." Regimental quarter-masters had already worked out a method for procuring rations. Thomas M. Coombs described the system in one of his letters: "Every morning the Captains of Companies would appoint a man for each mess to go ahead and furnish provisions. They would all go ahead of the command and scatter out to the farmhouses for miles on each side of the road, and by ten or twelve o'clock they would overtake us with sacks full of light bread, cheese, butter, preserves, canned peaches, berries, wine cordial, canteens of milk and everything good that the pantrys and closets of the hoosier ladies could furnish."

As on the previous day the forward parties saw very few people, but they knew the driving columns had been observed, and warnings passed on far ahead. From every village to the right and left of them, church bells were tolling urgently. By the time they sighted Salem, that town was a bedlam of church bells, fire bells, and shrieking whistles. It was as if the townspeople somehow believed that a vast amount of noise might frighten these devil raiders away.

The 2nd Kentucky won the hot dusty race into Salem. Lieutenant A. S. Welch of Company L led his platoon of twelve men in at a brisk gallop, their yells and fierce momentum scattering a force of frightened home guards. Before the defenders could re-form, Captain W. J. Jones brought his company pouring into a side street, over-turning an ancient swivel gun, which was loaded and ready to fire, in the public square.

By noon both brigades were swirling around the little town. They fed and watered horses, burned the railroad depot and a bridge over Blue River, ripped up tracks for several hundred yards, and then descended upon the Salem stores.

Basil Duke frankly admitted that his men pillaged Salem, "actuated by a desire to pay off all scores that the Federal Army had chalked up in the South. . . . Calico was the staple article of appropriation—each man tied a bolt of it to his saddle. . . . One man carried a bird cage with three canaries in it for two days. Another rode with a chafing dish, which looked like a small metallic coffin, on the pommel of his saddle, until an officer forced him to throw it away. Although the weather was intensely warm, another slung seven pairs of skates around his neck, and chuckled over his acquisition."

Morgan's provost marshal attempted to stop the plundering, but nothing short of mass court-martials would have been effective on that hot July day in Salem. The alligator horses literally cleaned out every drygoods store, saddle shop, and liquor store in town. "The ragamuffins were particularly delighted," commented the *New Albany Ledger* the next day, "with the style of Salem clothing and the quality of Salem whisky."

The only thing that stopped the mad celebration was an order to march out, and by two o'clock that afternoon the dusty horsemen were gone, vanished as quickly as they had come, leaving Salem, Indiana, its one day of Civil War to be talked about for years to come.

7

Under a blazing cloudless sky the raiders turned straight eastward now, marching to Canton, where they paused only long enough to wreck a stretch of railroad and tangle several sections of telegraph wire. "We then rapidly moved on," James McCreary recorded in his diary, "like an irresistible storm to Vienna." Here for the first time they found a town filled with women and children, the able-bodied men having departed northward to help guard Indianapolis from expected attack. Also for the first time the Kentuckians learned how deep ran the awesome dread of Morgan's "terrible raiders" among these people. "The women were soon crying," Sergeant Peddicord reported, "begging and imploring us to spare their children. The boys heard this with amazement, and asked the women if they thought we were barbarians that they should think we could hurt women and children. The men assured them that not a hair of their heads would be injured, nor would they wound their feelings in any way."

While the column continued on through Vienna in the dusk, George Ellsworth went to work in the telegraph office. He learned that Union forces were concentrating around Indianapolis, that home guard companies had been working through the day felling timbers and blocking roads south of the city, and that pursuing cavalry forces were still crossing at Brandenburg. Morgan was especially pleased that his Indianapolis ruse was working so well, and saw nothing alarming in reports of enemy cavalry still a day's march behind him.

Six or seven miles east of Vienna, near the village of Lexington, the advance companies began moving off the road for a short bivouac. They were only thirty miles due north of Louisville, yet for all that Union commanders anywhere knew of their whereabouts, they might as well have been on the moon.

That night John Morgan commandeered a house in Lexington and slept in comfort, guarded only by a small escort. Just before daylight a dozen or so Federal cavalrymen blundered into town, were challenged by Morgan's guards, and three of the Yankees were captured before they could gallop away.

Awakened by the clatter, Morgan decided he might as well start the columns moving again, and this day he chose to march north on a winding road through rolling country toward Vernon. A few miles above Lexington he sent Colonel D. Howard Smith's 5th Regiment east in a feint toward Madison. He also issued orders to seize every saddle horse in sight; the raiders' mounts were still holding up well, but he did not want to leave any replacements behind for his pursuers. Before noon, each regiment had a sizeable horse herd bringing up the rear.

It was midafternoon when the scouts sighted Vernon, and a cautious reconnaissance indicated that the town was prepared to fight. Sturdy barricades had been thrown up in the streets, and several hundred militiamen were waiting with rifles at ready. When Morgan sent in a truce party demanding surrender, the colonel in command flatly refused.

Morgan moved up to the front, joining Basil Duke and Adam Johnson for a conference. None of them liked the looks of the town. They believed they could force their way in, but feared the cost would be high, and to lose more men now might endanger the success of the raid. They decided to shift the brigades over to a side road leading back southeastward toward Dupont.

To gain time while his straggling columns were re-forming for the turnabout, Morgan sent in a second demand for surrender. In the meantime, however, a long railroad train had rolled in from the north, bringing General John Love and more than 1,000 volunteer troops. After taking command in Vernon, Love immediately sent out a reply demanding Morgan's surrender.

It was now late in the day, shadows of mounts and riders falling in tall black slants across the dusty roads. Morgan purposely delayed his answer until the sun was down. Then, about nine o'clock, he sent a message in to Love informing him that he would give the Federals thirty minutes to remove women and children, after which time the raiders would begin shelling Vernon with artillery.

While Love was frantically rounding up noncombatants and hurrying them to safety north of Vernon, Morgan's rear guard slipped away and, concealed by darkness, hurried on after the forward columns. The division was miles away to the southeast before Love, waiting for an artillery barrage that never came, realized he had been outbluffed by a master of military legerdemain.

"We traveled all night to Dupont," wrote James McCreary, "where we rested and fed our horses. Like an avalanche we are sweeping over the country. Man never knows his powers of endurance 'till he tries himself. The music of the enemy's bells is now as familiar and common as the caroling of the spring bird which, unknowing of death and carnage around, sings today the same song that gladdened our forefathers."

At midnight they went into camp, but Morgan had them in their saddles again by three o'clock in the morning. Since crossing the Ohio

River they had averaged twenty-one hours a day on horseback, and fatigue was beginning to take its toll. They were hungry, too, this Sunday morning, July 12, and after daylight, when they passed a meat-packing plant near Dupont, the boys could not resist falling out of column to "capture" some Indiana hams. Most of them slung the hams to their saddles and resumed march, but several laggards in the rear guard stayed too long and were captured by a band of militiamen.

Sunday morning church bells were ringing in all the villages—whether to summon worshipers or to warn them of the approaching raiders, the men could not tell. About noontime, Tom Hines' scouts and the 2nd Kentucky rode into Versailles at a walk, men and horses suffering from dust and sultry weather. After subduing a halfhearted force of home guards, they watered their horses and sought food and drink from the terrified householders.

While waiting for the rear regiments to come up, many men fell asleep on the streets beside their horses, but when a rumor was passed around that Frank Wolford's 1st Kentucky Union Cavalry had been reported only a dozen miles to the rear, they all mounted up willingly to resume march. The pursuing forces had closed the gap as a result of the division's delay and reversal of march at Vernon. All day Saturday the raiders' route of march had been like an inverted V, Morgan's men traveling both sides, the Union cavalry only the short base.

Leaving Versailles, Morgan put his columns on parallel roads again in an attempt to gain upon his pursuers, marching northeastward at a steady gait. Near Milan sheer weariness forced a halt, Bennett Young describing how he passed his dust-begrimed comrades "scattered along the fence corners for four miles." And James McCreary, the faithful diarist, was so weary that night when he tumbled off his horse, he could write but one sentence: "We moved rapidly through six or seven towns without resistance, and tonight lie down for a little while with our bridles in our hands."

The point where the two columns came together long after nightfall was just outside a village called Sunman. They bivouacked there, only fifteen miles from the Ohio state line.

8

While Morgan's main columns had been successfully eluding enemy forces in both front and rear, the detachment of two companies under Captain William J. Davis and Lieutenant George Eastin had not been so fortunate. After leaving Shepherdsville, Kentucky, this diversionary party of about 100 men marched rapidly around Louisville to Shelbyville, then swung north through Smithfield to Sligo, cutting telegraph wires, burning railroad bridges, and attempting to create the impression that they were Morgan's entire raiding force.

On the night of July 10, while their comrades were bivouacked scarcely twenty miles north across the Ohio near Lexington, Indiana, Captain Davis's men were approaching Westport on the river. The latter part of their march was over a corduroy road—poles laid crosswise on muddy earth—the clattering of their horses' hoofs breaking the stillness of the night.

About daylight of the eleventh, at the time Morgan's raiders were beginning their drive north toward Vernon, Davis's detachment reached the river. While his men were searching for boats, Davis stopped in at the residence of a Dr. Barbour, accepted an invitation to breakfast, and enjoyed making the acquaintance of the host's lovely daughter.

When Davis returned to the riverbank, Lieutenant Eastin reported that two small flatboats had been found opposite Twelve Mile Island. The bottoms not being particularly sturdy, Davis decided the safest method of crossing would be to use one boat to ply between the Kentucky shore and the island, the other between the island and the Indiana shore.

By eight o'clock all were off the Kentucky landing except Lieutenant Josiah B. Gathright of Company A, 8th Kentucky, and an eight-man platoon posted to guard the rear. As Gathright was calling the rear guard down to cross to the island, he saw three steamboats turning the river bend. A moment later puffs of white smoke rose from the decks, and shells roared toward the Indiana shore where Davis, Eastin, and about forty men were waiting along the grassy flats. About fifty other men were trapped on Twelve Mile Island with their horses.

Gathright acted promptly, taking the boat out quickly to the island. He made two turns to the island and back to the Kentucky shore, narrowly escaping a direct hit on the second run, rescuing thirty-four men before the gunboats moved up too close for risking another try. But in their haste, these men left not only their horses but also their arms and accouterments on the island.

And so at nine-thirty the morning of July 11, Lieutenant Gathright found himself the sole officer in command of forty-two men, only eight of them mounted and armed. They were cut off from their command across the river, and in their rear a dozen irate Federal patrols were searching for them. (As several of these men were of D Company, 2nd Kentucky, their subsequent adventures will be recorded in a later chapter.)

Meanwhile, Captain Davis and Lieutenant Eastin had moved away from their exposed position on the Indiana shoreline, and with their little band of forty set out to find John Morgan. If they had continued straight northward they might have overtaken the column's rear guard, but Morgan had underestimated by one day the time he expected to be in Salem. Unaware of this, however, and obedient to orders Davis turned west toward Salem, only to run into the hornet's nest stirred up in the wake of the swift-moving raiders.

"While crossing a small creek near Pekin," he later wrote to Frances Cunningham, "we were attacked by the 73rd Indiana Volunteers and a detachment of 5th U.S. Regulars in ambuscade." Outnumbered, Davis ordered a retreat into a nearby woods, where he hoped to make a stand. In the fight which followed, Davis's horse stumbled over a fallen tree, throwing its rider. Davis fell unconscious, and most of his men, believing him killed, surrendered.

Among those surrounded was George Eastin, still wearing the captured sword of Dennis Halisey. Aware that a price had been put on his head for the alleged murder of Halisey, and knowing that identification of the sword was certain, Eastin quickly hid the shiny blade under a log somewhere in that little patch of woods near Pekin, Indiana. He also concealed all articles of identity and marks of rank, and when the Yankee captors asked his name, he told them he was Private George Donald, and it was under this *nom de guerre* that Lieutenant George Eastin went into a Northern prison camp.

A few hours later Captain Davis was revived by a cool evening breeze. He was still lying beside the log which doubtless had concealed him from the victorious Yankees. Davis hid in a thicket until morning, then set out on foot, alone in enemy country. After walking about five miles he met a small boy in a field. The boy volunteered the information that a wounded Rebel soldier was in a house nearby. Davis walked to the house, entered, and surrendered to six militiamen who were carefully guarding the wounded captive. It would be fifteen months before Captain Davis could rejoin Morgan's raiders.

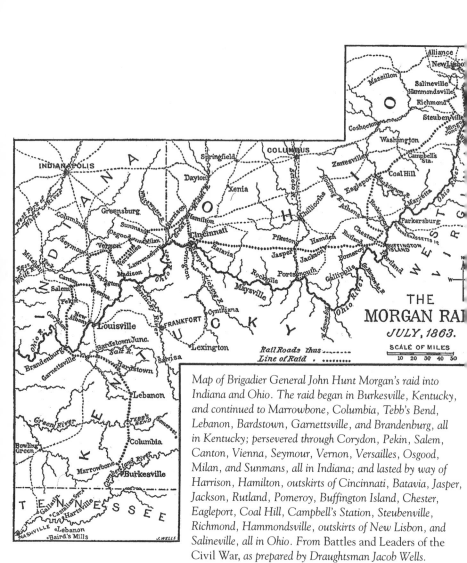

Map of Brigadier General John Hunt Morgan's raid into Indiana and Ohio. The raid began in Burkesville, Kentucky, and continued to Marrowbone, Columbia, Tebb's Bend, Lebanon, Bardstown, Garnettsville, and Brandenburg, all in Kentucky; persevered through Corydon, Pekin, Salem, Canton, Vienna, Seymour, Vernon, Versailles, Osgood, Milan, and Sunmans, all in Indiana; and lasted by way of Harrison, Hamilton, outskirts of Cincinnati, Batavia, Jasper, Jackson, Rutland, Pomeroy, Buffington Island, Chester, Eagleport, Coal Hill, Campbell's Station, Steubenville, Richmond, Hammondsville, outskirts of New Lisbon, and Salineville, all in Ohio. From Battles and Leaders of the Civil War, as prepared by Draughtsman Jacob Wells.

8

The Farthest Point North
(Morgan's Raid In Indiana and Ohio)

I'm sent to warn the neighbors, he's only a mile behind;
He's sweeping up the horses, every horse that he can find.
Morgan, Morgan, the raider, and Morgan's terrible men,
With Bowie knives and pistols are galloping up the glen.

1

Monday morning, July 13, 1863, the state of Ohio was invaded by Confederate troops for the first time in the war. The next two weeks for many Ohioans, particularly those in isolated farming areas and villages, was to be a time of self-induced terror which often approached the comical in its absurdities. As Bennett Young put it, the raiders in gray were pictured as "real sure enough devils, horns, hoofs and all. Even rhyme was put under conscription to help tell how awful Morgan's men were."

Actually, during most of their drive across Ohio the raiders were in flight. Rather than being bent upon destruction of the enemy, they sought to avoid him, dodging militiamen in front and racing to escape from an army of Union cavalry pounding at their heels.

About noon of the thirteenth, the 2nd Kentucky, heading Duke's brigade, rode into Harrison, Ohio, without resistance. "The most beautiful town I have yet seen in the North," James McCreary noted. "A place, seemingly, where love and beauty, peace and prosperity, sanctified by true religion, might hold high carnival. Here we destroyed a magnificent bridge and saw many beautiful women."

Waiting in Harrison for John Morgan was a man in rough civilian clothing, Sam Taylor, one of the captains who had captured Brandenburg and the steamboats. Taylor had been on another special mission—this time into Cincinnati. He reported to Morgan that Cincinnati was stampeded, the city under martial law and expecting attack, and Union troops were pouring in from Kentucky to defend it.

But Morgan had no intention of attacking Cincinnati, of risking disaster in its labyrinth of streets and hills. What he was looking for was an escape corridor between Cincinnati on the south and Hamilton on the north. As soon as the last of his companies was across the Whitewater bridge, he ordered the structure burned in order to delay his immediate pursuers, then marched out of Harrison on the road toward Hamilton. A few miles out he cut the telegraph lines, sent scouts north in a feint toward Hamilton, and turned his main column in the direction of Cincinnati. By thus threatening both points in the same afternoon, he kept his enemies waiting for him, leaving the intervening area free for his columns to slip through during the night.

The Union troops pursuing the raiders—including Wolford's Wild Riders—were so close behind that as they rode down the hill toward the river west of Harrison they could see a long line of Confederate cavalry stretching away toward the east. But the Federals could come no closer in the fading twilight; the bridge over the Whitewater was a mass of charred timbers.

2

On that afternoon of the thirteenth, the raiders started their longest continuous march, the severest test ever endured by Morgan's men and their horses. Yet it was not a rapid cavalry march, the dark night and unfamiliar roads holding them to a plodding pace much of the time.

To fight off sleep, the men talked, slow and easy, recalling events of their four days in Indiana. Already there were dozens of stories swapped back and forth among the companies of little incidents which would be forever remembered. . . . One of the boys entering the kitchen door of a farmhouse asking for food, the lady of the house flourishing a butcher knife in his face and shouting: "I'll let you know I'm from the State of Virginia and if you make any further attempt to enter here, I'll cut your heart out!" The cavalryman retreating, apologizing: "Ma'am, I know you Virginians will fight like the devil, and I have no doubt you mean what you say.". . . The hams captured at Dupont; some of the boys at a rest stop broiling theirs over a fire, the aroma tantalizing just as a warning of approaching Yankees came. "Mount up!" They strung the half-cooked hams to their saddles, galloping away at top speed, hams flapping, breaking loose, strewing the road, delectable suppers lost in the dust. . . . And Colonel Duke's story of the pies: everywhere they went they found bread and pies left in deserted kitchens like propitiatory offerings to fierce gods. The boys were suspicious of such gifts, uneasily passing them by until the day Duke rode up and caught several of his forward scouts standing around a table filled with apple pies cooling from the oven. "Why don't you eat them?" Duke asked. "They might be poisoned," replied one of the wary troopers. "I've always been fond of pies," said Duke. "Hand me one of the largest." The little Colonel downed the pie with relish, and when he appeared to be suffering no ill effects, the boys dived in and finished the lot. After that, Duke seldom arrived in time to find any pies left over by the ravenous scouts. . . .

As they rode eastward into the night they also worried aloud about the condition of their horses. Those who had already been forced to "swap" for Indiana farm horses grumbled over the sluggish movements of these "big-bellied, barefooted, grass-fed beasts." They would find as they moved across Ohio that these horses could endure no more than a day's march, sometimes less than that, Henry Stone reporting that he rode down eight horses before he was captured.

Another question they pondered was how much longer they could keep going. Nobody knew for certain how many men were left, but company sergeants comparing notes knew that about one out of

Members of Brigadier General John Hunt Morgan's regiments, although weakened from raiding in Kentucky and Indiana while eluding pursuing Union cavalry, had enough strength to continue their forays into Ohio. From Harper's New Monthly Magazine, August 1865.

every five of the men who had started the raid was no longer reporting for duty.

There was talk also of Butternuts, Copperheads, Peace Democrats, and Knights of the Golden Circle—those alleged friends of the Southern cause who, some had predicted, would rise up and take over Indiana and Ohio at the first strike of a Confederate invasion. The boys decided these people must be phantoms, for they had seen precious few friends on this raid. One of the stories going around concerned General Morgan and an Indiana farmer who wanted his horse returned, claiming that he was a Knight of the Golden Circle. "Good," replied Morgan, "then you ought to be glad to contribute a horse for the use of a Confederate soldier."*

Another topic of conversation as the raiders began that long night ride around Cincinnati was the whereabouts and strength of the enemy. They knew that Wolford's cavalry was in their rear, and could guess there were other Kentucky Union regiments. They could not know, of course, that Michigan, Ohio, Indiana and Illinois cavalry were also moving in on the chase, nor that 65,000 home guards in Indiana and 55,000 in Ohio were, or soon would be, armed and determined to kill or capture them. If they had known these awesome facts, the alligator horses doubtless would have considered this massive force a flattering lot of Yankees to be occupied with catching a few Kentucky boys out on a mild spree.

[*Although certain historians have hinted at a secret political link between Morgan's Indiana-Ohio raid and the so-called Copperhead conspiracy, there is little evidence to support such a theory. General Sherman, who understood his opponents better than most Union leaders, wrote on September 17, 1863: "They scorn the alliance with the copperheads. They tell me to my face that they respect Grant, McPherson, and our brave associates who fight manfully and well for principle, but despise the copperheads and sneaks who profess friendship for the South and opposition to the war as mere covers for their knavery and poltroonery." Eyewitness observers along the raid route confirmed Sherman's belief. For instance, Miss Attia Porter of Corydon, Indiana, recorded: "The rebs were pretty hard on the copperheads but they did not take a thing from us."]

3

After they crossed the Miami River, they burned another bridge behind them. "As the red flames created by the great burning timbers rose skyward," said Bennett Young, "they illumined the entire valley, and in the flickering shadows which they cast for several miles around . . . huge, weird forms, born, it is true, of the imagination, filled the minds and hearts of the invading horsemen for the moment with apprehensive awe and depressing forebodings."

Before midnight they were brushing the northern outskirts of Cincinnati, all houses darkened, the night extraordinarily black and airless. On this march, Duke's brigade followed Adam Johnson's, the 2nd Regiment bringing up the rear—where Morgan expected an attack would most likely come.

Because of the intense darkness it was impossible to keep columns closed up. Men could not see horses immediately forward, and several times Colonel Duke was uncertain as to which of the many roads and byroads Johnson's regiments had followed. He ordered flares lighted from paper or bolts of calico—still carried by many of the men—so that it would be possible to examine hoof tracks or see the direction of movement of suspended dust kicked up by the passing horses.

Sleep was the enemy now, stragglers falling from their saddles, awakening and stumbling after their mounts. Kelion Peddicord some- times saw in the light of flares "both, man and horse nodding together, and at such times the horse staggering like one intoxicated." Bennett Young said that men lashed themselves to their saddles, only to have their mounts collapse under them. "The crawl of the artillery and a large number of buggies bearing sick and wounded comrades over a hilly and woody country amidst almost absolute darkness, with here and there an unfriendly shot, made an ordeal which rarely if at all had come into soldier life."

General Morgan, who seemed to need less sleep than most men, rode up and down the line of march, "laughing with this one, joking with that one, assuming a fierce demeanor with another." As they moved through Glendale and crossed the Reading pike in the first gray of dawn, they surprised an occasional farmer out early for morning chores. One man described what he saw later that day for a newspaper reporter: "They were uniformed, many of them having linen dusters over their coats . . . appeared to be very much fatigued."

With daybreak came a welcome breeze and the first songs of morning birds. At convenient meadows and streams along the way companies dropped out of column for short halts to graze and water horses. But there could be no stopping for breakfast fires or sleep— so close to Cincinnati.

As regiments were re-forming, Duke's men hurrying through to the advance, the scouts ran into a militia outpost at a railroad bridge. They skirmished briefly, driving the enemy away and capturing a few fresh horses fully equipped. Hearing a train whistling, the scouts stacked crossties into a cattle gap, cut the telegraph wires, and concealed themselves in a cornfield near the tracks. The train's engineer, meanwhile, had sighted Morgan's main column on the road and put on a burst of speed.

"The train shot past us like a blazing meteor," said Lieutenant Peddicord, "and the next thing we saw was a dense cloud of steam above which flew large timbers. Our next sight startled our nerves, for there lay the monster floundering in the field like a fish out of water, with nothing but the tender attached. Her coupling must have broken, for the passenger carriages and express were still on the track, several yards ahead. Over three hundred raw recruits were on board, bound for Camp Dennison. They came tumbling and rolling out in every way imaginable. . . . All submitted without a single shot, and were sent under guard to the General."

The bridge defenders had been based at nearby Camp Dennison, and by the time Morgan's column crossed the railroad, the camp's complement of soldiers was in earnest pursuit. During the morning these untrained troops peppered away at the rear guard, but near Batavia they abandoned chase and began felling trees across the road to block the raiders in case they turned back. (Morgan of course did not turn back, and the felled trees only served to delay the regular Union cavalrymen when they arrived.)

About four o'clock that afternoon under a windless July sky, the weary, dusty raiders rode into Williamsburg—twenty-eight miles east of Cincinnati—ending the longest continuous march ever made by Morgan's men. They had covered ninety miles in thirty-five hours. As soon as the order was passed along to fall out for bivouac, the men tumbled from their saddles, tended briefly to their horses, and except for the unfortunate pickets all slept like dead men until bugles awakened them at dawn.

All day, July 15, as they continued eastward, forage parties scoured the countryside for food and horses, especially horses. A few miles out of Williamsburg, Dick Morgan and Tom Hines led the scouts off in a fast march twenty miles south to Ripley on the Ohio River, to search out possible crossings, but when they rejoined the main column late that evening at Locust Grove their report was negative. The Ohio was running full and ferries were under heavy guard. They would have to march on to Buffington Island, one of the fords selected by Captain Sam Taylor when he made his secret journey to Ohio back in the spring. And Buffington was almost a 100 miles to the east.

On Thursday, July 16, they were continually harassed by home guards, who ripped up bridges, felled trees across narrow roads, sometimes fired into the advance from concealment. "The enemy are now pressing us from all sides," James McCreary wrote that day, "and the woods swarm with militia. We capture hundreds of prisoners, but, a parole being null, we can only sweep them as chaff out of our way." At sundown they were in Jasper on the Scioto River. After ransacking the town they crossed the river to Piketon, breaking up a futile attempt by home guards to stand them off.

But behind them, Michigan and Kentucky Union cavalry regiments were regaining ground lost in the long ride around Cincinnati, and Morgan ordered another all-night march. For forty-five miles they rode steadily and at dawn on the seventeenth were in Jackson. Buffington Bar was still fifty miles away.

They halted in Jackson only long enough to take what they wanted from the stores. Some of the boys of the 2nd Regiment appropriated one drygoods establishment's stock of women's blue veils to use as sunshades. The veils proved to be useful accouterments as the troopers faced into the brilliant morning sun, but Ohioans were astonished when they saw this group riding by, looking for all the world like a company of harem ladies on parade.

During the past two days the column had acquired a number of odd pieces of rolling stock for transporting baggage and ailing members of the division—old lumbering omnibuses, a monstrous two-story peddler's wagon, a dozen or more hackney coaches used as ambulances, a number of barouches, top and open buggies, and several ordinary farm and express wagons. A Buckeye citizen forced to act as a guide reported after his release that he had ridden near the front with General Morgan in a barouche, and that the General was carrying "a pair of lady's fine kid boots suspended by their tiny silk lacings from one of the posts which supported the top of the vehicle." Morgan evidently had also visited a drygoods store to obtain a present for his young bride.

A short distance east of Jackson, the brigades took separate routes, Duke's men proceeding northeastward through Wilkesville, Johnson's following the southerly route through Vinton. Local militia again were felling trees in front of the 2nd Regiment, and the constant cry was "axes to the front" as the advance slowed down to cut away the blockades. At Wilkesville, there was token resistance in addition to log barricades, delaying Duke's column until long after midnight.

Day was breaking as the 2nd passed through Rutland, and when the advance joined Johnson's brigade near Pomeroy they found their comrades engaged in a sharp skirmish with regular Union troops. The latter were under command of General Henry M. Judah—Indiana and Illinois cavalry brought upriver from Louisville by steamboats to head off the raiders.

General Judah had arrived too late, however, to do more than brush Morgan's flanks. Shielded by hills, the raiders were around

Pomeroy at a trot before the pursuit could engage them. Major Webber marched the 2nd Kentucky in the rear, fighting off darting attacks from militia and units of regular Ohio troops.

Throughout the morning the column was virtually running a gantlet past strongly defended crossroads and hills, but Adam Johnson afterward recalled a reassuring meeting with General Morgan during a five-minute stop to rest horses. "I found him sitting on the gallery of a crossroads store, where there was a fine well; the boys were filling their canteens from the pump. The General greeted me with his bright smile, asking me to get down and rest a little, remarking: 'All our troubles are now over, the river is only twenty-five miles away, and tomorrow we will be on Southern soil.'"

About one o'clock that afternoon advance regiments were entering Chester. They quickly invested the town, preparing for an attack which never came. It was here that Morgan ordered a halt of about two hours—a delay which many of the men afterward believed was the turning point of their luck. The Ohio River was still eighteen miles away, and because of the long stop the raiders were unable to reach Buffington Island until after dark—forcing them to postpone their planned river crossing until the following morning.

Yet Morgan could scarcely have avoided a halt in Chester. Because of continual harassment from enemies along the way, his regiments had become intermixed, long gaps had broken the columns, men were marching in complete disorder, and horses were at the point of exhaustion.

By midafternoon they were out on the road to Portland, the sun scorching their backs, local militia active as hornets in their front. "Every bridge had been destroyed," said Lieutenant Peddicord, "and at every pass and ravine the road was blockaded and defended by troops in concealment. A large number of 'blockaders' were captured and compelled to clear away the obstructions that many of them had assisted in making. Poor fellows, they felt their time had come, so badly were they frightened. Oftentimes the boys would dismount, and go in pursuit of these bushwackers and command them to halt, but on they ran . . . never stopping until the boys laid violent hands upon them, holding them fast by main force. Even then they would strive hard to get away, just as some wild animals would do."

It was eight o'clock when the scouts fumbled their way into Portland on the Ohio River, under a sky veiled with a scud of clouds that brought early darkness. The first thing that most of the men wanted to do was stare across the liquid blackness of the river to vague shapes of hills that were Virginia.*

"All were now on the qui vive ," Major McCreary noted upon his arrival, "for the Ohio river is full of gunboats and transports, and an immense force of cavalry is hovering in our rear. . . . A dense fog wraps this woodland scene."

In the blackness of night and fog, the raiders could learn little more than that the approach to Buffington ford was defended by 300 Union infantrymen with two pieces of artillery, dug in behind a strong earthwork. Should they attack and try for the river? Or should they wait until morning? It was a difficult decision for Morgan and his officers to make. After some discussion they finally agreed that even if they could capture the earthwork without severe losses, the dark river probably would claim many lives. The Ohio was running much higher than normal because of unseasonably heavy rains upstream, and Buffington Island and its sand shallows were indiscernible.

Deciding to wait, Morgan ordered Warren Grigsby's 6th Kentucky, D. Howard Smith's 5th Kentucky, and Captain Byrne's battery to approach within 400 yards of the earthwork. At the first light of dawn these units were to storm the Yankee defenders. In the meantime, scouts moved out in both directions along the river, searching for other possible fords. One of these parties found a number of leaky flatboats about a mile and a half upstream, and as best they could in the darkness set about caulking the seams.

Most of the boys in the 2nd Kentucky had no special duties on this night. Junior officers and sergeants making a hasty check of ammunition supplies found that some men had no more than two or

---

[*Only a few weeks earlier this part of Virginia had become West Virginia, a Union state, but few of Morgan's men were aware of the change in status, nor would have accepted it, if they had known, as anything more than Yankee pettifoggery.]

three rounds left. But no one worried too much about that; Virginia and safety lay just across the ford. After engaging in rear guard action all day, they should have fallen into exhausted sleep, but somehow sleep would not come easily. Here and there musicians with guitars, banjos, and fiddles—confiscated from luckless Ohio merchants along the way—began playing sentimental tunes. In the darkness the musicians drew together, and a few of the boys came to listen. Soon they were all singing and playing "My Old Kentucky Home," the "Juanita," and "The Hills of Tennessee." To show off his dexterity a fiddler played a fast version of "The Arkansaw Traveler," and some of the listeners tried to dance a mock reel on the wet stubble of the wheatfield in which they were camped.

When weariness overcame the last of the music-makers, the foggy night lapsed into silence, broken only by the occasional snort of a horse, a soldier calling out in his sleep, and the muddy river murmuring unceasingly in the darkness.

4

"Everything important always happens to me on Sundays," John Morgan often said, and something very important was about to happen to him on the foggy Sunday morning of July 19, 1863.

The day began as planned, Grigsby and Smith starting their dismounted regiments cautiously through river mists toward the enemy earthwork. Not a sound could be heard on their front, and when the skirmish line dashed forward they found the earthwork abandoned, the two fieldpieces rolled over a nearby bluff.

Officers had just given the command to mount, when a rattle of musketry tore along the flank like a noise of ripping canvas. Fog still shrouded everything, but there was little doubt from the direction of firing that the attackers were General Judah's river-borne cavalrymen coming up after a night march from Pomeroy. A moment or so later, Judah's artillery boomed from behind the milky curtain of fog. And then as if on signal another fusillade of rifle fire broke from the opposite direction—revealing the presence of the raiders' constant pursuers in the rear, Union cavalry led by Generals Edward Hobson and James Shackleford, converging upon Adam Johnson's 2nd Brigade guarding the road from Chester.

While Morgan's forces formed to return fire from two directions, a gust of air "hot as the breath of an oven" rushed down the valley. The white fog lifted like a curtain going up, and for the first time the raiders could see the battlefield. They were in a V-shaped valley a mile long, about 800 yards wide, regiments scattered across meadows, cornfields, and among tan-colored shocks of wheat. Along one side of the V was a wooded ridge thick with Shackleford's cavalry; in the wide opening was Judah's mounted skirmish line. As they looked toward the other side of the V—the river running north and south— they were startled to see two menacing enemy gunboats. The raiders were trapped from three sides, the only way of escape being a narrow opening at the angle of the V.

As the 5th and 6th regiments began moving toward the river, the Union flagboat *Moose* opened fire with her powerful twenty-four-pounder Dahlgren guns. A minute later Judah's artillery in the valley and Hobson's on the ridge joined in the thunderous barrage. Now the raiders were caught in a three-way crossfire of exploding shells. In addition, several thousand dismounted Union cavalrymen were pressing closer, joining in with small arms fire. "The scream of the shells," Basil Duke wrote afterward, "drowned the hum of the bullets . . . and bursting between the two lines formed at right angles— a disposition we were compelled to adopt in order to confront both ground assailants—the air seemed filled with metal, and the ground was torn and ploughed into furrows."

There was little that Morgan's men could do to beat off the attacks. Although the 2nd Regiment was probably worse off than the others in regard to ammunition supply, a few companies averaged more than five rounds in cartridge boxes. As for Captain Byrne's battery, the bores of several pieces were so clogged they could scarcely be loaded with the few shells remaining, and the gunners in position to retaliate were quickly driven away by fire from the *Moose*.

Most disheartening of all was the rain-swollen river, its swift waters rippling over the sand shallows of Buffington Bar. A few men of Grigsby's and Smith's regiments rushed into the muddy current, tossing away their arms and stripping themselves of clothing, but less than thirty made it across, under close fire from the *Moose* and the *Allegheny Belle*. Farther upstream, some of the 9th Tennessee troopers managed to launch one of the repaired flatboats and crossed before the enemy discovered them.

The attack now heightened in fury, the Dahlgrens belching from the river, continuous small arms fire whining like an angry overtone. In the midst of this inferno, Duke and Morgan held a quick consultation. The only way of escape was through the narrow pass at the north end of the valley. Morgan would attempt to lead out as many men as possible, while Duke and Johnson made a last-ditch stand.

Duke galloped back to his brigade, and in the next few minutes watched his regiments break before one charge, rally to fight off another. He knew that many of the men had used their last cartridges. Several times he sent off couriers for the 2nd Kentucky, which had been camped about midway down the valley. But the 2nd was trapped in a maelstrom of men and horses, its companies being sucked off first in one direction and then the other, the men becoming hopelessly entangled with other regiments and separated from their sergeants and officers.

Farther up, Morgan was withdrawing rapidly through the narrow gap, his first companies in good order, the rear bunching, breaking ranks and clogging the road. Officers struggled vainly to re-form columns; bugles screamed quick urgent calls at cross purposes. Over all the field a thin blue haze of smoke was slowly spreading.

A shell struck the road where the 2nd was attempting to rally, throwing up a cloud of dust. A solid burst of shot danced around the heels of the horses; the pict-pict-pict-pict of bullets in flight made the men duck their heads clear to the saddle bows. A shell burst into a column, and then all around them was an eddy of men and horses in panic flight.

Troopers began unloading their booty of the raid—cutting loose

shoes, parasols, skates, sleighbells and birdcages, scattering them to
the winds. Long bolts of muslin and calico spun out in banners of
brilliant colors, streaming in the morning sunlight. "The upper end
of the valley," said Duke, "was filled with wagons and ambulances,
whose wounded and terror-stricken occupants urged the scared horses
to headlong flight. Often they became locked together, and were
hurled over as if by an earthquake. Occasionally a solid shot, or un-
exploded shell would strike one, and dash it into splinters. . . . The
remaining section of artillery was tumbled into a ravine, during this
mad swirl, as if the guns had been as light as feathers. The gunboats
raked the road with grape. . . . In a moment the panic was completed,
and the disaster irretrievable."

Among the last to escape through the jumbled gap were scattered
units of the 2nd Kentucky, Major Webber leading out the better part
of companies A, C, E, F, I and L.

5

As soon as he realized that further resistance was useless, Duke
ordered a flag of truce sent to the nearest of the Federal regiments,
the 7th Ohio Cavalry, under Colonel Israel Garrard. In a few minutes
firing ceased, and Garrard sent Captain Theodore Allen forward
with a platoon escort to accept Duke's surrender.

Shortly afterward a *Cincinnati Gazette* reporter, who had come
upriver with the gunboats, went ashore to see the captives. "The rebels
were dressed in every possible manner peculiar to civilized man. . . .
They wore in many instances large slouch hats peculiar to the slave
States, and had their pantaloons stuck in their boots. A dirty gray-
colored coat was most prevalent, although white dusters were to be
seen. . . . On the battlefield of Buffington Island, one could pick up
almost any article in the drygoods, hardware, house furnishing or
ladies' or gentlemen's furnishing—linen, hats, boots, gloves, knives,
forks, spoons, calico, ribbons, drinking cups, carriages, market wagons,
circus wagons. . . ."

Meanwhile Basil Duke and D. Howard Smith were meeting with Captain Allen of the 7th Ohio. "Colonel Duke," Allen recorded, "bore himself with great dignity, and I would not have known I had him if one of his own men had not accidentally disclosed his identity to me."

Of the approximately 700 men who surrendered at Buffington, 116 were of the 2nd Kentucky, a large part of G Company, the others representing almost every other company in the regiment. There are no accurate records to show how many of the 100 or so dead and severely wounded were 2nd Regiment men. The scouts—officially of the 14th Kentucky—also suffered heavy losses, both Dick Morgan and Tom Hines being captured. Hines was among those who surrendered to the 7th Ohio, and to show that he bore his captors no personal animosity he presented Captain Allen with a small Confederate flag.

While other Federal regiments were disarming scattered bands down the mile-length of the valley, the 7th Ohio moved its prisoners over to a tree-shaded strip beside the river. "As we sat on the river bank," Captain Allen said, "first one man and then another asked permission to go to the water's edge to wash his face, till pretty soon about one-half the men, both Union and Confederate, were at the river's edge, washing their faces, and digging the dust out of their ears, eyes, and nostrils. This proved to be such a halfway sort of business, and so unsatisfactory, that the men asked permission to go in swimming."

Allen decided to grant permission for one half the prisoners and one half the guards to swim together, the others to stand by and take turns later. The men stripped, plunging into the cool shallows. Only a few minutes before they had been enemies determined to kill each other; now they were splashing happily together in the water, ridding themselves of two weeks' accumulation of sweat and dust.

While the men were swimming together, one of Duke's officers standing beside Allen pointed to the naked soldiers and remarked philosophically: "It's difficult to tell one from the other when they're like that."

After the river bathing was finished, the Ohio boys shared the contents of their haversacks with Duke's troopers. "We spread out on the grass under the shade of the trees," said Captain Allen, "in regular picnic fashion, resting and waiting for orders." The captives soon fell asleep, sprawling like dead men. A few curious souvenir-hunting civilians wandered up to stare and search around, and when the guards were not looking they cut buttons off the uniforms of "Morgan's terrible men."

6

A few more than 1,100 men escaped with General Morgan, including about 250 of the 2nd Kentucky. They galloped away to the north, rounding a wide bend in the river, searching for another crossing. Close behind them came Shackleford and Wolford with Kentucky Union cavalry.

Fifteen miles upstream opposite Belleville, West Virginia, the river narrowed. It was deep for fording, but Morgan ordered the forward sections to plunge in and begin swimming their horses. Colonel Adam Johnson later told of leading the first group across: "Forming the men who were with me in columns of fours, I appealed to them to keep their ranks. . . . there was hardly a company in the whole division that was not represented in this body of men."

The first horses had scarcely touched hoofs upon the West Virginia shore when the gunboat *Moose*, like an unrelenting nemesis, shoved its ugly nose into view downstream. It was only a moment of bitter despair for the men on the Ohio shore. Only a few more minutes of precious time, and every man and horse could have been safely across! Without hesitation the gunboat opened fire, shelling columns forming on the Ohio shore, then dropping two or three heavy explosives into the stream where Morgan's men were swimming their horses four abreast.

"Looking back across the river," said Adam Johnson, "I saw a number of hats floating on the surface, and knew that each represented the life of a brave and gallant Confederate who had found a watery grave. . . . We reached the woods, where the men were now gathered, a little over three hundred."

When the gunboat opened fire, General Morgan was in mid-stream, swimming his prize steed, Glencoe. "He could have easily escaped," one of his officers declared afterward, "but seeing that the greater portion of his command would be left behind, he returned against the urgent protests of some of his officers and men, to share their fate."

Only 330 crossed safely, including two colonels, Adam Johnson of the 10th Kentucky and Warren Grigsby of the 6th. Two companies of the 2nd Kentucky were fairly well intact on the West Virginia side, F and L, with their captains, N. M. Lea and John Cooper. Captain Byrne, an artilleryman with no guns, rode ashore, and as might have been expected the always-nonchalant George Ellsworth also escaped with his portable telegraph. As quickly as possible these men mounted up and vanished into the West Virginia forest, bound south for the Confederate lines.

Driven away from the Ohio shoreline, Morgan's remaining force of 800 (about one-fourth of them were now 2nd Regiment men) gathered in the sheltering hills and quickly reorganized. Morgan named Major Tom Webber an acting colonel, combining the 200 men of his 2nd Regiment with about the same number surviving from other regiments of Duke's brigade. Roy Cluke replaced Adam Johnson as commander of the 2nd Brigade.

Webber assumed the duties of his new command with grim earnestness, still determined to escape and take his men out with him. For several days he had been painfully ill, disregarding his surgeon's advice to drop out of column and give himself up. Already the boys of the 2nd were calling him "Iron Man" Webber. As darkness fell over the Ohio hills, he set his men to work building large campfires, and when Morgan gave the signal all were lighted at once.

A few minutes later the reorganized companies mounted up, formed in columns of twos and rode quietly away. The old campfire trick was successful. Enemy patrols sighted the winking lights from afar, and all through the night Union cavalry units were moving into positions to surround what they believed was John Morgan's last camp of the raid.

But when morning came the raiders were far to the west, doubling back away from the river. For forty-eight hours they followed obscure trails through isolated hill country, avoiding all towns. Their whereabouts during this time were so much a mystery to Union pursuers that even General Burnside, who was commanding the entire pursuit operation, reached the conclusion that Morgan and most of his men had escaped into West Virginia.

Then suddenly, early in the morning of the twenty-second, they were reported sighted in a heavily forested section near the town of Zaleski, thirty-five miles west of the river. A few hours later the report was confirmed; several hundred Confederates were approaching Nelsonville. All of eastern Ohio, which had been breathing easier since the victory at Buffington, again became a bedlam of rumors and alarms. Never in the war had 800 poorly armed and badly mounted men frightened so many people over so large an area.

For three more days and nights, Morgan, Webber and Cluke kept their boys moving northeastward into the heart of the Union. On Thursday, the twenty-third, they crossed the Muskingum at Eagleport after fighting off some of Shackleford's cavalry, which had moved north across their front. "The enemy had fallen back on all the roads," Major Webber recorded, "guarding each one with a force in ambush much larger than ours—and to make our way out seemed utterly impossible."

The tireless Frank Wolford also got across their path, in the hills beyond the Muskingum, and captured more than 100 men, leaving Morgan with less than 700. According to Major Webber's account, the entire command narrowly escaped by climbing a high bluff "up which nobody but a Morgan man could have carried a horse."

Early Friday morning, the twenty-fourth, they rode boldly out upon the National Road, a few miles east of Cambridge. By questioning frightened farmers, they learned of an Ohio River ford called Coxe's Riffle a few miles below Steubenville. All day Friday and into the night the desperate horsemen marched eastward, through Harrisville and Smithfield.

Ten o'clock Saturday morning they were only five miles from the river, but their horses were utterly exhausted and a rest stop was ordered. The raiders sprawled under trees along the road near Wintersville, some of the officers entering a farmhouse and demanding breakfast. According to the terrified farmwife, Morgan and his officers collapsed upon her beds, stretching out for a few minutes of rest in their dusty clothes and boots. When a messenger brought Morgan warning of militia approaching from Wintersville, the General showed no concern. But a second report of regular cavalry moving up from the south—Shackleford and Wolford—caused a hurried departure.

Riding on toward Wintersville, the raiders charged the waiting militia, cleared the town, hurriedly collected foodstuffs from a general store, and swung away from Steubenville on the road to Richmond. A comedy of errors on the part of the Steubenville militia now saved them from immediate attack by Shackleford and Wolford.

As the Union cavalry came galloping after Morgan, Colonel James Collier was just arriving out of Steubenville at the head of 500 proud Minute Men. Sighting Shackleford's approaching dust cloud, the Minute Men immediately assumed it signaled the approach of Morgan's raiders. Forming a line of battle along a hill on the east side of Wintersville, Colonel Collier opened fire with a six-pounder loaded with scrap iron. The metal whistled through the air, one piece thwacking into the side of a Wintersville tavern and sending General Shackleford's troopers scurrying for cover.

As soon as Shackleford recognized the Minute Men for what they were, he sent an officer forward under a truce flag to enlighten their commander of his error. Approaching the militia's defense line, Shackleford's courier shouted: "What are you fools shooting at?" And then in colorful military profanity, he explained to the abashed Colonel Collier that he had been firing on Union soldiers.

All this delay won more than an hour of time for Morgan's raiders. They cut away from the main road, fended off two or three attacks from scouting parties during the late afternoon, and while Shackleford and Wolford were combing the countryside all night in search of them, they enjoyed a few hours of luxurious sleep, hidden in a patch of woods near Bergholz.

7

July 26 dawned bright and clear, a languid morning, the men rising without animation, wondering what another day would bring. It was a Sunday, the day on which everything important always happened to John Morgan, a week since the disaster at Buffington Island.

There were no more than 600 of them now, the ranks thinning daily as men dropped out for lack of horses or from sheer exhaustion. Most of them had no exact idea of where they were, and with Ellsworth and his telegraph gone the officers could only guess at the enemy's movements. From his tattered map, Morgan knew that Lake Erie was only sixty miles away, a hard two days' march, but even if they reached the lake their chances of escape by boat were poor indeed. And any hope of fighting their way around the shoreline to Canada was but a wild dream.

They had discussed surrender, rejecting it because they knew the Federals had suspended paroles and exchanges. Victories at Gettysburg and Vicksburg had surely filled the Northern prison camps with a surplus of Confederates, and if they surrendered now they could look forward to long periods of confinement. To a man they determined to fight on to the end.

What they did not know on this Sunday morning was that two fresh regiments of cavalry had entered the chase during the preceding twenty-four hours. Majors George W. Rue and W. B. Way had arrived at Mingo Station by rail from Cincinnati, each commanding about 375 veteran cavalrymen mounted on the speediest Kentucky saddle horses available.

Major Way and his 9th Michigan troopers struck Morgan's column at eight o'clock in the morning near Salineville and in a severe running fight inflicted about seventy-five casualties and captured 200 prisoners. Most of those captured were mounted on ungainly farm horses which failed miserably, the luckless riders firing off their last cartridges at the attackers and then surrendering. One group of Webber's brigade made their escape in front of a country church by hurriedly exchanging exhausted mounts for horses which had been hitched outside by the churchgoers.

At the time of the attack Morgan was riding in a carriage drawn by two white horses, and he escaped capture only by leaping out, mounting a led mare behind the carriage and galloping away. When the Michigan boys overtook the abandoned carriage they found inside "a loaf of bread, some hard-boiled eggs, and a bottle of whisky."

According to Major Webber's records, the surviving "old regulars" of C Company under Captain Ralph Sheldon made the last charge of the Great Raid during this Sunday morning fight. The troopers dashed valiantly down upon the enemy, but their tired horses breasted a fence without being able to clear it, knocking off the top rails. The boys of C Company stood their ground, firing their revolvers until chambers were empty. Some were killed, several wounded, and the most of them captured by the onrushing Michigan regiment.

With his command reduced to less than 400 men, Morgan broke away during this rear guard charge and continued northeastward. Riding parallel with him, however, on a secondary road, was another fresh enemy regiment—Major George Rue's assemblage of crack horsemen drawn from five different Kentucky and Michigan regiments, including a few of Frank Wolford's Wild Riders.

About noon the raiders collided with a small band of home guardsmen out of Lisbon. There was no fight, Morgan quickly sending forward a truce flag and promising to pass through the county without disturbing property if the Ohioans offered no resistance. Being completely outnumbered and unaware that Morgan's men were almost out of ammunition, the guardsmen agreed. When Morgan asked for a guide to the next county line, James Burbick, acting as a temporary captain, agreed to accompany the raiders as far as Elkton.

A few minutes later, his column in motion again, Morgan sighted the dust of Major Rue's troopers off to the right, across a broad valley. He turned immediately to Burbick and asked him if he would accept the surrender of the sick and wounded soldiers who were struggling to keep up with the fast pace. Burbick agreed to do so. While they were discussing terms, Rue's fresh horses pushed far ahead, swerving down a dry creek bed and cutting across Morgan's front.

John Morgan knew now that the end had come to his Great Raid. His men did not have enough ammunition to sustain a five-minute encounter; his horses could not outrun the force in his front, and he knew the pursuers in his rear would soon overtake him. But he had one more card to play—he wanted paroles for himself, his officers and men.

He ordered a halt and asked Burbick abruptly if he would accept his surrender. "On what conditions?" asked the astonished guardsman.

"On the condition that my officers and men be paroled to go home," replied Morgan.

"I don't understand the nature of a surrender," Burbick stammered. "I am not a regular officer."

"I have a right to surrender to anyone," Morgan insisted. "I want an answer right off, yes or no?"

"Yes," said Burbick.

Morgan took a handkerchief from his pocket, reached for Burbick's riding stick, and tied the white cloth to the end of it. He then ordered Burbick to ride out in company with two of the raiders' officers and inform the Federals that General Morgan had already surrendered.

It was two o'clock, July 26, 1863, a bright Sunday afternoon on the Crubaugh farm south of Lisbon, Columbiana County, Ohio, when Major George Rue, a six-foot-three Kentuckian, came riding up to John Morgan. Rue had to guide his mount through Morgan's troopers, who were lying in the grass along both sides of the road, some already asleep in the shade of fence corners. Morgan smiled when he recognized Rue; they had soldiered together in the war with Mexico.

Without preliminaries, Morgan informed Rue that he had already given his parole to Captain James Burbick. Then, as a sort of conciliatory gesture, he offered the Union commander a sorrel mare for a trophy.

Rue had little to say, but it was evident that he felt cheated over losing the honor of capturing General John Hunt Morgan. He ordered his officers to disarm the Rebels and collect their horses. He had 364 prisoners and almost 400 horses.

The endurance of the 2nd Kentucky Regiment is apparent in the records of Rue's prisoners. More than one-third of them were of that rugged organization. At the beginning of the Great Raid, one in five of Morgan's men was a 2nd Regiment trooper; after Buffington it was one in four; at the final surrender the ratio was better than one in three. The hard training given them by Basil Duke and St. Leger Grenfell had paid off for the veterans of the old 2nd. The Lexington Rifles, the Green River boys, the Lebanon Racers—they had shown the Yankees that Kentucky boys are alligator horses.

Years afterward a marker would be placed at the site of surrender, bearing the inscription:

> *This Stone Marks the Spot Where the*
> *Confederate Raider, General John H. Morgan*
> *Surrendered His Command to Major Geo. W. Rue*
> *July 26, 1863, and is the Farthest*
> *Point North Ever Reached by Any Body of*
> *Confederate Troops During the Civil War*

Whether Morgan surrendered to Rue, Burbick, or General James Shackleford is one of those moot points of history. To the end of his days Shackleford would claim the honor. Rue, he said, was operating under his command, and he even took away from Rue the sorrel mare given by Morgan, as well as the great Glencoe, which he shipped off as a gift to old General Winfield Scott. As for Burbick, Shackleford dismissed him as a mere civilian with no authority to accept a surrender from anybody.

Only a few minutes after Rue reached Morgan's side, Shackleford and Wolford arrived at a fast trot, and a strange reunion occurred there in the quiet Ohio farm country, all four men being Kentuckians. Wolford slid off his horse, limping with pain from the old wound Morgan's men had given him months before, his scorched meat-axe face breaking in a great grin at the sight of John Morgan disarmed.

Shackleford's manner, on the other hand, was cold and disdainful. Upon Morgan's insistence that Burbick had given him a parole, Shackleford declared that such a proposition was "not only absurd and ridiculous, but unfair and illegal." When Morgan saw that Shackleford had no intention of letting him go, he demanded to be put back upon the field to fight it out. "Your demand," Shackleford retorted, "will not be considered for a moment."

According to one of Wolford's men who was present at the meeting, "General Shackleford's passion got the upper hand of his judgement and he began to bestow some caustic epithets upon the conquered chieftain. Colonel Wolford interrupted, and rebuked the irate General, and told him that it was wrong to speak harshly to one whose hands were figuratively confined. Morgan as a token of appreciation of his kindness presented to Wolford his fine silver spurs."

During the afternoon the captives were marched down to Wellsville for transport by railroad to Cincinnati. Frank Wolford, in charge of the officers, put his prisoners at ease, and invited them all to share chicken and dumplings with him at the Whittaker House. "Gentlemen," he is reported to have said, "you are my guests. This hotel together with its bar, cigar stand, and other accessories is at your service and my expense. Do not go off the square in front of the hotel."

8

Basil Duke and the raiders captured at Buffington Island meanwhile had already been taken to Cincinnati. On that hot Sunday afternoon after the defeat at Buffington Island, they were marched ten miles on foot down the river to board two waiting transports. The overland march told severely on them, several almost fainting on the road from heat and exhaustion, and Duke himself became so lame he could hardly walk.

As the two boats bearing the prisoners approached Cincinnati, the levee filled with a throng of men, women, and children eager to see "Morgan's terrible men."

The sixty-eight captured officers disembarked, the boats then moving on down to the foot of Fifth Street, where the enlisted men were marched to a special train which would take them to Camp Morton at Indianapolis.

Duke, because of lameness, and Dick Morgan, because of an infected leg wound, were ordered into an open carriage. Their fellow officers formed in two ranks behind them and, with guards four deep on either side, were marched through Cincinnati to the City Prison on Ninth Street.

"Colonel Duke seemed to have many acquaintances in the city," one observer reported, "for as he rode up the street he was frequently recognized by persons in the crowd, to whom he would respond by lifting his hat."

For a brigade commander, the twenty-five-year-old Duke made a most unimpressive appearance, being dressed in plain blue jeans pants, a white linen shirt, and a dusty, wide-brimmed hat. He wore no marks of rank whatever. Yet he attracted the attention of every one, including a reporter for the *New York Post.* "He is of small stature, weighing scarcely 130 pounds, well built, erect, with angular features, dark hair brushed carelessly aside, sparkling and penetrating eyes of the same color, a low forehead, moustache and goatee. He has a sweet musical voice, a pleasant smile continually on his face, and is very free and cordial in his manner. There is nothing commanding in his appearance, though he has been termed by some the 'brains of the raid.'"

This same reporter also arranged to visit the other prisoners, "huge brawny men, most of them, while not a few of a more lithesome form, lying on blankets, jumped up and courteously greeted us, evincing in their manner good birth and education. They were dressed in all styles of costumes, but few Confederate uniforms being worn, as they were mostly clad in linen coats appropriated from the wardrobes of Ohioans or from clothing stores, the property of which they had confiscated. One huge six-footer was clad in a dressing robe, and sported a huge black sombrero, looped up at the side with a plume of the same color. His immense black whiskers, which reached nearly to his waist, and his heavy moustache, gave him a brigandish-looking appearance, as he strode in a theatrical manner around the room, smoking a cigar."

John Morgan's arrival after dark a week later, with Webber, Cluke and his other officers, provided another Roman holiday for Cincinnati. A mob of 5,000 milled around the railroad station, some brandishing pistols and shouting, "Hang the cut-throats!" But no effort was made to storm the glittering bayonets of the guard, Union regulars of the 111th Ohio Infantry, who formed a hollow square and marched the prisoners quickly through the crowds, the regimental band playing "Yankee Doodle."

At the jail, newspaper reporters were permitted to interview the prize captive of the raid. "Morgan appeared in good spirits," one wrote, "and quite unconcerned at his ill luck." He was dressed in a linen coat, white shirt, black trousers, and a light felt hat, "a well-built man, of fresh complexion and sandy hair and beard." The alert *New York Post* correspondent quoted a request Morgan made to General Mahlon Manson: "General, I wish you would intercede and get a drink for me. I'm terribly dry." After this remark, the reporter said, Morgan bowed courteously to the newspaperman, and with cigar in mouth walked away with his jailer.

9

And what did it accomplish—the Great Raid of July 1863? Militarily it forced General Burnside to delay his planned move into eastern Tennessee to join Rosecrans against Bragg at Chattanooga. Bragg never forgave Morgan for crossing the Ohio, but the absence of thousands of Burnside's troops occupied in pursuing Morgan's raiders enabled Bragg to win the battle of Chickamauga—the only great victory the Confederacy was to win in the western theater of war. In addition, during the crossing of Kentucky, Indiana and Ohio, the raiders inflicted almost 600 casualties and captured and paroled 6,000 enemy troops. They destroyed bridges, railroad equipment, telegraph wires and military stores, the total value of claims public and private approaching ten million dollars.

Yet neither Bragg nor the Confederate high command considered all this a fair exchange for 2,000 of the Confederacy's best cavalrymen.

As for the 2nd Kentucky Cavalry, it was never to regain its full strength. In late July the remnants of Company D, escaping from Twelve Mile Island, were making their way south by stealthy night marches through Kentucky and Tennessee. Sections of A, F and L companies and a scattering of men from other companies were with Adam Johnson in western Virginia, searching for the Confederate lines. Four hundred and ninety-three men of the 2nd Regiment were prisoners in Camp Morton, their officers locked in cells in the Cincinnati jail.

Almost two more years of war, however, were yet to come, and many 2nd Kentucky cavalrymen would play exciting parts in the struggle, even into the turbulent weeks following Lee's surrender at Appomattox.

Henry Morton Stanley at the time he joined the Confederate Army in 1861. Courtesy of University of Illinois at Urbana Champaign Library.

9

Oaths and Allegiances

1

Most famous of all the Galvanized Yankees was Henry Morton Stanley, a newspaper correspondent and African explorer, best known as the man who found David Livingstone on Lake Tanganyika and uttered the immortal words, "Dr. Livingstone, I presume."

Stanley did not serve in any of the six U.S. Volunteer Infantry regiments. He was among several captured Confederates who took the oath of allegiance and were inducted into a regular Union regiment—two years before the U.S. Volunteers were organized.

Stanley's real name was John Rowlands. Born illegitimately in northern Wales, he lived a precarious existence until the age of fifteen, when he sailed for New Orleans as a cabin boy. He jumped ship, and by chance met a wealthy Southern businessman whose name was Henry Morton Stanley. The elder Stanley gave John Rowlands employment and eventually adopted him, insisting that the boy take his name. Among other resolutions, young Stanley pledged himself never to drink intoxicating liquors, a promise which he was to break only once in his lifetime.

In 1860, the father placed his adopted son on an Arkansas River plantation to learn its management, and then sailed for Havana to attend to some urgent business matters. Young Stanley did not like plantation life, and he soon took a job as a clerk in a store at Cypress Bend, anxiously awaiting the return of his adopted father.

A few months later the Civil War began. At first, Stanley had no strong feelings about the war. He was then twenty years old and small for his age—he stood only five feet, five inches—and was shy and lonely. He considered himself an outsider, an Englishman; the war was an American affair and no concern of his. By early summer, however, he was caught up in the war fever and in July 1861 he joined the Confederate Army.

He saw no major action until the spring of 1862, when his regiment moved to northern Mississippi. On April 6 he was in the midst of the carnage at Shiloh. The next day, when Union forces pushed the Confederates back, Stanley was captured. A few hours later he was on a steamboat with hundreds of other prisoners bound for St. Louis. From there he was sent to a new but already overcrowded military prison, Camp Douglas in Chicago.

"Our prisons-pen," Stanley later wrote,

> was a square and spacious enclosure, like a bleak cattle-yard, walled high with planking, on the top of which, at every sixty yards or so, were sentry-boxes. About fifty feet from its base, and running parallel with it was a line of lime-wash. This was the "deadline" and any prisoner who crossed it was liable to be shot. . . . To whatever it was due, the appearance of the prisoners startled me. The Southerners' uniforms were never pretty, but when rotten, and ragged, and swarming with vermin, they heightened the disreputability of their wearers; and if anything was needed to increase our dejection after taking sweeping glances at the arid mud-soil of the great yard, the butternut and gray clothes, the sight of ash-colored faces, and of the sickly and emaciated condition of our unhappy friends, were well calculated to do so.

At one end of the prison enclosure was the office of the commandant, Colonel James A. Mulligan, a considerable hero at that time to the numerous Irishmen of Chicago. The long-haired, droopy-moustached Mulligan had earned a reputation as a wild fighter at Lexington, Missouri, even though he and most of his Irishmen had been captured there. After being exchanged for a Confederate colonel, Mulligan returned to Chicago as commander at Camp Douglas, but he was only marking time until he could organize another Irish regiment.

Among the Confederate prisoners captured at Fort Donelson in February 1862, Mulligan had discovered a number of Irish-born prospects who seemed willing to fight for the Union in exchange for their freedom. Before Stanley's arrival, Mulligan had sent a message to General H. W. Halleck asking if it were permissible to enlist prisoners of war into the Union Army. Halleck did not know. On March 4 he informed Mulligan that he was passing the query on to General McClellan. A week later Halleck wrote again to Mulligan: "As the War Department does not answer my letter in relation to your enlisting prisoners of war I shall take the responsibility of authorizing you to immediately fill up your regiment in that way. Great caution, however, must be used as to the character of the persons so enlisted. You should make yourself personally acquainted with the history of each recruit received and exercise a sound discretion in the matter."

Mulligan of course was delighted. He virtually converted Camp Douglas from a prison camp into a recruiting station and began mustering in Irishmen and other foreign-born recruits. A few days later, however, he received another message from Halleck, dated March 15: "I have just received instructions from the War Department not to permit the enlistment of prisoners of war. You will be governed by these instructions."

Evidence indicates that Mulligan conveniently "lost" that second message, and because of poor communications between various divisions of the burgeoning and far-flung U.S. War Department, several months passed before Washington authorities discovered that the fiery Irishman had gone blithely ahead with his enlistment of prisoners. Not until October did the Commissary General of Prisoners discover a roll of 228 Confederate prisoners "who while in charge of Colonel Mulligan at Camp Douglas, Ill., were permitted to enlist. . . . All this was done without authority and in violation of Colonel Mulligan's special duty."

Sometime in April, at least a month after Mulligan was ordered to discontinue recruiting, a Camp Douglas official informed Prisoner Henry M. Stanley that he could be released "by enrolling as a Unionist, that is becoming a Union soldier." Although Stanley debated the matter for six weeks, he finally volunteered as a recruit on June 4.

Harsh as were conditions in the prison, it was no easy decision for young Stanley to make. In his autobiography he described his feelings with his customary vivid style:

"We found it to be a dreary task to endure the unchanging variety of misery surrounding us. I was often tempted with an impulse to challenge a malignant sentry's bullet by crossing that ghastly "deadline" which I saw every day I came out.

In our treatment I think there was a purpose. If so, it may have been from a belief that we should the sooner recover our senses by experiencing as much misery, pain, privation, and sorrow as could be contained within a prison; and, therefore, the authorities rigidly excluded every medical, pious, musical or literary charity that might have alleviated our sufferings. . . .

Left to ourselves, with absolutely nothing to do but to brood over our positions, bewail our lots, catch the taint of disease from each other, and passively abide in our prison-pen, we were soon in a fair state of rotting, while yet alive. . . . Everything we saw and touched added to its pernicious influence—the melancholy faces of those who were already wearied with their confinement, the number of the sick, the premature agedness of the emaciated, the distressing degeneration of manhood, the plaints of suffering wretches, the increasing bodily discomfort from ever-multiplying vermin, which infested every square inch. . . . The men began to suffer from bilious disorders; dysentery and typhus began to rage. Day after day my company steadily diminished; and every morning I had to see them carried in their blankets to the hospital. . . . Those not yet delirious, or too weak to move unaided, we kept with us; but the dysentery . . . was a peculiary epidemical character, and its victims were perpetually passing us, trembling with weakness, or writhing with pain,

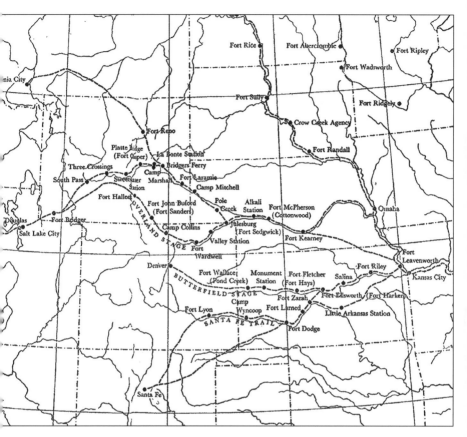

Map identifying military posts occupied by the 1st to 6th U.S. Volunteers, from October 17, 1864, to November 13, 1866. From an unknown source.

exasperating our senses to such a degree that only the strong-minded could forego some expression of their disgust.

The latrines were all at the rear of our plank barracks, and each time imperious nature compelled us to resort to them, we lost a little of that respect and consideration we owed our fellow-creatures. For, on the way thither, we saw crowds of sick men, who had fallen, prostrate from weakness, and given themselves wholly to despair; and, while they crawled or wallowed in their filth, they cursed and blasphemed as often as they groaned. In the edge of the gaping ditches, which provoked the gorge to look at, there were many of the sick people, who, unable to leave, rested there for hours, and made their condition hopeless by breathing the stenchful atmosphere. Exhumed corpses could not have presented anything more hideous than dozens of these dead-and-alive men, who oblivious to the weather, hung over the latrines, or lay extended along the open sewer, with only a few gasps intervening between them and death. Such as were not too far gone prayed for death, saying, 'Good God, let me die! Let me go, O Lord!' and one insanely damned his vitals and his constitution, because his agonies were so protracted. No self-respecting being could return from their vicinity without feeling bewildered by the infinite suffering, his existence degraded, and religion and sentiment blasted.

Yet, indoors, what did we see? Over two hundred unwashed, unkempt, uncombed men, in the dismalist attitudes, occupied in relieving themselves from hosts of vermin, or sunk in gloomy introspection, staring blankly, with heads between their knees, at nothing; weighted down by a surfeit of misery, internal pains furrowing their faces, breathing in a fine cloud of human scurf, and dust of offensive hay, dead to everything but the flitting fancies of the hopeless!"

When Stanley was first presented with the possibility of escaping this desolation by taking an oath of allegiance and enlisting in the Union Army, he refused. "Every American friend of mine was a Southerner, my adopted father was a Southerner."

Perhaps it was his bunk mate, W. H. Wilkes of Mississippi, who unintentionally helped the young English-born prisoner to make his decision. Wilkes was a nephew of the Union admiral, Charles Wilkes, who had forcefully taken Confederate commissioners James Mason and John Slidell off a British vessel. The young Confederate Wilkes did not seem to think it strange that his family should be divided by the war, and Stanley may have reasoned that changing allegiances could not be so reprehensible after all.

Six more weeks of prison horrors, the useless flight of time, the fear of being incarcerated for years, led Stanley to the belief that he was going mad. "Finally I was persuaded to accept with several other prisoners the terms of release, and enrolled myself in the U.S. Artillery service, and on the 4th June was once more free to inhale the fresh air."

Two or three days later he fell ill from dysentery, but sought no medical aid for fear he might be returned to prison. On the day he arrived at Harper's Ferry, he collapsed, was taken to a hospital, and on June 22 was mustered out of service, a physical wreck.

Stanley's career in the Union Army was brief, but he was not yet finished with the American Civil War. He left Harper's Ferry on foot, and spent almost a week walking twenty-four miles to a farm near Hagerstown. There a kindly farmer took care of him until he regained his health. He worked in the Maryland harvest, went to Baltimore and took a job on an oyster schooner, and eventually found a berth on a seagoing ship. He was determined to make his way to Havana and rejoin his father, but when he reached Cuba he learned that the elder Henry M. Stanley was dead.

Once again he was alone in the world. Returning to New York, Stanley enlisted in the U.S. Navy, and thus probably became the only man ever to serve in the Confederate Army, the Union Army, and the Union Navy. By now a fine sailor, he soon earned a rating on the *Minnesota* as ship's writer, his duties being to transcribe the log and other ship records.

While the *Minnesota* was off Fort Fisher, North Carolina, Stanley witnessed at close hand several sea and land battles, and while writing these up for the ship's records, an idea came to him to compose some narratives of the exciting events and send them to newspapers. Thus began Stanley's career as a journalist and writer.

He became so interested in writing that he wanted to do nothing else. After the *Minnesota* docked in Portsmouth, New Hampshire, Stanley became so bored that he decided he had had enough of the U.S. Navy. On February 10, 1865, in company with another young sailor, Stanley deserted.

Stanley's three failures as an American soldier and sailor seem a strange beginning for a man who in a few years was to become one of the great figures of the nineteenth century.

There was one final piece of irony in his American adventures. After he deserted the navy, Stanley felt a compulsion to see the West. He reached the frontier in the spring of 1865, just as the organized regiments of Galvanized Yankees were marching out from Fort Leavenworth to help hold together the breaking lines of communication between East and West. He visited many of the same places where these men soldiered—stations along the Platte, Salt Lake City, Denver. In Colorado he built a flat-bottomed boat and floated down the Platte, stopping occasionally at camps and forts manned by the 5th and 6th U.S. Volunteers. When he reached Omaha, for some inexplicable reason this sober young man got gloriously drunk. He roamed the streets all night, singing and yelling, and next morning swore he would never become intoxicated again.

Stanley was a Galvanized Yankee before that epithet was even invented—and then only for a brief time—but he surely met and talked with some of the men who had made the same hard choice he had made back in 1862 in Camp Douglas prison. One can but wonder what his emotions were toward these erstwhile brothers-in-arms. Sympathy, pity, envy? Or was it remorse? Why, when he reached Omaha, did he feel compelled to break a pledge he had made to himself as a youth never to touch intoxicating liquors, a pledge he did not break again as long as he lived?

—➤◆◄—

2

In the first year of the Civil War, military leaders were too much occupied with other matters to give any deep thought to conversion of allegiances. No large-scale battles were fought in that preparatory year and comparatively few prisoners were taken. In 1862, however, events moved on a grander scale. Many thousands of soldiers were engaged across half a continent; captives began to crowd each other in dreadful prison pens.

Because the Union did not recognize the Confederacy as a sovereign nation, the business of exchanging prisoners presented a tricky problem, but eventually a cartel was devised for the parole and exchange of captured soldiers. The system never was very satisfactory to either contender; one side or the other would suddenly change the rules or suspend exchanges altogether.

Not long after this exchange system was put in operation, Northern prison commandants—such as Colonel James Mulligan— discovered that some of their prisoners had no desire to be exchanged. In the spring of 1862 these defectors were few, and most of them were foreign-born, with no strong sense of allegiance to any country. Yet they were there and something had to be done with them.

After Colonel Mulligan audaciously arranged to enlist Henry M. Stanley and 227 other Confederate prisoners into the Union Army, leaders in the upper echelons of the War Department began to ponder the problem of loyalties. Americans had inherited the English ideal of natural allegiance to one's country, yet they had also endured a long period of travail from the Revolutionary War through the War of 1812 during which they had rejected that doctrine. By the 1860s, however, loyalty to the Union was a sacred thing to millions of Americans, and there was something repellent in the idea of lightly transferred fealties.

The fact that the Confederacy was not recognized as a legitimate government, but only as an erring group of states, made it possible for Union leaders to reason that *nemo potest exuere patriam*, the doctrine that no one can cast off his country, was not applicable to

Major General John Pope demonstrated great ability in successfully quelling the Indian uprising in Minnesota as commander of the Department of the Northwest. From Frank Leslie's Illustrated History of the Civil War, 1861–65, page 342.

captured Confederate soldiers. If there was no Confederate States of America then a captured Confederate soldier was not committing an act of treason if he took an oath of allegiance to the United States. In the spring of 1862 the policy makers could reason that far but no farther; the idea of enlisting former enemies was still too uncomfortable to accept. Prisoners were permitted to take the oath on condition that they would remain north of the Confederate lines, and they were required to give a bond of $1,000 as security for this condition. For the next two years, the War Department would approach and retreat from the idea of enlistments with great caution and suspicion—until at last in 1864 President Lincoln gave it his endorsement.

The most powerful man in the cabinet, Secretary Edwin M. Stanton, was one of those who seemed unable to make up his mind on the question. As early as July 10, 1862, Stanton authorized United States Marshall Robert Murray to interview prisoners of war in New York "for the purpose of ascertaining whether any and how many are willing to enter into the military service of the U.S." About the same time, the commissary general of prisoners, William Hoffman, informed Adjutant-General Lorenzo Thomas that some prisoners had expressed a wish "to remain at the North and enter our service." On August 5, the governor of Indiana wrote General Halleck that a number of rebel prisoners in Camp Morton "desire to volunteer into our Army instead of being exchanged. I am in favor of accepting them, believing they can be trusted and it will have a good effect."

Stanton could not bring himself to take definitive action on any of these openings, and the final steps toward enlisting prisoners might never have been taken had not the Sioux Indians started their war along the Minnesota frontier in late summer of 1862.

Under the fierce generalship of Little Crow, the Sioux attacked the Minnesotans at a time when most of their soldiers were away fighting Confederates, and in a few days slew more than 1,500 settlers. Governor Alexander Ramsey of Minnesota bombarded the War Department with pleas for help at a time when one Confederate Army was thrusting north into Kentucky and another was driving General John Pope back upon the defenses of Washington. No troops could be spared for fighting Indians. After Pope was dismissed from command, Stanton transferred him out to Minnesota to redeem himself, and gave consideration to a suggestion made by Governor Ramsey: "The 3rd Regiment of Minnesota Volunteers is on parole at Benton Barracks, St. Louis. We need a well-drilled force of which we are now utterly destitute to resist the overwhelming force of Indians now attacking our frontier settlements. Cannot you order the 3rd Regiment to report at once to me, with arms and ammunition, of which we are in great need? This service would not be in violation of their parole. The exigency is pressing. Reply immediately."

Stanton was inclined to agree with the governor of Minnesota. The parole system as originally arranged between the Union and Confederacy provided that when one side had an excess of prisoners they were to be paroled and sent home, not to engage in further military activities until exchanged. In 1862 both sides stopped the practice of permitting parolees to go to their homes, and established parolee camps so that men awaiting exchange could be drilled and kept under military discipline. Such was the condition of the 3rd Minnesota, and after studying the parole agreement, Stanton convinced himself that it would not be in violation of the cartel to send these men back to Minnesota to fight Indians. Orders to that effect were issued, but a test of whether or not this was in violation of the parole agreement was avoided because the regiment was declared exchanged on August 27.

On September 9, Governor David Tod of Ohio telegraphed Stanton: "If the Indian troubles in Minnesota are serious and the paroled Union prisoners are not soon to be exchanged would it not be well to send them to Minnesota? It is with great difficulty we can preserve order among them at Camp Chase." Stanton immediately replied that this was an excellent suggestion, and a week later he sent General Lew Wallace to Camp Chase, near Columbus, to organize the paroled Union soldiers into regiments "for service against the Northern Indians." He also arranged for several thousand other parolees in camps at Annapolis and Harper's Ferry to be transferred to Camp Chase for ultimate service against Indians.

By the end of September, so many parolees were pouring into

Camp Chase that Wallace could not handle them. "Do not send any more paroled prisoners here," he wired Stanton. "It is impossible to do anything with those now at Camp Chase. They generally refuse to be organized or do any duty whatever. Every detachment that arrives only swells a mob already dangerous. The Eastern troops are particularly disinclined to the Indian service."

In a lengthy report to Adjutant-General Thomas, September 28, Wallace explained that almost every man in camp was "possessed with an idea that because he was paroled he was until exchanged exempt from duty of any kind. . . . A large number in fact hold paroles which they have sworn to, obligating them not to go into camp or take arms for any purpose in behalf of the United States. . . . When I announced my purpose in camp that I was to organize them for service against the Northwestern Indians a very few received it with favor. Nearly the whole body protested. Especially was this the case with the Eastern troops. Every objector intrenched himself behind his parole."

To further complicate Lew Wallace's difficulties, the Confederate Army got wind of the scheme to use parolees against Indians, and immediately attempted to block it by adding a no-Indian-fighting clause in their paroles. This came to President Lincoln's notice on October 3, and he asked the War Department to rule on its validity "based upon the general law and its cartel. I wish to avoid violations of law and bad faith." After deliberating for twenty-four hours, Stanton and Halleck telegraphed Lincoln "that the parole under the cartel does not prohibit doing service against the Indians."

But this was not the end of the matter. The very next day, October 5, the Confederate government through its prisoner exchange agent dispatched a message to the Union exchange agent, protesting the sending of

> officers and men of the U.S. forces who have been paroled and not exchanged . . . to your frontiers to fight the Indians now in arms against you. This is in direct conflict with the terms of the cartel. Its language is very plain. It says: "The surplus prisoners not exchanged shall not be permitted to take up arms again, not to serve as military police or

*constabulary force in any fort, garrison, or field work held by either of
the respective parties, not as guards of prisons, depots or stores, not to
discharge any duty usually performed by soldiers, until exchanged under
the provisions of this cartel."*

In Minnesota by this time, General Pope had scraped together
enough volunteer soldiers and militia to put down Little Crow's
Sioux. Two years later when a more widespread Indian war broke out
across the Plains, the War Department had reached a position where
it could accept without too many qualms the principal of enlisting
former enemies into its armies.

The steps by which it arrived at this rationalization were gradual,
and make an interesting study of the pragmatics and absurdities of
civil wars. The question of foreign-born prisoners, for example, was
forever arising. In February 1863, the commandant at Camp Butler,
Illinois, reported the presence of a large number of Irish, German, and
Polish prisoners of war, some of whom had gone from Illinois to the
South for employment before the war, and who claimed they had been
conscripted by force. "They are willing to take the oath of allegiance
and fight for the Union, and but for the misfortune of locality would
ere this be found in the ranks of loyal regiments." Colonel Christian
Thieleman, who was organizing a German cavalry regiment, the
16th Illinois, became interested in enlisting these men and brought
pressure to bear on the War Department.

At this time Stanton was firmly against such action and forbade
enlistment of former Confederates, even though foreign-born. A
month later, however, after receiving notices from other camps of
many more such prisoners who were about to be exchanged and
returned to the South, he softened his attitude: "The rule is not to
permit Confederate prisoners to join our Army. But in any case in
which you are satisfied a prisoner is sincerely desirous of renouncing
all connection with the rebels, you may on his taking the oath of
allegiance send him to Fort Delaware, to be released there after
further investigation as to his sincerity and sent North to reside."

Meanwhile, commanders at various camps were occasionally

taking matters into their own hands and permitting small groups of prisoners to swear allegiance and enlist in Union regiments. (Prison commanders changed frequently, and some had no knowledge of War Department policy in the matter.) At Camp Douglas in March 1863 a few former Confederates were inducted into Illinois regiments. At Camp Morton in June, fifty Tennesseans enlisted in the 71st Indiana, 155 in the 5th Tennessee Union Cavalry. "Quite a parade was made of the departure of this last group for Lexington [Kentucky] on June 13. With an escort from the 71st Indiana they marched down Pennsylvania Street to Market and through the heart of the town [Indianapolis] to Union Station where they entrained with rousing cheers."

Oddly enough this latter incident occurred on the very day that Confederate General John Morgan was starting his columns North for his great raid through Indiana and Ohio, a raid which would result in the capture of a number of his cavalrymen, some of whom later became Galvanized Yankees and served with the 11th Ohio Cavalry in the West.

In that same month events had moved far enough for Stanton and the War Department to take one more official step toward enlistment of Confederates. Union armies were sweeping up so many prisoners that there was not room for all of them in Northern camps, and commanders in the field began requesting permission to enlist those who expressed a desire to transfer their allegiances to the Union. Reacting to these demands, Stanton directed on June 20 that "when it can be reliably shown that the applicant was *impressed* into the rebel service and that he now wishes in good faith to join our army, he may be permitted to do so on his taking the oath of allegiance."

This ruling was so loosely administered, however, and so many of the freed and enlisted Confederates deserted at the first opportunity, that Stanton reversed himself on August 26: "The Secretary of War directs that hereafter no prisoners of war be enlisted in our Army without his special sanction in each case." The order of course virtually halted enlistments in the field. Stanton gave General William Rosecrans special permission to enlist a few foreign-born

Confederate conscripts, and in September he authorized Governor Morton of Indiana to muster more than 100 Irish Catholic prisoners into an Indiana Irish regiment.

About this time someone—probably General Gilman Marston at Point Lookout prison—conceived the idea of enlisting captured Confederates into the U.S. Navy. Stanton turned this proposal over in his mind for several weeks, consulted with the Secretary of the Navy, and at last on December 21, 1863, issued instructions to prison camp commanders to make arrangements to enlist into the Navy prisoners willing to take the oath of allegiance.

There was no great rush of prisoners desiring Navy service. Not many of them had any sea experience, and in at least one camp, Rock Island, loyal Confederates organized themselves to block the efforts of the camp commandant to so enlist them. The leaders of this movement secretly enlisted 1,300 fellow prisoners into a paper cavalry regiment of ten companies, which held steadfast until the autumn of 1864, when a few were beguiled into the Galvanized Yankees with the offer of freedom for going West to fight the Indians. The majority of this group remained loyal to the Confederacy until freed by exchange or the end of the war.

Near the end of 1863, one of the most controversial figures of the Union Army, General Benjamin Butler, entered the listings of those in high command who were interested in converting Rebels into Yankees. Butler was a shrewd politician, a poor military leader, a good hater with genius for creating enemies as well as whipping his followers into line, ruthless and possessed of such abounding energy that few could ignore him. As Commander of the Department of Virginia and North Carolina, he was responsible for the operation of one of the largest of all prison camps, Point Lookout, a Maryland sandspit thrusting into Chesapeake Bay.

Late in December, Butler began an earnest correspondence with Stanton, in which he expressed the opinion that many more prisoners could be enlisted into the army than into the navy. As Butler was a political power in Massachusetts, the Secretary of War decided to bring the matter to President Lincoln's attention. On January 2,

1864, Lincoln addressed himself directly to the general, informing him that enlistments of prisoners of war into either the army or navy would be permissible under certain conditions. These conditions, the President added, would be explained by his secretary, John Hay, who was to deliver the letter in person. That same day Stanton sent a telegram to Butler stating that the President was sending Hay "to Point Lookout with a letter to you. . . . You will please meet him there, if convenient, and come to Washington for the purpose of explanations and further instructions." Evidently no effort was to be spared by the administration in gaining Butler's good will; 1864 was a presidential election year.

John Hay met Butler on January 9, presenting him with a questionnaire which Lincoln had composed, four questions which were to be asked in privacy to every prisoner at Point Lookout. In addition to the questionnaire, the President had sent a large blank book in which each prisoner was to sign his name and his replies to the interrogation:

1. Do you desire to be sent South as a prisoner of war for exchange?
2. Do you desire to take the oath of allegiance and parole, and enlist in the Army or Navy of the U.S., and if so which?
3. Do you desire to take the oath and parole and be sent North to work on public works, under penalty of death if found in the South before the end of the war?
4. Do you desire to take the oath of allegiance and go to your home within the lines of the U.S. Army, under like penalty if found South beyond those lines during the war?

With characteristic dispatch, Butler appointed one of his protégés, Lieutenant F. M. Norcross, a lamed war veteran of the 30th Massachusetts, to direct the questioning of prisoners and recruit those who answered the second questions in the affirmative.

On March 1, Private Bartlett Malone, a Point Lookout prisoner from North Carolina, noted in his diary: "Our Company was examined on the Oath question evry man was taken in the House one at a time and examioned; the questions asked me was this: Do you wish to take the Oath and join the U.S. Armey or Navey; or work at government work or on Brestworks or Do you wish to take a Parole and go to your home if it be insied of our lines or do you wish to go South." I told him I wished to go South." This answer kept Malone in prison until a few days before the end of the war.

The interrogation of some 8,000 prisoners individually was a slow process, and it was late in March before Butler informed Stanton that he had "more than a minimum regiment of repentant rebels, whom a friend of mine calls *transfugees*, recruited at Point Lookout. "They behave exceedingly well, are very quiet, and most of them I am certain are truly loyal, and I believe will make as efficient a regiment as there is in the service. I should like to organize and arm it at once."

Four days later Butler received his final authorization "to recruit and organize a regiment at Point Lookout, Maryland, to serve for three years or during the war." On March 28, the regiment was officially designated as the 1st U.S. Volunteer Infantry. This was the culmination of the War Department's two years of circling the sensitive question of allegiances—a complete acceptance of all erring brothers who were willing to repent.

In the early months of 1864, about one in eight of the prisoners at Point Lookout took the oath and became Galvanized Yankees. Many of them had been there on that flat stretch of sand, which was bare of trees, shrubs, or vegetation of any kind, for two years or more. They had endured scorching summers "whose severity during the day is as great on the sandbarren as anywhere in the Union north of the Gulf," and hard winters "more severe at that point than anywhere in the country south of Boston." Surrounded by a fifteen-foot board enclosure, they were "confined in open tents, on the naked ground, without a plant or a handful of straw between them and the heat or frost of the earth."

Private Malone recorded the deaths of five men from freezing, hunger so acute "that they caught a Rat and cooked him and eat it." He also made three entries in April and May 1864, referring to guards shooting into prisoners' tents, killing and wounding several, and then on June 14 noted briefly that "500 rebels taken the Oath and went outside."

To remain loyal to the Confederacy, they had to resist not only their physical discomforts, the brutality of guards, rumors of a collapsing South but also pleading letters from home. Evans Atwood, captured in Virginia, wrote his wife of the opportunity to take the oath, and she urged him to do so—anything to escape the debilitating prison life.

"Since the receipt of your letter," he replied,

> *ten thousand thoughts have wearied my mind, my soul, my very life. . . . After calm, sober and serious meditation, I have weighed, wondered and re-examined your request and excuse me for so saying— I must follow the path of duty to my country, for which I am now a prisoner. I have gone through many dangers, have passed often by the gates of death . . . but amid all this I ever thought that your prayers, your sympathy, and your love followed me; but now what must I say? What must I do? I must not disgrace friends, character and more than all, kindred—wife, child! No . . . I do not think you desire this. Let me stay in prison until released honorably; let me discharge my duty.*

Lieutenant Atwood did not become a Galvanized Yankee. We have no record of his emotions as he watched 1,000 of his former comrades board the convoy ship *George Henry* late in April 1864 to sail to their first duty assignment at Norfolk, Virginia. "We arrived at Norfolk," Captain Robert Benson of the *George Henry* noted in his diary of April 24, "with our load of soldiers, all Confederates— soldiers who have been as prisoners but are now Federal soldiers, having gotten tired of the Rebel side are disposed to try Uncle Abraham a short time."

Thus far in the War Department's game of oaths and allegiances, nothing had been said about sending the 1st Regiment to the frontier to fight Indians. The regiment was assigned to routine police duties at Norfolk, but under the hard driving of young Colonel Charles Dimon and his eager New England officers, the 1st U.S. Volunteers quickly became a first-class body of soldiers. It was inevitable that

Butler and Dimon would want to test them in the field, and on July 27 the regiment was marched down to Elizabeth City, North Carolina. The mission was of no military consequence; they seized a few horses and some bales of cotton, fired a few shots at some fleeing guerrillas, and returned to Norfolk.

When General Grant heard of the incident, however, he was disturbed. He had no enthusiasm for trifling with loyalties. Very likely he viewed the experiment as an extremely unmilitary business conceived by three civilians—Lincoln, Stanton, and Butler—who were too much inclined to meddle in military matters which none of them properly understood.

On August 9, Grant as general in chief of the armies, informed the War Department that he was ordering the 1st Regiment U.S. Volunteers to the Northwestern frontier. "It is not right," he explained, "to expose them where, to be taken prisoners, they must surely suffer as deserters." From that date to the end of the war, Grant was firmly opposed to using former Confederates against Confederates; in fact, he was opposed to enlisting prisoners for any kind of military service. [See note, pages 186–187.] On August 28 he issued an order forbidding assignment of military duty to Confederate deserters in the field, but permitting them to be employed as civilians in the quartermaster department, provided they took the oath of allegiance.

As late as January 1865, Grant's opposition to permitting former Confederates to fight Confederates undoubtedly led the War Department to forbid enlistments of North Carolina prisoners by a Union officer from that state. A considerable number of North Carolinians, the would-be recruiter claimed, "have written from time to time to me to come and get them out of prison" for enlistment in the 2nd North Carolina Union Mounted Infantry. The War Department's ruling was brief: "It is not believed to be expedient to adopt the policy here urged."

Again on February 19, after it was apparent that Galvanized Yankees were the only troops immediately available for service against Indians and that several regiments would probably be organized, Grant wrote Stanton to protest the payment of bounties to these enlisted prisoners. "The most determined men against us," he said, "would be the first to enlist for the sake of the money and would return with it to their friends. I would make no special objection to trying the experiment of one or two regiments raised without bounty, but even this would be risky. The men who want to enlist are those whom really it is most desirable to exchange first."

Although the organization of the Galvanized Yankee regiments was not a military secret, those responsible for the operation apparently never made any announcements to the press. The fact that recruiting was carried on in prisons served as a cover until the regiments appeared on public view. The first notice of their existence appeared in a few newspapers at the end of August 1864 when "the 1st U.S. Volunteers, one thousand strong, passed over the New York Central Railroad *en route* for the West. . . . The train which carried the regiment numbered 29 cars." The report was erroneous in that it stated they were to be employed against hostile Indians on the Overland Stage route. The 1st Regiment was bound for Minnesota and the Missouri River forts.

This brief item apparently attracted little attention, and not until six months later, when the 2nd and 3rd Regiments moved out upon the Plains, did the Congress of the United States take notice of this unusual military activity. On February 25, 1865, the actions of the War Department were questioned in the House of Representatives, which passed a resolution directing the Secretary of War "to inform this House whether rebel prisoners have been enlisted into our service, have received bounties, and have been credited to quotas of one or more States; and if so how many have been enlisted and credited, and when and to what States."

Stanton made a hasty attempt to satisfy the House's demands, but his listing was far from complete. He included the men of the 1st and 4th Regiments at Point Lookout, and the 2nd and 3rd at Rock Island, which had been paid Pennsylvania bounties, but he made no mention of preparations then under way to recruit the 5th and 6th, nor of the numerous "special permissions" his department had given to various governors, commanders in the field, and organizers of regiments to induct prisoners here and there for service in Union organizations. Perhaps he had forgotten most of the latter; certainly the records were scattered and far from complete.

No doubt Congress eventually would have launched an investigation and become engaged in a series of debates on the difficult subject of oaths and allegiances, but the war was rushing to its end. After Lee surrendered on April 9, nobody of authority in Washington, except Ulysses Grant, gave any more thought to the origins of the 6,000 Galvanized Yankees soldiering on the faraway Western frontier.

[NOTE: In a note for Lieutenant Colonel Henry S. Huidekoper, 150th Pennsylvania Volunteers, President Lincoln, on September 1, 1864, wrote:

> *"It is represented to me that there are at Rock Island, Ill., as rebel prisoners of war, many persons of Northern and foreign birth, who are unwilling to be exchanged and sent South, but who wish to take the oath of allegiance and enter the military service of the Union.*
>
> *Colonel Huidekoper, on behalf of the people of some part of Pennsylvania, wishes to pay the bounties the Government would have to pay to proper persons of this class, have them enter the service of the United States, and be credited to the localities furnishing the bounty money. He will therefore proceed to Rock Island, ascertain the names of such persons (not including any who have attractions southward), and telegraph them to the Provost-Marshal-General here, whereupon direction will be given to discharge the persons named upon their taking the oath of allegiance; and then, upon the official evidence being furnished that they shall have been duly received and mustered into the service of the United States, their number will be credited as may be directed by Colonel Huidekoper."*

Learning after a meeting with Secretary of War Stanton that General Grant opposed enlisting Confederate prisoners into the Union Army, Lincoln, on September 22, 1864, sent the following explanation to Grant:

> *"I send this as an explanation to you and to do justice to the Secretary of War. I was induced, upon pressing application, to authorize the agents of one of the districts of Pennsylvania to recruit in one of the prison depots in Illinois, and the thing went so far before it came to the knowledge of the Secretary that, in my judgement, it could not be abandoned without greater evil than would follow its going through. I did not know at the time that you had protested against that class of thing being done, and I now say that while this particular job must be completed no other of the sort will be authorized without an understanding with you, if at all. The Secretary of War is wholly free of any part in this blunder."*

Yours, truly
A. Lincoln

With the plan now in motion, Secretary Stanton, on September 25, 1864, queried Grant for suggestions:

"The President some time ago authorized a regiment of prisoners of war at Rock Island to be enlisted into our service. He has written you a letter of explanation. It was done without my knowledge and he desires his arrangement to be carried into effect. The question now arises, how shall they be organized, officered, and assigned to duty? Shall they be formed into one regiment by companies as other troops, or assigned in companies or squads to other organizations? Please favor me with your views on the subject. . . ."

On that same day, Grant replied:

"Your dispatch in relation to the organization of troops from prisoners of war is just received. I would advise that they be placed all in one regiment and be put on duty either with Pope [on the Northwest frontier] or sent to New Mexico."]

Major General Nathan Bedford Forrest, one of the greatest and most daring cavalry leaders of the Confederates in the West. From Harper's Weekly, February 18, 1865.

10

Battle of Brice's Cross Roads

"Here, on June 10, 1864, Nathan Bedford Forrest inflicted the most decisive defeat of the Civil War on the Union army."

"The battle of Brice's Cross Roads was the most complete and crushing defeat sustained by Union arms. . . . If this disaster to our army had occurred in the early months of the war, the North would have been profoundly shocked; but coming at a period when the country had become accustomed to the details of great battles, with corresponding loss of life, and occurring away down in Mississippi, far from news centers, it caused no particular sensation."
—Colin McDonald, Color Bearer of the 9th Minnesota Volunteer Infantry.

By late spring of 1864, the armies of Major General William T. Sherman were driving deep into Georgia. With every hard-won mile of progress, however, Sherman's extended supply line became more exposed. His concern over this vulnerability was directed mainly at one Confederate general, Major General Nathan Bedford Forrest. "There never will be peace in Tennessee," said Sherman, "till Forrest is dead." To keep Forrest off his supply line, Sherman repeatedly ordered expeditions sent into Mississippi and Alabama for the purpose of either destroying the Confederate cavalry commander or diverting him from raids.

On June 1, 1864, Forrest started his forces from their base at Tupelo, Mississippi, to raid Sherman's railroad supply line in Tennessee. By coincidence on that same day, Major General Samuel D.

Sturgis marched out of Union headquarters near Memphis with an army of about 8,000 men, bound for Tupelo in search of Forrest.

From the very first day, as these journal entries indicate, the Union expedition was dogged by bad weather:

> June 2, rain fell at intervals all day and part of the next. June 3, rain during the day. June 4, rained heavy until 1 P.M., making the roads almost impassable. June 5, showers during the afternoon. June 6, commenced raining at 5 A.M. and continued at intervals all day. June 7, several showers during the afternoon and the roads very bad.

At Ripley on the night of June 7, General Sturgis called a staff meeting to discuss abandonment of the expedition. "The artillery and the wagons were literally mired down," Sturgis said later, "and the starved and exhausted animals could with difficulty drag them along." Brigadier General Benjamin H. Grierson, commanding the cavalry division, was emphatic in urging a return to base. Just one year earlier, Grierson had made his great raid through Mississippi, and he credited its success to surprise and rapidity of movement. Now, bad weather and a train of 306 wagons made surprise and rapid movement impossible; Grierson feared an ambush. Colonel William L. McMillen, commanding the infantry division, was equally determined to go ahead. To turn back would be a disgrace, he said. Sturgis, although filled with forebodings, finally agreed with McMillen. They would go on to Tupelo.

Not present at the meeting was another worried officer, Colonel De Witt Thomas, commander of the 93rd Indiana Infantry. On that evening, Colonel Thomas was camped on the W. C. Falkner plantation near Ripley, and he had a pleasant conversation with the wife of the absent Confederate colonel who owned the place. "A very intelligent person, Mrs. Falkner," Colonel Thomas said afterward. (Her great-grandson would become a famous author, William Faulkner.) In answer to Colonel Thomas's inquiry as to where Bedford Forrest was, Mrs. Falkner replied that Forrest had been away from Mississippi but had returned and would give the Union soldiers plenty to do in a few days.

Brigadier General Samuel D. Sturgis was no match for the brilliant strategies of Major General Nathan Bedford Forrest and was decisively beaten at Brice's Cross Roads. He closed his military career in 1888 as a colonel of the 7th Cavalry. From Frank Leslie's Illustrated History of the Civil War, 1861–65, page 102.

"How many men does Forrest have?" Colonel Thomas asked. Without blinking an eye, Mrs. Falkner replied: "28,000."

This information did not worry Colonel Thomas because he did not believe it then, but he was much concerned over the leadership of Sturgis and his division commander, McMillen. Thomas knew that Sturgis was a West Pointer with a splendid war record in the East. At Antietam Ferrero's brigade of his division had made the charge that carried the strategic bridge. On the night before the expedition left Memphis, however, several officers had seen Sturgis roaring drunk at the Hotel Gayoso, and on the next day Colonel McMillen was so intoxicated that he had fallen prone in the presence of enlisted men. Thomas had to get him to a house and put him to bed.

After the slow-moving column left Ripley, Colonel Thomas's distrust of his commanders continued to grow. Instead of placing the cavalry on the flanks, Sturgis sent them ahead so that horses' hoofs churned the rain-soft roads into mire, making it almost impossible for men to march or wagons to roll. Little effort was made to repair bogs in the road. Forage and ration supply was so poorly organized that some regiments had surpluses, while others had acute shortages.

On the morning of June 10, at Stubbs's Plantation, the Union column was slow in getting into motion. Grierson started his cavalry at 5:30, but the infantry did not follow until seven o'clock, leaving a considerable gap between the two divisions. At officers' mess, Colonel Thomas noted that General Sturgis and Colonel McMillen each took a strong slug of whiskey before breakfast. This early morning drinking did not bother him nearly so much as the slow start.

Only a few miles east of Stubbs's Plantation, three separate columns of Confederate cavalry had been in motion since four o'clock that morning. As Mrs. Falkner informed Colonel Thomas at Ripley, General Forrest had returned to Mississippi. Within a few hours after the Union expedition left Memphis on June 1, intelligence reports began coming into the Confederate department headquarters of Major General Stephen D. Lee at Tupelo. After weighing the relative advantages of raiding Sherman's supply line or doing battle with Sturgis's army, General Lee summoned Forrest back to Mississippi.

On the night of June 9, Forrest knew exactly where the Union column was camped, and he estimated that before noon of the tenth the advance elements would reach Brice's Cross Roads. Forrest's major problem was to assemble enough Confederate cavalry strength from scattered camps along the Mobil & Ohio Railroad to stop his enemy at the crossroads.

On the morning of the tenth, while Sturgis's column moved slowly southeastward along the Ripley road toward Guntown, Forrest's three mounted units were moving swiftly southwestward along the Baldwyn road toward Pontotoc. Two brigades under Colonels W. A. Johnson and H. B. Lyon were only six miles from Brice's Cross Roads; Colonel Edmund Rucker's brigade was eighteen miles away; Colonel Tyree Bell's brigade was twenty-five miles distant at Rienzi.

Forrest that morning was riding with Colonel Rucker. An hour after the sun rose, jungle-like heat began steaming from the rain-drenched earth. "It's going to be hot as hell today," Forrest remarked to Rucker. He went on to describe the country around Brice's Cross Roads. "Densely wooded and the undergrowth so heavy that when we strike them they won't know how few men we have. Their cavalry will reach the crossroads three hours ahead of the infantry. We can whip their cavalry in that time. They'll send back to have the infantry hurried up. In this heat, and coming on at a run, five or six miles over a muddy road, their infantry will be so tired we will ride right over them." This was only hopeful conjecture on Forrest's part, of course, but it turned out to be a remarkably accurate prediction.

Meanwhile Grierson's advance brigade under Colonel George Waring was already skirmishing with Confederate scouts. At Tish-omingo Creek about nine o'clock, Waring's cavalrymen charged a group of pickets who were destroying a bridge. Colonel Waring ordered the bridge repaired and followed the Confederates to Brice's Cross Roads, where they turned left on the Baldwyn road.

Around the Brice plantation house was a six-acre clearing looking out over an undulating, heavily timbered landscape, with an under-growth of blackjack and scrub oak in full leaf. When Grierson arrived, he immediately saw the strategic advantages of the crossroads; he brought his artillery up and sent patrols out on the different forks. Along the Baldwyn fork went the 4th Missouri Cavalry; 600 yards from Brice's house this road cut through a cornfield with rail fences along each side. The 4th Missouri was about halfway along the stretch of road when two companies of whooping Confederates came charging out of the fields.

These Confederates were the advance of Colonel Lyon's 700-man brigade, which had just arrived from Baldwyn. After their dashing charge they swung back into the woods, dismounted, and formed a skirmish line. Farther up the road, Forrest heard the firing and galloped to the front.

When he observed the numbers of Union cavalry streaming into Brice's Cross Roads, Forrest realized that the odds were against his holding them in check until his main force under Tyree Bell arrived from Rienzi. He dispatched a courier with orders to Bell to hurry forward, and then began his familiar game of bluffing his enemy into believing that he was there first with the most men.

For an hour Forrest took advantage of his woods cover, keeping the Union cavalry off balance with feigned attacks from both sides of the road. During this time Rucker's and Johnson's brigades began arriving, and Forrest soon had enough men to lay the groundwork for attacks on both right and left flanks of the Union cavalry.

Although Bedford Forrest never studied military science, the trial and error of three years of war combined with a natural aggressiveness had made him into a superior tactician in the use of cavalry. He used horses to move his men rapidly from one point to another, dismounted them quickly, and concentrated their firepower in surprise attacks from flanks and rear. Only when caught in desperate situations such as encirclement did he use the slashing saber charge.

On this morning he sent Colonel Johnson out to the right of Lyon's brigade, toward Tishomingo, and Rucker far to the left, toward the Guntown road. Johnson struck first at Waring's left flank, the 4th Missouri, but quickly withdrew when the Missourians opened up with their four mountain howitzers. By eleven o'clock Grierson's 2nd Brigade, under Colonel E. F. Winslow was moving into positions on the right of Brice's Cross Roads. Although Bell and his 2,800 Confederates were still some distance away, Forrest decided that he must now risk an attack in earnest.

Riding along his extended line, Forrest shouted assurances to the dismounted troopers and ordered his officers to lead them in a coordinated charge across the cornfield. At the sound of the bugle, they rushed out of the dense blackjack thickets. Rucker's 7th Tennessee was the first unit to overrun the Union skirmish line. Colonel Waring immediately brought up the 7th Indiana, and a fierce hand-to-hand fight began along a rail fence on the Union side of the field.

"It was very hot and sultry," one of the Tennessee troopers recalled afterward. "As we approached, the fence seemed ablaze with crackling breechloaders. The fire was so terrific that the regiment staggered for a moment, and some of the men fell flat upon the earth for protection. They again pushed forward, reached the fence and began to pull the brush away in order to close with the Federals. So close was this struggle that guns fired were not reloaded, but used as clubs; and pistols were brought into play, while the two lines struggled with the ferocity of wild beasts. Never did men fight more gallantly for their position than did the determined men of the North for this blackjack thicket on that hot June day."

After taking the brunt of the Tennesseans' assault, the Indianians began retreating. A member of the 9th Illinois, a regiment just to the left, said the Indianians "being armed with an inferior carbine were compelled to fall back." This break in the line exposed the 9th Illinois to enfilading fire and they too had to withdraw. Waring now threw in his last reserves, the 2nd New Jersey, and was able to form a second line of defense.

So furious was the Confederate attack, Grierson believed he was heavily outnumbered. He sent couriers racing back to General Sturgis, who was with the infantry column. "I had an advantageous position," Grierson later said in his report of the action, "and could hold it if the infantry was brought up promptly." Grierson failed to explain why he did not consider taking his cavalry back to the infantry; perhaps he did not know they were still five miles from the crossroads. He was quite aware, however, of the intense heat in which the foot soldiers were marching and should have guessed they would be ordered into a double-quick step. His horses were well-rested, and according to testimony of several officers there were as good or better battle positions where the infantry was marching, west of the bottomlands of Tishomingo Creek.

In response to Grierson's messages, Sturgis ordered McMillen to double-quick his forward brigade to the front. Sturgis then hurried forward with his mounted escort to the crossroads. "When I reached the crossroads I found nearly all the cavalry engaged, and the battle growing warm, but no artillery had opened on either side. . . . Frequent calls were now made for reinforcements, but until the infantry should arrive I had, of course, none to give." It did not occur to Sturgis, either, that it might be advantageous for the cavalry to fall back on the infantry.

The Union cavalry regiments, pressed on their flanks, now began falling back on their own account. "I was compelled to occupy the line [in front of Brice's house] temporarily with my escort," Sturgis said. "This handful of troops . . . behaved very handsomely, and held the line until the arrival of the infantry. About 1:30 P.M. the infantry began to arrive."

Sturgis did not describe the dead-beat appearance of those first infantry arrivals. They were the 113th Illinois of Colonel George Hoge's brigade. According to their commander, Lieutenant Colonel George Clarke, they had double-quicked for four miles. "One-third of my men were so completely exhausted as to be scarce able to stand; several were sun struck." Colonel Hoge himself said that some of the Illinois men collapsed as they were going into battle; others were so exhausted they could not load their rifles.

As fast as the wilted infantry regiments arrived to man the front lines, the cavalry regiments withdrew. "General Grierson now requested authority to withdraw the entire cavalry," Sturgis reported, "as it was exhausted and well-nigh out of ammunition. . . . He was directed to reorganize his command in the rear and hold it ready to operate on the flanks."

Colonel De Witt Thomas, who was bringing up his 93rd Indiana

Infantry at this time, was appalled by the confusion of cavalry at the Tishomingo Creek bridge, but he managed to get his troops to their assigned position on the Guntown road at the extreme right of the line. "I relieved the 3rd Iowa Cavalry," he said. "Colonel Noble of the 3rd Iowa remarked as he passed out that he had received no fire there at all, but that I would have a hot time of it pretty soon."

Meanwhile the long, cumbersome train of 300 wagons was bumping along the narrow earthen causeway toward the Tishomingo Creek bridge. No orders had been given to halt it at a safe distance from the battlefront. Its escort of soldiers from the 59th U. S. Colored Infantry, four men to a wagon, was commanded by Colonel Edward Bouton, and he discovered two lieutenants quarreling over where and how to park the train. Each claimed to have orders direct from General Sturgis. They made the fatal error of taking the train across the creek bridge and parking it in a field within range of Forrest's artillery.

From Forrest's viewpoint the situation was even better than he had hoped for that morning. Before the newly arrived Union infantry regiments could open an attack, Colonel Bell's full brigade arrived at a gallop. With these troops were Morton's and Rice's artillery, twelve fieldpieces manned by some of the most accurate gunners in the Confederate Army. After more than twenty miles of sticky roads, mounts and teams were spent, their bellies blood-slashed from spurs.

With no wasted motion, Captain John Morton unlimbered his guns and started shelling the crossroads. "They fired very rapidly," Captain Henry Lee of the 7th Wisconsin Battery later testified. "They had our range exactly."

Forrest meanwhile assigned command of his right wing to Brigadier General Abraham Buford and extended the line by ordering Colonel Clark Barteau to move down Tishomingo Creek, within striking distance of the bridge. He then mounted his escort and led Bell's troopers off in a swinging arc eastward. At the Guntown road he positioned Bell on the right flank of the Union infantry.

During this period of readjustment by both armies, a comparative stillness fell over the green land. Occasionally a sharpshooter fired off a single shot; a rabbit or a squirrel would rustle the leaves of the blackjack, but there was no bird song in the heavy humid air of the June afternoon. No wind stirred, not even a breeze. The sky was a cloud-less, washed-out blue. Under their thicket cover, the sweat-drenched men of both armies welcomed the respite. They wiped moisture from their faces, nibbled at cold rations, drained their canteens.

Bedford Forrest, however, had no intention of permitting the Yankees to catch their breaths. About three o'clock he ordered Bell to start advancing through the blackjack. The foliage was so thick that the men had to stoop or crawl, trailing their rifles as they pushed forward. One of the first Union regimental commanders to discover their presence was Colonel Thomas of the 93rd Indiana, on the flank of the second line of defense.

In the opening exchange of volleys, the Confederates drove back the Indiana skirmishers and partly turned their right flank. "I imme-diately opened fire," Colonel Thomas said, "and drove the enemy back a little." On Thomas's left were five Illinois regiments; Colonel Hoge, commanding the forward brigade, now ordered this whole force to attack.

Observing that Bell's right and Rucker's left were being turned back by the Union assault, Forrest dismounted his escort (115 men) and dashed into the breach. Pistol in hand, the determined general led the way through the brush, firing into the fixed bayonets of union infantrymen. (This may have been a unit of the 81st Illinois, which had exhausted its ammunition.) In a few more minutes, Hoge's center began to waver. About the same time, the Confederates on Hoge's right struck with sudden fury, swinging around the 81st Illinois and striking the 93rd Indiana.

"One of the hardest contested battles I have ever witnessed," Colonel Thomas recorded. "The enemy flanking me every few moments and my men changing their front, contesting for every foot of ground. . . . I pressed forward again upon the enemy . . . was again outflanked and had to again give back, which I did by retreating and firing, changing my front as often as it was necessary to prevent my men from being surrounded."

While Sturgis's right was thus being rolled back, Johnson and

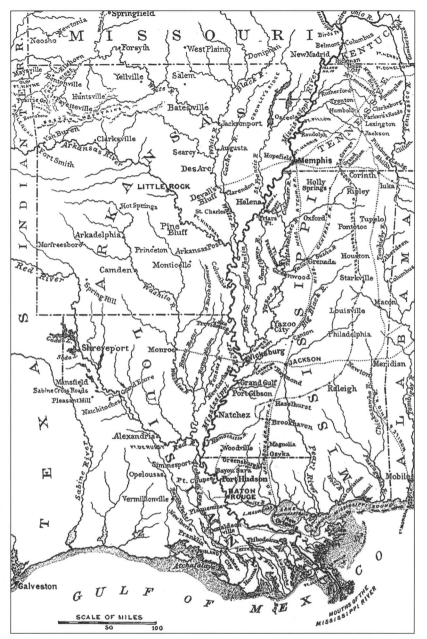

The Battle of Brice's Cross Roads took place just north of Tupelo, Mississippi, and was one of many engagements and campaigns that occurred in areas noted on this map of the Mississippi Valley. From Battles and Leaders of the Civil War, *as prepared by Draughtsman Jacob Wells.*

Lyon, on the left, drove between the 95th Ohio and 113th Illinois, enfilading the Ohioans from both sides. Lieutenant Colonel Jefferson Brumback of the Ohio regiment described the action: "I retired my line in as good order as possible forty or fifty yards and made another stand, holding the position until again flanked and compelled to retire. This time my men fell back perhaps seventy-five yards, still in the timber and brush, when they again withstood the enemy until my right was again turned."

Still farther to the right, Colonel Clark Barteau was moving his 2nd Tennessee Cavalry down Tishomongo Creek. One year earlier Grierson had successfully eluded Barteau on his raid through Mississippi. In front of Barteau this afternoon, Grierson's cavalry was re-forming and preparing to come to the aid of the hard-pressed Union infantry. "I succeeded in reaching the Federal rear just as the fighting seemed heaviest in front," Barteau said afterward. "I at once deployed my men in a long line, had my bugler ride up and down sounding the charge at different points, and kept up as big a show as I could and a vigorous fire upon the Federals until their complete rout was evident."

Barteau thus evened the score. This time he outfoxed Grierson, who reported it this way: "Scarcely had I succeeded in mounting and re-forming my command after their desperate fight of four hours, when the enemy rushed forward in overwhelming numbers." Barteau had only 250 men, but he succeeded in immobilizing Grierson's cavalry just long enough for Forrest to put the Union infantry to flight.

About four o'clock Forrest mounted his escort and started on a hurried circuit of his lines; as he rode along he shouted encouragements to his troops to make one more mighty effort to drive the Yankees from the crossroads. When he reached the artillery position, Captain John Morton warned him sharply to get back down the slope. Union artillery shells had been coming in dangerously close, Morton explained. Forrest turned his horse back into the trees; at the same time he called Morton to follow him. The long-jawed, beardless, twenty-two-year-old artilleryman obeyed instantly. Forrest's usually sallow face was red as "a painted Indian warrior," and Johnny

Morton wondered if he was in for a tongue-lashing from his quick-tempered commander.

Forrest dismounted and reclined against a tree trunk. His uniform was soaked with perspiration, and he was breathing heavily. The tired general and the alert young captain might have been father and son. "Well, John," Forrest said, "ten minutes from now I'm going to order a charge all along the line and double the Yankees up on the crossroads, right up yonder where their artillery is. I want you to take four guns, double-shotted with canister, and when the bugle sounds, hitch your horses and gallop forward on the road as close as possible to the enemy, and give 'em hell right up yonder where I'm going to double 'em up."

"Yes, sir," Morton said.

Forrest was already on his feet, ready to mount. "You'll have no infantry support, captain."

Morton afterwards admitted that Forrest's last words had scared him, but he hurried back to his guns and prepared to follow orders.

The Confederate attack began with a furious discharge of small arms and artillery. Morton's guns bounced forward, pouring canister into the Union lines along both sides of the road. Believing that his artillery was surely supported by heavy forces of riflemen, Union officers began drawing their men back. Lieutenant Colonel George Clarke of the 113th Illinois: "We were compelled to retreat, knowing it would be useless to contend against odds of four to one. I am sorry to say that our retreat was in great confusion."

Similarly convinced of enemy superiority, the infantry division commander, Colonel McMillen, hurried a messenger back to General Sturgis, informing him that he would have to fall back on the crossroads unless reinforcements were sent immediately. "I have none to send you," Sturgis replied, and ordered McMillen to hold his positions until a line of cavalry could be formed to protect his retreat.

About 4:30 P.M. the rout began. Companies of Union infantry cut off from their regiments came streaming back into the crossroads, but McMillen was unable to form a resistance line there. Colonel De Witt Thomas combined his 93rd Indiana with the 9th Minnesota, and they made a stubborn fight of it back to the crossroads, where elements of the 10th Missouri Cavalry and 95th Ohio joined them. But by this time Forrest's men were attacking them on both flanks and from the rear.

Confederates from both wings of Forrest's army now swept out of the blackjack into the cleared space around the Brice plantation house. They swarmed over the artillery positions, captured the guns, and turned them upon the fleeing Federals. Half a mile back down the road to Ripley, ambulances, wagons, cavalry, and artillery were beginning to pile up in an inextricable jumble around the narrow bridge over Tishomingo Creek. Captain Henry Lee of the 7th Wisconsin Battery, who had been ordered back to protect the wagon train, described the scene as a stampede. "A rebel battery opened fire on us and shells were falling rapidly. The wagon train continued to move out. As it did so, it came directly in front of our pieces. In consequence of this and the large number of our own men who were engaged in cutting their teams loose and mounting themselves, we could not fire. I so reported to General Grierson. He said, 'Then limber up and go on.' I did so."

Just to the north of the creek bridge, Colonel Edward Winslow ordered horse-holders of the 4th Iowa Cavalry to take the regiment's mounts across the stream while the dismounted troopers made a desperate stand. "Two infantry regiments which were retreating in disorder were by this maneuver saved from destruction or capture," Winslow said. "The enemy now vigorously shelled with our own guns the dismounted men and the bridge." At the same time Colonel McMillen ordered Bouton's Colored Infantry brigade to form a line of support for the 4th Iowa. Bouton's riflemen managed to catch the onrushing Confederates with oblique fire, inflicting severe casualties, but Johnson's Alabamians splashed across the creek in a swift flanking movement and forced the line back 300 yards. Finally, the 59th Colored Regiment rallied and made the last Union charge of the day. It was a futile, bloody encounter of bayonets and clubbed muskets.

After that, as Sturgis said, the Union regiments "drifted toward the rear, and were soon altogether beyond control. The road became crowded and jammed with troops, the wagons and artillery, sinking into the deep mud, became inextricable. No power could now check or control the panic-stricken mass as it swept toward the rear."

At the bottleneck of the bridge, wagons were overturned and horses were left struggling in harness. In frantic efforts to escape, soldiers pushed each other into the stream. Others jumped voluntarily into the flooded creek; some drowned or were shot while they floundered in the muddy water. The first Confederate units reaching the bridge cleared it immediately by shoving wagons and horses into the creek, opening it for quick passage of a mounted pursuit force.

Forrest himself led this band of horsemen, several hundred men who had been serving as horse-holders in rear of the battlefront. Horses and men were fresh and ready for action. As the sun was setting, Lieutenant Colonel Charles Eaton of the 72nd Ohio Infantry glanced back and saw a line of Confederates a mile in length. "They advanced in beautiful style and with their banners flying."

On through the dark night, made even blacker by thick-foliaged trees on both sides of the road, the demoralized Union army sought vainly for sanctuary. Every time an attempt was made to form a rear defense line, Forrest's pursuing horse soldiers would dart out of the darkness. With a stinging crackle of fire and a whooping Rebel yell, they attacked and then vanished as quickly as they struck.

Judging from evidence given later by his officers, General Sturgis now gave up all hope of stopping the retreat. In his report he said: "The enemy pressed heavily on the rear, and there was nothing left but to keep in motion." When he gave Colonel Winslow orders to push on for Ripley, Winslow replied that this would require abandonment of what was left of the artillery and wagons. "The artillery and train have already gone to hell," Sturgis told him. "My soldiers are nothing but a mob."

In the darkness the retreating column took the wrong road across a creek bottom known as Hatchie Swamp. Ambulances, wagons, and artillery pieces were soon sinking into deep mud. In spite of the protests of Winslow and Colonel Bouton, Sturgis ordered the bogged vehicles abandoned. "General, don't let us give it up so," Bouton cried. He believed that his Negro regiment could extricate the vehicles. "I will stake my life that I could save the whole of them," Bouton declared.

"For God's sake," Sturgis replied, "if Mr. Forrest will let me alone I will let him alone. You have done all you could and more than was expected of you, and now all you can do is to save yourselves."

When Forrest's men reached the swamp at three o'clock in the morning, burning wagons illuminated an eerie scene of desolation—scores of drowned and dying horses and mules; an endless line of half-burned wagons; several pieces of artillery, a row of tilted ambulances filled with wounded men begging for water and medical attention. Some pieces of abandoned artillery had been spiked, rammers and wheels broken; others were only buried deep in the bog.

Between the swamp and Ripley the road was better, but Forrest's cavalrymen continued their harassment until daylight. On the march down from Ripley to Brice's Cross Roads, the Union column had spent two and a half days; the survivors made it back in twelve hours, but they had left all their wagons behind them. They left hundreds of rifles and cartridge-boxes, thrown away after they expended their last ammunition upon darting shapes in the night. They also left hundreds of straggling comrades too weary to keep up with the rapid flight.

Four miles below Ripley, Grierson managed to assemble several scattered cavalry detachments. Most of the men had only a few rounds left, and their ammunition supply was now in Confederate hands—back on Tishomingo Creek or in Hatchie Swamp. They made a gallant stand, but Bedford Forrest, refreshed by an hour of sleep, came galloping up with his escort troop and the 7th Tennessee. In a matter of minutes, Grierson's defense line collapsed.

All through the day Forrest harried his enemy relentlessly, driving his men and himself as hard as he drove the soldiers of the Union. By day's end on the eleventh, Sturgis's army was without food or ammunition, the infantrymen's feet were so blistered and swollen they began discarding their shoes. But Forrest could go no farther. Near Salem, where he had lived as a youth, he fainted from exhaustion and lay unconscious for almost an hour.

Brice's Cross Roads had cost the Union expedition 2,240 of its

8,000 men—223 killed, 394 wounded, and 1,623 missing. All its artillery, ambulances, wagons, baggage, ammunition and camp equipage, 184 horses and mules, and 2,000 rifles were gone. The Confederates had lost 492 men killed and wounded.

Until long after the war, Sturgis and most of his officers believed they had been beaten by superior forces. Their estimates varied from 8,000 to as high as 20,000. General Sherman accepted the low figure, but still could not understand "how Forrest could defeat Sturgis with 8,000 men . . . but Forrest is the devil, and I think he has got some of our troops under cower."

When Colonel De Witt Thomas brought his Indiana infantrymen back through Ripley on the retreat, he stopped briefly at the Falkner Plantation to pay his respects to Mrs. Falkner. After taking a look at his beaten regiment sprawled along the road, she invited him in to breakfast. "I believe you asked me the other day, Colonel," she said, "how many men Forrest had, and I told you he had 28,000. Did you not find my words very nearly correct?"

No one can be certain exactly how many men Forrest did have at Brice's Cross Roads, but the most reliable high count brings the total to 4,875. No one can be certain, either, whether Forrest ever said: "I git thar fustest with the mostest men." Brice's Cross Roads proved, however, that he had a genius for convincing his enemy that he had the most, and more importantly it proved that he was a master tactician in the use of cavalry, mounted and dismounted.

Former Ohio Congressman Clement L. Vallandigham became an unofficial leader of the Copperheads and was very critical of the war effort in the North. Courtesy Library of Congress [Brady Collection], LC-BH82-4408.

11

The Northwest Conspiracy

"One of the most misunderstood episodes of the war was centered around a plot that never came off to free Confederate prisoners in the North, and foment revolt."

For both the Union and the Confederacy, 1864 was unquestionably the darkest year of the Civil War. The North was war-weary, frustrated because its bloody victories seemed to change nothing, while at the same time across the nation Democrats and Republicans were engaged in a bitter presidential campaign that brought long-simmering internal dissensions to the surface. The South was facing military disaster: Sherman was marching to the sea; Grant was closing in on Richmond. The Confederacy had exhausted its sources of military manpower, and the Union refused to exchange any of the thousands of Rebel soldiers held in Northern prison camps.

To stave off defeat, Confederate leaders searched for some means of forcing Sherman to turn back north from Atlanta, anything which might prolong the war until aid could be secured from Britain or another foreign country. In a move of desperation, the Confederate high command on March 16 ordered Captain Thomas Henry Hines to make his way through the Union lines to Canada. While en route, Hines was to confer with Northerners known to be friendly to the Confederate cause and to encourage them to organize and prepare themselves to "give such aid as circumstances may allow." In Canada,

Hines' mission was to assemble all Confederate soldiers who had escaped there and employ them "in any fair and appropriate enterprises of war against our enemies."

Six weeks later this venture was considerably enlarged when President Jefferson Davis sent Jacob Thompson and Clement Clay to Canada with several hundred thousand dollars to finance the organization and arming of Confederate sympathizers in the North. Captain Hines would now report to Thompson, and would be responsible for military operations directed principally toward the freeing of Confederates in prison camps. Money was also to be spent in influencing the Northern press, sabotaging supply bases, blowing up steamboats and railroad trains, and upon various other schemes.

Out of this came a vague plan to attack prison camps in Illinois, Indiana, and Ohio, free thousands of Confederate prisoners of war, supply them with arms and horses, and then sweep across the Northwest, seizing arsenals and gathering recruits from among local sympathizers. The ultimate objective was to overthrow the state governments and form a Northwestern Confederacy. If this failed, the army would cross the Ohio and Mississippi rivers and link up with Confederate cavalry forces.

Tom Hines, who was to direct this fantastic operation, had served in Brigadier General John Hunt Morgan's famed 2nd Kentucky Cavalry Regiment. During the summer of 1863 he was an advance scout for Morgan's raid into Indiana and Ohio, and after he and Morgan were captured, it was Hines who engineered their astounding escape from the Ohio state penitentiary at Columbus. In 1864 Hines was a lithe young man of twenty-five, with black, curly hair, a thin moustache curving over a determined mouth, cold blue eyes set wide apart. In Canada he found several of his old comrades who had also escaped from prisons. One of them, twenty-three-year-old John Castleman, had enlisted Hines into Morgan's regiment, and Hines immediately made Castleman his partner, with equal rank in the leadership of the conspiracy.

Hines and Castleman could not, of course, carry out their great plan without assistance from sympathizers in the Northwestern states.

Jacob Thompson, a former U.S. Secretary of the Interior under President James Buchanan, was appointed Confederate Commissioner to Canada in 1864 and became involved in the Northwest Conspiracy, St. Alban's raid in Vermont, and the plot to burn New York City. Courtesy Library of Congress, LC-USZ62-12082.

The most promising sources of aid seemed to be state and local organizations, which early in the war were known as Knights of the Golden Circle but which had been reorganized as the Sons of Liberty. The membership of these organizations was made up largely of Democratic party supporters, especially those who had family or commercial ties with the South, and of men who opposed the war for one reason or another, who disliked Lincoln and his policies, or who were simply attracted to the romantic mysteries of secret societies, with their elaborate handgrips, signs, and passwords. Supporters of Lincoln and the Republican party called them Copperheads or Butternuts.

As the organizations were secret, the memberships were also secret; estimates of the total in the Northwestern states ranged from a few thousand to half a million. When Jacob Thompson was told that 340,000 members of the Sons of Liberty were ready for action against the Union, he was realistic enough to reduce the number by half. Recent historians have concluded that the number of militant antiwar Democrats in Illinois and Indiana was probably not more than 35,000, and much fewer than that in the other states.

Opposition to the draft was especially strong in southern counties of Illinois, Indiana, and Ohio. Groups of war opponents invaded draft offices and destroyed the records. The more militant ones physically attacked enrolling officers. They formed secret committees to aid draft resisters in escaping to Canada, and made strong efforts to persuade soldiers to desert and also flee to Canada. They devised propaganda campaigns to convince soldiers that the war was meaningless and could never be won. Even as far north as Syracuse, New York, draft protesters scrawled graffiti on walls and carried placards with legends such as these: *We Will Not Be Conscripted In a War For The Emancipation of Slavery, Crush The Tyrant Lincoln Before He Crushes You.*

In January 1863, Colonel Henry B. Carrington, mustering officer for Indiana, reported 2,600 deserters and stragglers arrested around Indianapolis within a very few weeks. Union military officials such as Carrington, as well as a number of Republican politicians, attempted to link the Sons of Liberty and other Democratic organizations with all these activities.

The national hero of the anti-war Democrats was Clement L. Vallandigham, a congressman from Ohio. Vallandigham bitterly opposed the war, charging that it was being fought for the benefit of Eastern capitalists and to the detriment of the Northwest. He called for a cease-fire and the beginning of peace talks while both armies were being gradually withdrawn from the battlefields. In 1863 he charged the Lincoln administration with destroying civil liberties and the Constitution. After delivering an especially vigorous speech in Ohio in May 1863, Vallandigham was arrested by military authorities and sentenced to prison. Lincoln commuted the sentence to banishment to the Confederacy. Not wishing to be identified with the Confederate cause, Vallandigham made his way to Canada. During February 1864, officials of the Sons of Liberty visited him in Windsor, Ontario, and persuaded him to become Supreme Commander.

Early in June, Jacob Thompson and Tom Hines met with Vallandigham and several officials of the Sons of Liberty. One of the latter, a Chicagoan, told Hines that he had "two regiments organized, armed and eager for uprising." How much of the Confederate conspirators' plans was known to Vallandigham probably will never be known. Vallandigham refused to take any of Thompson's money, but during these meetings the Democratic leader announced that he would return to Ohio in a few days, fully expecting to be arrested by Federal authorities. The Confederates were delighted, of course; if an arrest were made, Vallandigham could become a martyr, creating a situation which might lead to a general uprising of his followers in the Northwest.

Vallandigham's surprise appearance on June 15 at the Ohio state Democratic convention in Hamilton caused quite a sensation. He made one of his impassioned speeches, virtually daring the Lincoln administration to arrest him again, but at the same time warning his followers not to begin any act of violence or disorder. Then he launched into an attack upon the Republican party, accusing it of fostering a dangerous secret society known as the "Loyal Union League." He charged that the men who controlled the League were a treasonable organization. Vallandigham insisted that the latter served only as a countermovement to the Union League, that there was no conspiracy against the government except to overthrow the Lincoln administration in November, not by force but through the ballot box.

If the Confederate conspirators were counting on an arrest to start an uprising, they were acutely disappointed. The Federal government did not entirely ignore the exile's return; agents followed him everywhere making notes of his remarks, but he was left free to travel and speak as he pleased.

Hines and Thompson meanwhile continued their negotiations with Sons of Liberty leaders. As the national Democratic convention to nominate a candidate for president was scheduled for July 20 in Chicago, the plotters decided that date and place would be propitious for the start of an uprising. Before a detailed plan could be worked out, however, the Democratic party postponed its convention to August 29.

At this point in the conspiracy only a handful of Sons of Liberty officers were involved in the plot with the Confederates in Canada. They called themselves the Committee of Thirteen. Of the men in this group, the motives of Charles Walsh, a Chicago Democratic leader, are most difficult to comprehend. Early in the war he had devoted much of his time and money to raising two regiments of Irishmen to serve in the Union Army, the 23rd and 90th Illinois Volunteers. He owned a prosperous livery business, and for weeks his earnings had suffered while he used his teams and stables for assembling and housing recruits for Mr. Lincoln's Army. He ran so short of money that he had to remove his daughter from an expensive private school. Walsh was a loyal Democrat, however, as loyal to his party as he was to the Irish and his church. By 1864 he was bitterly angry over the forceful methods the high-riding Republicans were using against Democratic voters in Chicago. Yet it is doubtful if Walsh fully understood how far Hines meant to go, or if Hines understood the limits to which Walsh was willing to go.

In mid-July a secret committee of the Sons of Liberty met with the Confederates in Canada and obtained a considerable amount of money to be used in buying arms. A few days later they held another meeting in Chicago to choose a new date for the uprising. They chose August 16, but once again postponed action—this time until August 29, the eve of the Democratic national convention.

On August 24, Hines and Castleman set their plan in motion. From the Confederates in Canada they carefully selected fifty-eight men, many of them tried and true comrades from John Morgan's shattered cavalry regiments. Among them was Colonel George St. Leger Grenfell, a British soldier-of-fortune who had served with Morgan in 1862–63. Grenfell later had joined Jeb Stuart; then made his way to Washington to take the amnesty oath so that he could travel in the North. In New York, Grenfell had met some old friends who persuaded him to join them on an excursion to Canada. While visiting Toronto he found the Morgan men and apparently could not resist the tantalizing Chicago adventure proposed by Tom Hines.

There was also George (Lightning) Ellsworth, the audacious telegrapher who had tricked the Yankees time and again while on raids with Morgan. Others were Ben Drake, one of the most daring of the scouts, and George Eastin, who loved sword-fighting on horseback and had already been memorialized for posterity in a ballad.

When Jacob Thompson allotted $23,000 for the Chicago invasion, he asked Hines to take twelve more "men with good connections." Hines was dubious. He did not suspect the loyalty of the new recruits, but he had had no opportunity to study their reliability. One weak man could destroy everything. Hines accepted them, but only at Thompson's insistence.

Thompson appeared to be especially impressed with the credentials of Maurice Langhorn, a former Confederate artillery sergeant who had made his way through the lines from Kentucky to Canada. Langhorn became the unofficial quartermaster for the expedition, assisting with arrangements for railway travel from Toronto to Chicago, and the issuance of six-shooters, ammunition, and $100 in cash to each man. Beginning on August 24, a few Confederates left Toronto each day by train. Upon arrival in Chicago they went to the Richmond House and registered as members of the Missouri delegation to the

Democratic convention. Grenfell, Langhorn, and Hines were among those who left on the twenty-sixth. Observing that Grenfell was wearing a gray uniform suit, Langhorn warned him: "Colonel, if you go in those clothes to Chicago, they will arrest you." "No," Grenfell replied, "this is an old uniform that was worn in an English battalion I once belonged to. I have my English papers, and my gun and dog, and if they ask me what I am doing, I will say I am going hunting."

Traveling on one of these trains from Canada was Thomas Keefe, a United States secret agent, who was busily memorizing faces and gathering information to report to the commander at Camp Douglas, Colonel Benjamin Sweet. Camp Douglas held 8,000 Confederate prisoners near the Chicago lake front, and during the past several weeks Colonel Sweet had successfully penetrated the Chicago Sons of Liberty with informers. He had also been reading his prisoners' incoming and outgoing mail and was aware of a plot against Camp Douglas. He had noticed that the prisoners from John Morgan's regiments seemed unusually brash and restless. Anticipating some sort of incident during the Democratic convention, Colonel Sweet had requested an additional 2,000 troops to guard his 8,000 prisoners, and the last week of August these Federal reinforcements were quietly moved into position.

During the weekend of August 27–28, thousands of visitors poured into Chicago. Most came by rail, but one observer reported as many as 300 wagons rolling into the city from downstate Illinois and Indiana. It was not unusual to see men carrying sidearms, and some carried shotguns.

Colonel Grenfell was carrying a hunting rifle and was accompanied by his yellow-spotted dog when he entered the Richmond House and boldly signed the register: "G. St. Leger Grenfell, Gt. Britain." When Tom Hines arrived he signed as "Dr. Hunter." Sergeant Maurice Langhorn registered as "George Langley."

The Sons of Liberty were also meeting in Chicago, and were hopeful of being addressed by their hero, Clement Vallandigham. Some historians have stated that Vallandigham attended a secret meeting of the Sons of Liberty, but this would have been difficult for him to accomplish. "Vallandigham is here and excites as much curiosity as a loosed elephant would in our streets," one newspaper reported. "Crowds follow him everywhere he goes." He did make one speech to his admirers from the balcony of the Sherman House, where he was staying, and delivered another in Chicago's Court House Square.

On Sunday evening, August 28, Hines and Castleman met with a group of Sons of Liberty officers in the Richmond House. Hines described his plan for the assault on Camp Douglas, adding that a few trusted men among the Confederate prisoners there were ready to lead an uprising from within. He then asked how many men were available in Chicago to help his little band of Confederates launch the attack. The Sons of Liberty were evasive. Charles Walsh made vague remarks about a thousand good Irish fighters, but he was not sure when they could be ready.

What was worrying the Sons of Liberty were some stories that had appeared in Chicago newspapers a day or two before—not lead stores but bare references to red signal lights that had been seen one night outside Camp Douglas, some conjectures that there might be "a demonstration to release the rebel prisoners at Camp Douglas." Although the Chicago Police Commission had laughed off the rumors, assuring the press that fears of a breakout at the prison camp were groundless, the Sons of Liberty were nervous because there had been public mention of the possibility. Many more soldiers certainly were in evidence around Camp Douglas, which indicated that the authorities knew something about Hines's plan. In spite of this, Hines declared himself willing to lead the attack at any time during the Democratic convention, provided the Sons of Liberty could give him 5,000 men.

Next day the Peace Democrats, who were opposed to the nomination of General George McClellan, held a demonstration outside the Richmond House. Speakers denounced the war, called for the nomination of Horatio Seymour, and flaunted banners which read: *Blessed Are The Peacemakers. War Is Disunion—Sheathe The Sword And Save The Union. Peace And Union.*

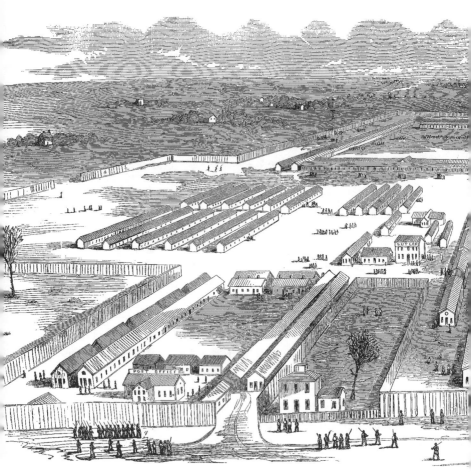

Camp Douglas as shown in 1862 covered approximately 80 acres and was located about four miles southeast of downtown Chicago. From Frank Leslie's Illustrated History of the Civil War, 1861–65, page 306.

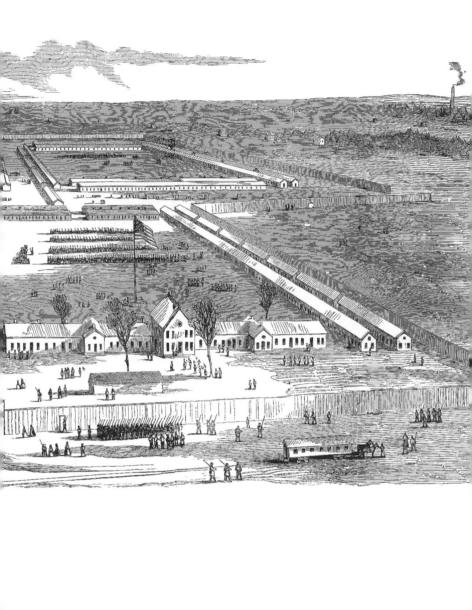

By Tuesday afternoon, Hines knew he was not going to get 5,000 men. There was, however, a possibility of switching to an alternate plan to seize Rock Island arsenal, 200 miles west of Chicago, and free several thousand Confederate prisoners there. Castleman and twenty of the most reliable Morgan men, with 500 Sons of Liberty assisting, would board the regular night passenger train to Rock Island and take possession of it en route. Hines with the remaining fifty Confederates, meanwhile, would take control of "all wires and railroads out of Chicago, preventing any truthful telegraphic news, or any transportation, and convey to the outside world the breaking up of the National Democratic Convention by assault of United States troops." While Hines and his men were startling the nation with their false alarms, Castleman and his band would free the prisoners at Rock Island, then move on to Springfield and take possession of the Illinois state capital. The only element missing in this plot was the little army of 500 from the Sons of Liberty.

To the great disgust of Hines and Castleman, the Sons of Liberty could not furnish them with even 100 men. The organization's leaders had taken a considerable amount of Jacob Thompson's money for buying arms and for recruiting, but now at the showdown they could offer only apologies, lame explanations, and requests for more time. "Impractical dignitaries," Castleman labeled them, and neither he nor Hines believed them when they promised to be between organized and ready for action at the time of the presidential election in November.

For another twenty-four hours, Hines and his men stayed close to the Richmond House, hoping until the last moment for something favorable to develop. They heard that Vallandigham was the hero of the convention, enthusiastically cheered whenever he appeared, and that he had been given a free hand in writing a peace platform for the Democrats. But on Wednesday the thirty-first, when McClellan beat out Seymour for the party's nomination for President, it was Vallandigham who moved that the vote be made unanimous. The Chicago newspapers that evening made dismal reading for the Northwest conspirators. The headlines not only told of McClellan's nomination, *A Man of War On a Peace Platform*, but the news from the front was even more depressing: *Atlanta Falls to Sherman's Army.*

The Chicago convention was now over and the thousands of visitors were preparing to depart. With them must go Hines and his Confederates. "Another day in Chicago," Castleman remarked, "would be fraught with great danger." Hines called his men together and offered them the options of returning to Canada, trying to make their way south to the Confederacy, or going with him and Castleman to southern Illinois and Indiana, where they would organize an army from the ranks of the Sons of Liberty. This time they would bypass the "impractical dignitaries," Castleman said, "and get in touch with subordinates who were often in real earnest." Twenty-three men chose to return to Canada, twenty-five said they would go south; twelve went with Hines to Mattoon, Illinois, and ten with Castleman to Marshall, Illinois, where they established bases in preparation for a second invasion of Chicago on the eve of the presidential election. They were determined to make one more try at freeing the prisoners in Camp Douglas.

One of those who decided to head southward was Colonel Grenfell, but he and his spotted hunting dog went only as far as Carlisle, Illinois. There he stopped at the Hunter's Home, an inn favored by sportsmen in pursuit of prairie chickens. For several weeks he "mixed in the highest society, acted like a gentleman, talked of nothing but hunting," and spent some time with a doctor who treated him for diarrhea and rheumatism.

Another who chose the southward route was Maurice Langhorn. Instead of crossing into the Confederacy he went to Washington, D.C. On October 10 he took the oath of allegiance to the Union, and a few days later started back to Chicago.

On Saturday afternoon, November 5, Langhorn called upon the commander of Camp Douglas, Colonel Benjamin Sweet. He introduced himself by showing Sweet a letter bearing the signature of Secretary of State Seward, which indicated that he was a former Confederate soldier who had taken an oath of allegiance to the Union. Langhorn then revealed to Sweet that he had been one of the

Chicago conspirators in August, had since repented, and was now devoting his time to canvassing for the election of Abraham Lincoln. Not more than an hour before, Langhorn continued, he had met one of his former comrades on a Chicago street. The conspirators were back in Chicago 500 strong, Tom Hines was their leader, and they were planning to storm Camp Douglas on the following Tuesday, election day.

Langhorn could not have chosen a more opportune time for a betrayal of his former associates. During the past week, Colonel Sweet had been desperately seeking some evidence of a conspiracy so that he could move against the Sons of Liberty, arrest a few prominent leaders and link the whole affair with the Democratic party on the eve of the elections. The resulting roorback would not only help the Union candidates, but might bring Sweet a promotion to brigadier general.

Throughout the autumn Republican leaders in Indiana had successfully created an image of disloyalty around that state's Democratic party by linking it with the Sons of Liberty in a spectacular trial of several officers of the organization who were arrested in September on charges of treason. While the trial was in progress, John Castleman was arrested in a second roundup. A few days later, a Confederate raid from Canada against the St. Albans bank in Vermont added fuel to the fire.

Colonel Sweet and other loyal Union men in Illinois were eager to trap the anti-war Democrats in similar fashion and frighten the regular party members into voting for Lincoln on election day. Langhorn therefore was just the man Sweet needed. Sweet did not trust the turncoat, but Langhorn seemed to know all the Confederate conspirators, and he offered the valuable information that some were staying at the Richmond House, some at the Tremont House. Sweet suggested that Langhorn register at the Tremont House; next day the colonel would meet him there for a further report.

Only forty-eight hours before Langhorn walked into Sweet's office, the colonel had put out a feeler for a conspiracy in the person of John T. Shanks. Shanks was a sallow-faced Texan in his mid-thirties who was captured during Morgan's raid into Ohio. In civilian life, Shanks had been a forger and embezzler; during his military career he had always kept one eye out for the main chance. In prison he naturally gravitated into an easy clerkship in the camp hospital, with light duties and special privileges. Shanks had applied to take the oath of allegiance so that he might join a "Galvanized Yankee" company for service on the Western frontier. Colonel Sweet knew that Shanks was a shifty character, but the colonel decided the Texan might be useful in tracking down conspirators in Chicago.

On the evening of November 3, Sweet arranged for Shanks to "escape" from Camp Douglas. In company with Detective Thomas Keefe, the Texan went to the home of Judge Buckner Morris, a well-to-do Kentucky-born lawyer who had lived in Chicago for many years and always voted the straight Democratic ticket. Morris frequently referred to President Lincoln as "Abraham the First"; he publicly advocated his impeachment and wanted the war settled by compromise. He was treasurer of the Chicago Sons of Liberty. Colonel Sweet sent Shanks to Morris's home because the colonel suspected him of aiding escaped Confederate prisoners. Late in October five prisoners had tunneled out of Camp Douglas, and no trace of them had been found. Sweet suspected that they might have joined the Chicago conspirators, and he hoped that Shanks might find his way to them through Morris.

While Detective Keefe waited down the street, Shanks knocked on Judge Morris's door, secured admission, and convinced the judge and his wife that he was a genuine escaped Confederate prisoner. Mrs. Morris gave him $30 to cover his railroad fare to Cincinnati, and the name and address of a man there who would help him through the lines into Kentucky. Shanks departed, rejoined Keefe, and together they went to report to Colonel Sweet. After marking each bill with an X, Shanks turned the money over to the colonel for future evidence. Shanks of course had failed in his mission to penetrate the conspiracy, and Sweet had to put him temporarily under cover.

Two days later, however, when Maurice Langhorn unexpectedly appeared with his voluntary information, Sweet decided to try his luck again with Shanks by sending him to the Richmond House. On Sunday afternoon (November 6) Shanks strolled into the Richmond House and registered as John Thompson, Springfield, Illinois. On the registry he found Colonel Grenfell's name. Shanks had known the Englishman while he was with Morgan's cavalry. Grenfell was not in his room, but Shanks waited in the lobby until he recognized the soldier-of-fortune as he came limping in about seven-thirty with his spotted hunting dog. Shanks approached him, identified himself as a former comrade who had escaped from Camp Douglas, and then accompanied Grenfell to his room.

Grenfell was cordial, but told Shanks that he was short of funds and could not help him escape from Chicago. About 8:30 Shanks excused himself and went out to report to Detective Keefe. Shanks had found Colonel Grenfell, but had learned nothing of any conspiracy. Keefe told him to go back and try again.

Shanks returned to Grenfell's hotel room about 9:30, and stories of what occurred there, what was said, who were present, are based entirely upon the Texan's testimony. Much of it could have been invented by Shanks to please Keefe and Sweet, or all of it could have been true. According to Shanks, Grenfell introduced him to two other men, Fielding and Ware. (Fielding's real name was John Bettersworth.) Shanks sent down for a bottle of brandy and soon the four men were sipping the liqueur and talking of an attack upon Camp Douglas. Grenfell's arthritis was troubling him; frequently he would rise from his chair to hobble about the room, but at the same time (Shanks testified) he talked enthusiastically of setting fires all over Chicago while the attack was proceeding against Camp Douglas. During the course of the evening, Shanks volunteered to join the enterprise and sketched out a map of the prison's interior for them. About ten o'clock Ware excused himself; he said he was going to see Tom Hines to help formulate the final plans.

Just before midnight Grenfell announced that he was "quite unwell" and would like to go to bed. Shanks picked up his half-empty brandy bottle, and he and Fielding (Bettersworth) went to the latter's room. During the next hour, according to Shanks, Fielding laid out the entire plan of attack upon Camp Douglas. About 1,500 men would be available, he said, from Sons of Liberty groups in Illinois and Indiana. At 4:00 P.M., Tuesday, November 8, election day, they would start from various points in Chicago and by seven o'clock would assemble on three sides of the prison camp. After assuring Fielding that he would see him the following morning, Shanks went to his own room in the hotel. The time was between one and two A.M., Monday, November 7. An hour or so later, Shanks was rudely awakened by policemen, who informed him that he was under arrest.

Late Sunday evening, after hearing from Shanks through Detective Keefe, and after receiving additional information from Maurice Langhorn, Colonel Sweet decided to strike with several raids during the night. Instead of telegraphing his commanding officer, Brigadier General John Cook in Springfield, to secure approval for the raids, Sweet sent a dispatch by messenger: "I am not entirely sure of the telegraph," he explained. "I have every reason to believe that Colonel Marmaduke, of the rebel army, is in the city under an assumed name, [as well as] Captain Hines, of Morgan's command, also Col. G. St. Leger Grenfell, formerly Morgan's adjutant-general, as well as other officers of the rebel army. . . . I must also arrest two or three prominent citizens who are connected with these officers. . . . These arrests may cause much excitement. . . . I regret that I am not able to consult with you on my proposed action before acting without letting an opportunity pass which may never again occur."

As he set his forces into action, Colonel Sweet remarked to a member of his staff: "If things come out all right, I'll be a brigadier general." The "prominent citizens" arrested on his orders were Judge Morris and Charles Walsh, both members of the Sons of Liberty and leaders of the Democratic party. Langhorn's "valuable assistance" had led Sweet to Walsh. The net also brought in Grenfell, Colonel Vincent Marmaduke, and two former officers of Morgan's command, Charles Daniel and James Cantrill. In addition, about 100 men were picked up from grog-shops and flop-houses, or from among drunkards in the streets, all being charged with conspiracy against the United States government. As usual, Tom Hines managed to escape.

Thus ended the myth of the Northwest Conspiracy. The charges and arrests, however, made a splendid roorback for Republican newspapers that afternoon. On the following morning, election day, the story was spread across the nation. The Democrats had no time to defend the party from the charges of complicity. The exposure of the "conspiracy" also provided an excuse for placing armed soldiers near ballot boxes to guard them from "disloyal" Democrats, and on November 8, 1864, good Union men everywhere suspected all Democrats of disloyalty.

The arrest of John Shanks, of course, was a deception to enable the shifty Texan to gather further evidence while in confinement with his fellow prisoners. The trial of the conspirators began the following January and dragged on until the war ended. Judge Morris and Vincent Marmaduke were acquitted; Charles Walsh was sentenced to five years in prison. Charles Daniel, being a Morgan man, found a way to escape to Canada before the trial ended. (John Castleman, another Morgan man, also escaped from his jail in Indiana.) James Cantrill turned state's evidence and was allowed to take the oath of allegiance. Colonel Grenfell, who was probably the least guilty of all, was sentenced to death; later the sentence was reduced to life imprisonment. Colonel Sweet received his promotion to brigadier general; Shanks was given command of a "Galvanized Yankee" company and sent out west to fight Indians; Langhorn was awarded a government clerkship. Tom Hines returned to Kentucky and after the war became a respectable lawyer and judge.

The Northwest Conspiracy may well have been the most enormous fraud of the entire Civil War period. The Confederate leaders vastly inflated the size of their forces in order to draw the Sons of Liberty into the conspiracy. In turn, the Sons of Liberty exaggerated the size of their following in order to obtain funds from the Confederates to build up their organization. Topping both of these magnifications was the crude hyperbole of Union military and political leaders who hoped to split the Democrats and frighten that party's loyal members into voting for Union candidates in the crucial election of 1864. Above all, the Confederates misread the surface evidences of disloyalty in the Northwest. When opportunities for action were provided, few of those who spoke so fervently for revolution were willing to take the final step, to use the bullet and the gun against their government.

Brigadier General Stand Watie was the highest-ranking Indian in the Confederate Army. After Pea Ridge in 1862, he fought mostly in the Indian Territory. Courtesy of National Archives [Brady Collection], III-B-4914.

12

The Million-Dollar
Wagon Train Raid

"The prize: 205 Union army wagons laden with all kinds of valuable supplies. The locale: The Indian Territory (later Oklahoma). The cast: Hundreds of [Indian] soldiers on both sides."

At Fort Scott, Kansas, on September 12, 1864, Major Henry Hopkins of the 2nd Kansas Cavalry made a final inspection of a Union supply train under his command and ordered it to start moving south for Fort Gibson, Indian Territory. The mule-drawn train consisted of 205 Army wagons, ninety sutler wagons, and four ambulances—loaded with perhaps a million dollars' worth of clothing, boots, shoes, arms, ammunition, blankets, foodstuffs, liquor, and medicine. In motion, the train stretched for four or five miles across the Kansas plain, a rich prize for plundering by any Confederate force daring enough to attack it.

To guard his wagons, Major Hopkins had an escort of 260 men detached from the 2nd, 6th, and 14th Kansas Cavalry Regiments. "On leaving Fort Scott," he later reported, "I sent orders to the commanding officers of stations on the road . . . to thoroughly scout the country in their vicinity and notify me if the enemy be there and their movements; and also to reinforce me with as many troops as they could spare, being fully convinced that the enemy intended an attack on the train at some point on the route between Scott and Gibson."

On that same day, 200 miles to the south in the Choctaw Nation, three Confederate leaders were completing plans for a raid on

Major Hopkins' wagon train. They were Richard M. Gano, Stand
Watie, and Charles DeMorse. Colonel DeMorse, 29th Texas Cavalry,
had just returned from a mission to headquarters of the Trans-
Mississippi Department at Shreveport, Louisiana. DeMorse carried
secret orders from General Kirby Smith authorizing a raid against
Union supply lines north of Fort Gibson. Originally the raid was
meant to be coordinated with a massive invasion of Missouri by
General Sterling Price late in September.

In August, however, Brigadier General Stand Watie's reliable
Cherokee spies had reported that an unusually large wagon train was
assembling at Fort Scott for movement south early in September. The
timing of the raid, therefore, was advanced several days, and on
September 13, Watie, Gano, and DeMorse joined forces at Camp Pike
on the Canadian River.

In more conventional theaters of war there probably would have
been a wrangle over who was to command this expedition. General
Watie, a three-quarter-blood Cherokee in command of the 1st Confederate Indian Cavalry Brigade, was the ranking officer, but he and
Colonel DeMorse had been operating for two years as separate though
allied brigade leaders. They were good friends, both having been
editors of newspapers in civilian life. DeMorse had started his military career with only his 29th Texas, but when the 5th Texas Brigade
was formed he became its leader. After receiving a serious wound in
1863, DeMorse went home to Clarksville, Texas, to recuperate, and
Richard Gano replaced him. Gano was Kentucky-born, but had
moved to Texas before the war. Early in the war he went back to
Kentucky to join John Morgan's cavalry, rising rapidly to regimental
command; then he volunteered to return to Texas to help defend
his adopted state. When Gano was assigned to DeMorse's brigade,
Kirby Smith named him "acting brigadier general." This situation
might have rankled a smaller-minded man than Charles DeMorse,
who was fifteen years older than Gano and had fought alongside
Sam Houston for Texas independence. Colonel DeMorse, however,
was more interested in victory than command, and he had the highest regard for Acting Brigadier General Gano.

With only the objective of the prized train in mind, Gano, De-Morse, and Watie led their troops across the Canadian River early on September 14 and rode northward. Watie's brigade consisted of 800 Cherokees, Creeks, and Seminoles; Gano's brigade was made up of 1,200 Texans, including DeMorse's 29th Texas Cavalry Regiment, the 30th Texas, four fragmented companies of Texas cavalry, and Captain Sylvanus Howell's Texas battery of six artillery pieces.

The combined force totaled about 2,000 men, all veterans of two or three years of fighting in Arkansas and Indian Territory. They were well mounted and armed, but being so far from Confederate supply bases they had to make do with a hodgepodge of uniforms. Some men possessed only an official uniform hat to indicate their military allegiance; others wore trousers and blouses that were frayed or patched at knees and elbows. Some wore boots or parts of uniforms captured from the Union Army, and if a man owned a blanket it probably did double duty as a saddle blanket. Naturally the men looked forward to capturing new military supplies before winter set in.

On September 15 the column reached the Arkansas River. "It required six hours to cross the river; hard work," Gano reported. "All the artillery ammunition had to be packed over by hand, and many of our brave boys were plunged beneath the waves in consequence of quicksands." Unobserved by Federal patrols, they camped only thirteen miles west of Fort Gibson.

Meanwhile, Major Hopkins' train had passed Baxter Springs, Kansas, and started across the Cherokee Nation. Here he was joined by 100 Union Cherokees led by Captain Ta-la-lah. The train now had 360 men guarding its passage.

On the morning of September 16, the Confederate column's advance scouts reported a detachment of Union soldiers cutting hay at a camp near Flat Rock. Gano's 30th Texas and Watie's 1st Cherokee were sent circling to the rear of the hay camp, while the main force of Confederates moved forward to a small mound. With the aid of a field glass, Gano "could see them at work making hay, little dreaming that the Rebels were watching them." About 175 soldiers of the 2nd Kansas Cavalry and the 1st Kansas Colored Infantry were in the camp.

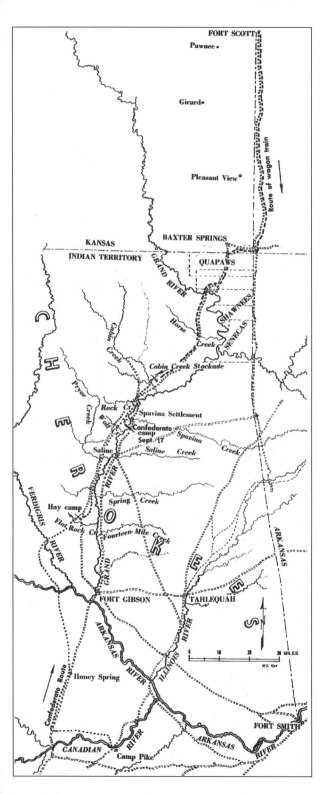

The Union wagon train route from Fort Scott, Kansas, to Fort Gibson, Indian Territory, is depicted on this map, showing roads and localities that once existed. Errors in topography and scale. Courtesy of Dee Brown Collection.

As soon as the Confederates sighted the dust of the Texans and Cherokees coming up to block the Union rear, Watie led his Indians to the left. DeMorse took the 29th to the right, and Gano made a frontal charge with the remainder of the Texans. They had the Union hay camp completely boxed in and outnumbered ten to one.

For a few minutes the Kansas soldiers made a running fight of it; then the officer in command led his men in a desperate saber charge to escape the encirclement. Only about twenty cut their way to safety. The remainder were captured or killed, Gano reporting that he counted seventy-three dead upon the field. Gano said that he offered the defenders an opportunity to surrender. One of his staff officers, Major E. M. Stackpole, went forward with a flag of truce, but when it was fired upon, the Texans charged in and overran the last defense position.

As the sun was setting, the Confederates heaped hay over captured wagons and mowing machines and set it to blazing. They burned Fort Gibson's winter forage supply, 3,000 tons of it, and at sunrise of the seventeenth rode northward toward Rock Creek. "Hearing nothing of the train," Gano said, "we feared lest they might have taken the road east of Grand [Neosho] River. We encamped on Wolf Creek midway between the roads; scouted both and learned that the train had not passed."

That same evening thirty miles to the north, Major Hopkins' million-dollar wagon train halted at Horse Creek. Around midnight a courier arrived with a message from the commanding officer at Fort Gibson warning Hopkins of a strong Confederate force heading in the direction of Cabin Creek. Hopkins was ordered to move with all possible speed to the protection of a stockade on Cabin Creek and there await further orders. "I immediately moved the train in double column," Hopkins reported afterward, "and arrived at 9 A.M. on the 18th."

Early that morning, the Confederate officers were holding a council of war. They knew that if they remained camped on Wolf Creek, within easy striking distance of both military roads, eventually the wagon train would come to them. If they stayed too long, however, they would be discovered and attacked by Union forces in the area. They decided the best course of action was to find the train quickly, capture it, and start moving it rapidly toward Confederate territory.

Gano's final decision was to take 400 of his best-mounted Texans and two guns of the battery north for a reconnaissance along the parallel roads. General Watie would command the camp, keeping his Indians and the remainder of the Texans in concealment until he heard from Gano.

By noontime the reconnaissance force was moving up Cabin Creek. About three o'clock they halted in a timbered hollow less than two miles from the Union stockade. "From this distance," Colonel DeMorse said afterward, "the tents of the enemy were discernible with the naked eye, but not a single man could be discovered." Gano took a small detachment forward to a rise in the prairie, and when he raised his field glass he could see the stockade atop a low bluff beside the creek. It was strongly fortified with timbers set upright in the ground. On the right was a solid wall of hayricks, probably protecting a corral. Along the bluff to the left was an enormous train of wagons parked close together, with hundreds of mules grazing nearby on the grassy flats. Certain that this was the train they had come to capture, Gano immediately dispatched a courier to General Watie to bring up the remainder of the Confederate force.

The presence of Gano's reconnaissance party had not gone unnoticed. About four o'clock, a patrol from the regular Union detachment at Cabin Creek returned to the stockade to report sighting about 100 Rebels a few miles to the south. Major Hopkins immediately ordered a platoon of his 2nd Kansas Cavalry to saddle up. "Moving south from the station at Cabin Creek three miles," he later reported, "I found the enemy strongly posted in a hollow on the prairie."

Assuming that the troops in the hollow composed the total Confederate raiding force, Hopkins turned his platoon back to Cabin Creek station. He was confident that he could defend his train with the soldiers at his disposal. In addition to the men with his wagons, he had the support of Union Cherokees at Cabin Creek, so that his total command numbered about 600 men. Late in the afternoon, Hopkins ordered the wagons formed into a quarter-circle along the bluff, posted soldiers behind them, and doubled his outer pickets. Night fell, with no sign of Confederates anywhere on the horizon.

During the early hours of the night General Watie brought the Confederate main force up to join Gano's reconnaissance party. This was Watie's home territory, the heart of the Cherokee Nation, but he and his soldiers had retreated south to the Choctaw Nation after joining the Confederacy. In 1863, he had lost a battle along this same Cabin Creek, and was eager now for revenge, especially against the Union Cherokees, known as "Pins" because most of them were full-bloods and members of the secret Pin Society. The Cherokees were fighting a civil war within a civil war.

Soon after midnight, Watie reached Gano's position in the hollow. While the horses were resting, the Indians and the Texans worked out a plan of attack. Gano would form his brigade on the left, with Watie on the right, their lines joining at center on Sylvanus Howell's six cannons. Under a bright moon they moved out, silent as ghosts.

By two o'clock in the morning, the Confederates were aligned on a low ridge looking down upon the silvery creek. Campfires glowed yellow behind the curve of wagons, and from inside the stockade came occasional shouts and laughter. The celebrating Union soldiers evidently expected no attack before daylight.

To draw their blood enemies into the open, Stand Watie's Cherokees began taunting the Pins with turkey-gobble challenges, and in a minute or so the sounds came back as though echoed, the throaty repetitive calls of the native male turkey. Watie turned in his saddle, glancing at the moon, which was low in the sky and still shining very brightly. *Our enemies, he noted, have the double advantage of firing up hill with the moon and the sky light.* Suddenly out of the shadows of the slope before him, he saw a stumbling figure coming up from the stockade. The lone enemy soldier stopped to give a turkey call, and then came on clumsily again. A Pin, probably drunk. "Halt!" one of the forward Cherokees called out, and then after a moment or so fired his rifle.

Gano ordered half his men to dismount. Horse-holders steadied the mounts where they were. The lines swung forward, mounted men in front, the dismounted men a few paces to the rear. From the bluff came sounds of men shouting and running, the rattle of harness metal. A hoarse voice called out then from the Union picket line, demanding to know who had fired the shot.

"An officer came out of the darkness to hold converse," Gano said afterward, "and having informed us that they were Federals and learned that we were Rebels, he called on God to damn us, and invited us forward. I asked him if he would receive a flag from us. He said he would answer in five minutes. I waited fifteen and hearing some wagons moving I advanced my line about 3 A.M. and when within 300 yards or less of their fortifications they opened fire."

The Confederates immediately replied with small arms, and then as the engagement became general along the line from right to left, Howell's battery opened with a crashing salvo. As the roar of artillery swept away across the plains, Gano heard the creak of wagon wheels. He ordered Howell to detach two guns and hurry them around to the right so as to put a crossfire on the train.

Colonel DeMorse, who sent regular dispatches of his 29th Regiment's exploits to his newspaper at Clarksville, Texas, described the night battle in vivid style: "The bright flashes of musketry along both lines, the white smoke of the bursting bombs, the whistle of the Minie ball, accompanied by the guttural sound of Howell's artillery as it belched forth its iron messengers of death, under the brilliant lustre of the moon and stars . . . rendered the scene sublime."

Until sunrise the Confederates would not know how badly the unexpected artillery shelling had demoralized the Union teamsters. They could hear shouting and pounding hoofbeats, the braying of mule teams, and the occasional splintering crash of a wagon tumbling off the bluff. "It was difficult to ascertain the enemy's exact position and strength excepting from his fire," General Watie said afterward. "His line seemed to extend the length of ours. For a considerable length of time the firing was heavy and incessant. Our forces steadily advanced, driving the enemy to his cover." During this advance, a company of Watie's Indians overran one end of the train, captured several wagons, and quickly moved them to the rear.

Gano now decided to pull his men back and wait for daybreak. In his report he explained that he did this because of the confusion of close night fighting and because he was convinced that he had stopped the train from moving out. Colonel DeMorse's newspaper account gave another reason: "Ammunition being a serious matter with us, the troops were withdrawn to a position secure from danger, to await the dawn of morning. We were not long in this position before the enemy, under the impression that we had suffered considerably in the attack, again endeavored to remove the train." To stop the movement, Gano sent two Texas battalions forward. For an hour they exchanged harassing fire with the Union defenders. While this action was in progress, General Watie sent Lieutenant Colonel C. N. Vann with two mounted Cherokee regiments around to the rear of the Union position to block any possible escape of the train north on the Fort Scott road.

When the sun rose the Union commander, Major Hopkins, was dismayed to find his train in complete disarray. He later explained to his superiors that at the beginning of the attack he had expected an enemy force of not more than 800 men. "I was not informed that they had any artillery until it was opened upon my lines," he said. "They numbered not less than 2,000 at the very lowest," he accurately estimated, "and four to six pieces of artillery." It was the artillery that demoralized the defenders of the wagons. "The teamsters and wagon masters, with very few exceptions, stampeded, taking with them one or more mules out of each wagon, leaving their teams and going in the direction of Fort Scott. This rendered it impossible to move any part of the train."

From their position at dawn, the Confederates were within rifle range of the line of hayricks, the log barricade, and the canvas-covered wagons scattered behind a screen of timber along the bluff. After studying the scene for a few minutes, Gano and his staff officers agreed that their first move should be to secure the wagons. They would worry about the stockade later.

This illustration depicting the destruction of a sutler's train in Virginia may very well replicate the attack on the wagon train at Cabin Creek, Indian Territory. From Harper's Weekly, *September 5, 1863.*

DeMorse's 29th Texas and a battalion of Seminoles and Creeks led by John Jumper and George Washington Grayson were assigned the task of enveloping the train while the remainder of the force kept the Federal defenders pinned down. Lieutenant Colonel Jumper was half Seminole—a tall and dignified warrior who wore a thick, black, down-curving moustache. Captain Grayson was half Creek—nineteen years old, well-educated, and disdainful of the medicine-making habits of the men he commanded.

They went in to the left of Howell's battery while the 30th Texas gave close support and, as DeMorse described it, "wrested from them the bank of the creek and a large number of wagons. . . . Conspicuous for his daring and gallantry was Col. John Jumper. His towering form was always to be seen in the thickest of the contest, a conspicuous mark for the enemy, as he mingled among his braves, encouraging them, and setting for them a noble example."

The attack doubled back the Union right, but Major Hopkins was finally able to make a stand. In an attempt to finish off the fight, Gano took two of Howell's guns and, using his tactics of a mounted line supported by men on foot, drove in from the flank. The guns were unlimbered only 100 yards from the Union position. Gano himself led the 30th Texas and was about to overrun the Federal line when a small band of 6th Kansas cavalrymen surged out of concealment in a ditch. They stopped the Texans temporarily, inflicting the heaviest Confederate casualties of the fight. Attempting to capture the Confederate battery, Captain Henry Ledger with twelve men made a desperate mounted charge, but all were cut down. Ledger's horse fell within fifteen feet of the guns but the captain managed to make his escape.

"Our forces were compelled to fall back in disorder, leaving the train," Major Hopkins said in his report. "I collected all the scattered troops possible together and moved in a direction east of Cabin Creek." Behind them rose a boiling black cloud of smoke from tons of hay already set on fire by the Confederate victors.

Gano described the Union retreat as a rout: "All with a loud shout rushed on to victory, driving the enemy behind their fortifications from where they fled in wild confusion to the densely timbered bottoms. At nine o'clock (six hours after the first volley was fired) the field was ours with more than $1,000,000 worth of Federal property in our hands. We burned all the broken wagons and killed all the crippled mules. We brought off 130 wagons and 740 mules."

From the wagons almost every man in the expedition took Union uniforms or civilian clothing and discarded their ragged outfits. With winter approaching, the new woolen pants and coats, flannel underwear, and shiny leather boots more than compensated for the long, hard riding and dangerous fighting. As an added bonus, there was a bottle of brandy or whisky for all.

Considering the number of men engaged, Confederate losses were light—nine killed and forty-two wounded. Twenty-six Union soldiers were captured, and twenty-three dead were found on the field; the number of wounded Federals was never accurately determined because of the scattered flight of the teamsters.

The Confederates had the million-dollar train, but now they must move it across 100 miles of dangerous territory. Strong Union forces from Forts Gibson, Smith, and Scott would be in pursuit of them, and the wagons must be crossed over two formidable rivers, the Arkansas and the Canadian. To add to Gano's difficulties, some of the Indians had drunk too freely of captured spirits, and they were slow in getting the train started.

Within an hour after moving out, the raiders' scouts sighted a Union column of infantry, cavalry, and artillery coming north from Fort Gibson. Gano halted the train and took a regiment of Texas cavalry and Howell's artillery out in a screening maneuver. He drew the Federals into a long-range artillery duel until darkness fell, and then ordered the train to roll out swiftly in a westerly direction while he held off the attackers.

"What a ruse we played upon the enemy that night," DeMorse wrote his newspaper, "to induce them to think the train was still with us, it might not be politic to state, as we may have use of it again." The ruse, revealed afterward by Gano, was to run an empty wagon back and forth over a slab of rocky ground so as to make the Federals believe the train was being corraled in the darkness. The raiders, however, never had an opportunity to use that deception again.

After three days and nights of hard driving, they succeeded in getting the train safely to their base. From Indian Territory to Richmond the feat was hailed as a great victory for the combined Texan-Indian brigades. A month later, however, Sterling Price's important Confederate raid across Missouri met with sudden disaster at Westport. Had Gano and Watie not advanced their timetable in order to capture the wagon train, and instead had followed Kirby Smith's original plan to make a coordinated raid into Kansas and draw off Union forces from General Price, the Trans-Mississippi Confederacy might have gained a great deal more than the spoils of a rich wagon train.

Major General John S. Marmaduke, who commanded a division during the Battle of Westport, was captured the following day, October 25, 1864, while fighting a rearguard action at Mine Creek or Little Osage River, in Kansas. He was imprisoned until July 1865. Although ranked in this article as a major general, Marmaduke did not officially receive his second star until March 18, 1885, with date of rank to the previous day. From Battles and Leaders of the Civil War.

Major General Alfred Pleasonton organized a Provisional Cavalry Division in Missouri and kept the pressure on Major General Sterling Price throughout the battle, ultimately leading Price to abandon and burn his supply wagons. From Frank Leslie's Illustrated History of the Civil War, 1861–65, page 230.

13

The Battle of Westport

"Sterling Price's bold raid across Missouri ended here in the biggest battle of the war west of the Mississippi."

On September 7, 1864, after a summer campaign against hostile Indians on his western frontier, Major General Samuel R. Curtis, commanding the Department of Kansas, returned to headquarters at Fort Leavenworth. Among the stacks of paper on his desk were reports that a strong force of mounted Confederates under Major General Sterling Price had crossed the Arkansas River bound for St. Louis.

Curtis was confident that if Price became entangled with Major General William S. Rosecrans around St. Louis, he would never be able to bring his army all the way across Missouri to Kansas. As he said later, he "deemed it both monstrous and impossible that a Rebel army could march unchecked . . . for over 200 miles into the very heart of our territory." He telegraphed to Rosecrans the report of the river crossing, which had come from his spies (one of them being Wild Bill Hickok), and kept a wary eye on Price's movements far to the east.

Three weeks later, after Curtis heard that Price had bypassed St. Louis, he began preparing for the worst. As his army numbered only 4,000 Regular volunteers, he asked Kansas's governor, Thomas Carney, to call up the militia, and thereby suddenly found himself embroiled in political controversy. National and state elections were only a month away, and Governor Carney suspected that Curtis was in league with his political enemies. Calling up the militia, he thought, might be a scheme to transport voters outside their polling districts and somehow defeat him in the elections. Carney replied that a band of raiding Confederates 200 miles away in Missouri offered no threat to Kansas. Curtis knew better, but he was inclined to move cautiously. Politics had been his undoing in Missouri in 1862; he had been exiled to Kansas and replaced by Rosecrans (who had been exiled from Tennessee after Chickamauga).

Not until Price's columns passed Jefferson City and were halfway across Missouri did Governor Carney issue a call to arms: "Let each man come with such arms as are at hand and a full supply of ammunition. As this campaign will be a short one, no change of clothing will be necessary." Next day, October 10, Curtis declared martial law in Kansas and began organizing his Army of the Border into two wings: a cavalry division under Major General James G. Blunt, a militia division under Major General George W. Deitzler.

For his main line of resistance, Curtis chose the Big Blue River which ran eastward across the Kansas line below Westport, Missouri, and then turned north to Independence. He summoned civilian volunteers to assist the soldiers in fortifying the stream; at the main fords they felled trees and built barricades.

On October 13 Curtis learned that Rosecrans was in full pursuit of the invaders, but the latter's forward elements were already reported to be near Lexington. Curtis immediately ordered Blunt and Deitzler to move on parallel roads toward Lexington to feel out the enemy's approach.

General Price meanwhile was mainly concerned with the problem of escaping with his immense wagon train. After invading the southeastern part of Missouri he had taken heavy casualties in the Battle of Pilot Knob, then had moved within forty miles of St. Louis. From spies sent ahead he received warnings that the city was strongly defended; General Rosecrans had acquired 4,500 infantry reinforcements from Cairo, Illinois. Although some of Price's officers were willing to risk an attack, he decided to turn west toward Jefferson City, the state capital.

The orders which Price had received in August had specifically instructed him to "make St. Louis the objective point of your movement." The major purpose of the raid originally was to "rally the loyal men of Missouri" and recruit soldiers for the Confederacy, but after Brigadier General Joseph O. Shelby's division of Missourians joined Price in north Arkansas, the raid became a political as well as a military force. On Shelby's staff was Thomas C. Reynolds, a former lieutenant governor of Missouri, who hoped that the raid would swing his state back to the Confederacy, and that he would be inaugurated governor after the November election.

Price, a former governor of Missouri himself, sympathized with Reynolds's desires, and on October 7 the raiding army was camped so close to Jefferson City that Reynolds could look longingly upon the dome of the capitol above the autumn-colored trees. During the morning, forward elements skirmished with Federal forces, driving them into the city's fortifications about midafternoon. From scanty intelligence reports, Price estimated that the capital's defenders numbered 12,000 (actually there were only 7,000). In a council of war that evening he decided that Jefferson City was impregnable. Reynolds was angered by this decision, and never forgave Price for his "hesitating generalship." Next morning as the column faced westward toward Kansas, it was no longer a political force but an army seeking recruits, supplies of war, and an escape route back to the Confederate lines. The raiders were prepared to give battle if necessary, but were no longer seeking a fight.

When he entered Missouri, Price's army consisted of 12,000 men, and although one-third of them had no arms they formed the most powerful body of cavalry ever mounted west of the Mississippi River. The three divisions were led by Major Generals James F. Fagan and John S. Marmaduke, and Brigadier General Joseph O. Shelby. Fourteen pieces of artillery were distributed among them.

As they marched in separate columns across the state, they gathered up sixteen additional pieces of artillery, large numbers of small arms, much ammunition, hundreds of horses and cattle, stores of flour, bacon, and coffee, blankets, overcoats, and underclothing. By the time they reached Boonville, October 10, they had recruited enough men to form a brigade of two regiments. (They had also temporarily lost hundreds of men, Missourians who had dropped out to visit their families.) Their train of captured goods had grown to 500 wagons and 5,000 cattle, accompanied by 1,500 recruits still unarmed.

Although Sterling Price had led Confederate forces twice before in Missouri, he was not a cavalryman and seemed to have little concept of the principles of speed and deception essential to the success of a cavalry raid. He was in his middle fifties and was losing the vigor which had attracted Missourians to his banner in 1861. They still called him "Old Pap," but discipline was weakening. In the latter stages of the raid, he abandoned his saddle for the comforts of a carriage. Each day his subordinates grew more critical of him, especially Shelby and his hardbitten veterans, who foresaw disaster if they continued their slow fifteen-miles-per-day march "in the atmosphere of a prolonged picnic."

Shortly after sunrise, October 17, Brigadier General M. Jeff Thompson, one of Shelby's brigade commanders, reported that Federal cavalry had dashed into Lexington and forced his pickets back from the town. The Federals were 300 troopers of Blunt's 2nd Colorado. Blunt himself arrived the next afternoon, and skirmishing continued for twenty-four hours. On the nineteenth, Shelby's main force drove Blunt out of Lexington, fighting Colonel Thomas Moonlight's 11th Kansas in stubborn retreat back toward the Little Blue River.

At dawn of the twentieth, the Union regiments were stretched precariously along the Little Blue. Both Shelby and Marmaduke were forming for an attack across that stream and against Independence. If Blunt could hold long enough, however, the Confederates would be trapped between Curtis's Army of the Border and Rosecrans' pursuing Army of the Missouri.

Rosecrans' cavalry commander was Major General Alfred Pleasonton, a veteran of the eastern theater of war who had been sent west to prevent such raids as the one now in progress in Missouri. Pleasonton was forty years old—handsome, sinewy, dynamic. Instead of carrying a saber, he wore a whip on his wrist.

On October 8, the day after Price turned west from Jefferson City, Pleasonton arrived there to begin assembling a provisional cavalry division. The task was not easy. Most of Rosecrans' mounted troops were scattered over the state in small detachments, and Pleasonton realized that if he hoped to overtake Price he would have to depend largely upon 4,000 cavalrymen in the vicinity of Jefferson City, and 4,500 infantrymen coming up by boat from St. Louis. He soon had two brigades under Brigadier Generals John McNeil and John B. Sanborn in pursuit. During the following week he assembled two more mounted brigades, and on the evening of October 20, Pleasonton's advance galloped into Lexington only one day's march behind Price's army, which was readying itself for a crossing of the Little Blue and an attack upon Independence.

The following morning General Curtis, at his headquarters on the road between Kansas City and Independence, could hear the booming of guns along the Little Blue. After ordering General Deitzler to move his Kansas militia to fortifications along the Big Blue, he went forward with Blunt's cavalry to see how well his front lines were holding.

For the first time, many Kansas militiamen now crossed the border into Missouri. Most wore civilian clothes, with red badges pinned to hats or sleeves to identify themselves as soldiers. Among them was Sam Reader, a farmer with an artistic bent. He later painted a watercolor of the march to the Big Blue, captioning it "Second Kansas State Militia Invading Missouri." Reader's outfit, under Brigadier General M. S. Grant, camped near Hickman Mills on the escape route for Price's wagon train. The next forty-eight hours would provide Reader with plenty of material for dramatic art.

Meanwhile along the Little Blue, Blunt's seasoned volunteers were giving the Confederates a hard fight. At noon Colonel Moonlight's brigade repulsed an attempted bridge crossing by Marmaduke's division, then was forced back to a line of stone walls and farm houses. Colonel Charles Jennison's 3rd Wisconsin and 15th Kansas cavalry regiments came up on the right and were pressing Marmaduke until Shelby came to the rescue. Moonlight found himself outflanked

Driven from their homesteads by the Confederates, these refugees from southern Missouri seek comfort and safety near a Union troop encampment. From Frank Leslie's Illustrated History of the Civil War, 1861–65, *page 97.*

by General Jeff Thompson's and Colonel Sidney Jackman's brigades, but fought a stubborn rear-guard fight back to Independence.

Curtis now ordered a complete withdrawal behind the fortifications of the Big Blue, abandoning Independence to the Confederates. At five o'clock that afternoon he telegraphed Rosecrans: "Confident I can stop Price," adding that if Pleasonton's forces would press forward from the rear "we will bag Price." Curtis believed that Price had 30,000 men, outnumbering him two to one. Actually the reverse was true. Price now had only 7,500 fighting men, and although he rested that night in Independence, he ordered his precious wagon train to start moving southward at once along the road to Hickman Mills.

Early Saturday morning, October 22, Shelby's division marched south out of Independence to engage the Federals along the Big Blue. The action was designed primarily to cover the passage of the wagon train. After reconnoitering the formidable entanglements at Byram's Ford, Shelby ordered companies of Jackman's and Thompson's brigades to dismount and try a frontal attack against Jennison's Kansas and Wisconsin cavalry. By two o'clock that afternoon, Shelby was convinced that a direct attack would be too costly; he sent mounted men south and north to try other crossings. Not far from Hickman Mills, one of Jeff Thompson's regiments forded the river, reached the crest of a ridge, and wheeled north, flanking Curtis's line of defense. As soon as this was accomplished, Jackman's dismounted men charged across Byram's Ford, rolling back Jennison's brigade. Thompson later described the chase: "We drove the enemy so fast that the axes they had used to fell the trees were left by them, and they were speedily put to use opening a road for our artillery and train to cross." Remounting his men, Thompson pressed Curtis's army back northward across Brush Creek into Westport. In the rout, Jackman's men captured a twenty-four-pounder brass howitzer.

While this operation was in progress, two of Shelby's regiments were attacking General M. S. Grant's raw militia at Hickman Mills. It was another disaster for the Federals. Curtis's entire right wing was now demolished; a hundred militiamen were dead, more than a hundred captured. Among the prisoners was Sam Reader, the amateur artist, who later escaped and painted the scene of his capture.

Although victorious, Price's army had halted just long enough for Pleasonton's advance to overtake the rear guard. In the afternoon, Marmaduke had to come to Fagan's assistance to form a new rear. Fighting was furious until nightfall, when the last of the Confederates crossed the Big Blue and dug in behind the abandoned fortifications which had been built to stop them. The train, escorted by regiments of Fagan's division, was also safely across the river.

By nightfall, Blunt's 1st Brigade under Colonel Jennison had formed a new line running east and west just north of Westport. Shelby and Fagan were bivouacked on a ridge south of Brush Creek, close enough to Westport to see lights blinking in the town. At right angles to their divisions, Marmaduke faced Pleasonton across the Big Blue.

General Curtis, visibly shaken by the failure of his army to hold the Big Blue, was pessimistic. He was almost sixty, and like his adversary, Price, was feeling the toll of three years of war. Not even a reassuring message from Pleasonton and the dull booming of the latter's guns beyond the Big Blue gave any lift to his spirits. Had it not been for the younger and more vigorous James G. Blunt, the Army of the Border would have withdrawn into the defenses of Kansas City that night.

After a long council of war at the Gillis House in Kansas City, Curtis finally agreed to make a stand before Westport, directing Blunt to personally supervise preparations for the battle. Somewhat as Shelby had taken command of the fighting from the weary Price, Blunt now took over from Curtis. It was two o'clock in the morning when the council of war ended; by three o'clock Blunt had troops and supply wagons moving through Westport to form a line along Brush Creek. "As night wore on," Colonel Jennison recorded, "we seemed encircled by the camp fires of the Rebels which gleamed menacingly from the woods, as if mocking the anxiety which prevailed throughout our lines."

Across the creek, the Confederates were no less anxious. According to one of Shelby's officers, Shelby sent a major to Price to suggest a night withdrawal to save the army. No reply came. The night was bitter cold, below freezing, the air thick and hazy until a chill wind began blowing. "A fitful, gusty, moaning night," one of the men later described it. Dawn would bring a Sunday morning, but it would not be a quiet one.

At first daylight, Blunt deployed his three available brigades (Colonel Charles W. Blair's 3rd had not yet arrived) and at sunrise ordered skirmishers of Jennison's 1st and Colonel James H. Ford's 4th to move through the woods and across Brush Creek. The morning was clear and cold, with a bluish mist hovering over the bottomland, hindering visibility. The advance horsemen splashed across the ice-rimmed stream and through the opposite woods. Not until they came out upon the frost-browned field beyond could they see Shelby's gray line of cavalry approaching.

With a rattle of small arms the fighting began. Jennison's men, coming up in the center, ran into a maze of rail and stone fencing. They dismounted, took cover behind the fences, and turned a galling fire upon the charging Confederates. By this time, Captain W. D. McLain had emplaced his Colorado battery, and the day's artillery dueling began. Within a few minutes "clouds of dense and sable smoke" mingled with the fading mist.

About this time, General Curtis—somewhat more cheerful after three hours' sleep—arrived at the Harris House in Westport, where Blunt was observing the battle through a telescope from the rooftop. Not long afterward, the Confederates began driving the Federals back across Brush Creek, and Blunt hurriedly started for the battle-field. Both Ford and Jennison were outflanked, and Moonlight's 2nd Brigade on the right received such a fierce fire that he had to wheel and retreat across the Kansas line. As Jennison's brigade moved back almost into Westport, Colonel Blair arrived with his 3rd Brigade of Kansas militia supported by Captain James Dodge's Wisconsin battery.

During pauses in the cannonading, Curtis on the hotel rooftop could hear the distant booming of Pleasonton's guns along the Big Blue. He also noted that Shelby's lines had become ragged; they were slowing up to re-form—just as Blair's fresh troops were preparing to enter the battle. Suddenly the old warrior in Curtis came to life. After hastily dispatching a message to Pleasonton, he called for his horse and galloped forward to join General Blunt. He would lead the next attack himself.

Colonel Blair, however, had already moved into the right side of the line, his over-eager Kansans dismounting and charging across the creek without orders. Curtis immediately ordered the remainder of the line forward, and the onrush of Federals broke through Shelby's skirmishers. But before the Kansans could gain the ridge, Jeff Thompson's brigade stormed upon them, and once again Curtis's army withdrew to cover of woods and fences.

Regrouping his forces, Curtis reached for a weak point in the Confederate line. "I tried to get through the timber with Dodge's battery . . . but the roads were not favorable." At that critical moment, luck brought him a local farmer searching for a lost horse. The farmer showed the general a narrow gulch that led out upon the high ground held by Shelby.

In a few minutes, the Wisconsin battery, escorted by 11th Kansas cavalrymen, was up the ravine and on Jeff Thompson's flank, pouring a withering fire down the startled Confederates' line. At the same time, General Blunt ordered Jennison and Ford to charge on the left. Hundreds of blue-coated soldiers swarmed out of the woods, firing and cheering. "Their movement was steady, orderly, and gallant," Curtis later wrote. "We steadily advanced all arms over a beautiful prairie where both armies were in full view. It was at this time about 11:30 A.M."

After withdrawing to another elevation, the Confederates made several stabbing attacks, one of the more dramatic being a cavalry clash between Captain Curtis Johnson's Kansans and Colonel James McGhee's Arkansans. In the melee the two leaders singled each other out for combat and like medieval knights dueled until both men fell from their horses. Johnson was severely wounded; McGhee was dead.

About noon the Confederate lines seemed suddenly to break, and the Army of the Border drove in for a victory. Curtis did not know until later that Price had ordered Shelby and Fagan to turn eastward, support Marmaduke's withdrawal from Pleasonton's attack, and then concentrate around the wagon train. The Union leaders were certain they had put Price's army into a two-mile rout until they saw the long blue line of Pleasonton's cavalry on their left. At this point Blunt stampeded the Confederates with enfilading fire from twenty pieces of artillery.

Marmaduke had been fighting hard all morning. Although he had the advantage of fortifications, he was outnumbered more than two to one, and it was only a question of time until Pleasonton's cavalry broke across the Big Blue. After two hours of furious battling Captain Edward Dee led a battalion of the 4th Iowa Cavalry across the north side of Byram's Ford, while Colonel John Philips crossed on the south. While this enveloping movement was in progress, Lieutenant Colonel Frederick Benteen (who twelve years later would ride with Custer at the Little Big Horn) dismounted his 10th Missouri Cavalry and charged the center.

Marmaduke had placed a heavy gun to sweep the ford where Philips crossed, and it inflicted heavy casualties upon horses and men in the stream. After the Federals reached the west bank, they had to cross an open field under fire of sharpshooters concealed behind logs and in treetops. Union Missourians and Arkansans were fighting Confederate Missourians and Arkansans, and the hand-to-hand combat was bloody. When Marmaduke received orders to withdraw on the rear of the train, his ammunition was nearing exhaustion.

Although Marmaduke sent couriers to Shelby and Fagan, notifying them that he was withdrawing, his messages failed to get through. Fagan swung eastward first but, instead of finding Marmaduke, was almost overwhelmed by an unexpected charge from Pleasonton's cavalry. Only the timely arrival of Shelby's advance brigade under Colonel Jackman saved him from disaster. As soon as Jackman saw Union cavalry sweeping over a ridge before him, he dismounted his men, ordering them to run 200 yards in front of their horses and kneel there on a broad open plain without cover, weapons at ready. Jackman described the approach of the Federals: "They came on in a swinging trot, and when within eighty yards at the command a destructive fire was poured into them, killing and wounding a large number of men and horses, and causing their line to reel and break."

Shelby now became aware that he was caught between two on-rushing armies. In the rear, Blunt's artillery was shattering his lines; everywhere he turned riderless horses careened among wounded Confederates who were crawling all over the prairie. "Nothing was left but to run for it," he wrote. "My own men fighting, every one, on his own hook, would turn and fire and then gallop away again. Up from the green sward of the waving grass two miles off, a string of stone fences grew up and groped along the plain—a shelter and protection. . . . The fences are lines of fire, and the bullets sputter and rain thicker upon the charging enemy. . . . My command was saved, and we moved off after the army, traveling all night."

Shelby not only wrote his reports in the style of his favorite author, Sir Walter Scott, he frequently played the role of a Scott hero. One of his officers described him coming out of the fight at Westport "without a hat on his head, his sandy locks streaming on the wind, his six-shooter in his hand . . . still not whipped." But Shelby's division left 800 men—killed, wounded, or captured—on the fields before Westport.

Along the road to Little Santa Fe the fleeing Confederates left a screen of smoke from burning prairie grass and grain stacks. They also left behind them the last Confederate hopes of winning anything in the West. The Battle of Westport was the biggest Civil War engagement west of the Mississippi—20,000 Federals against 9,000 Confederates (including 1,500 unarmed men with the wagon train). Dead and wounded on both sides totaled about a thousand.

And the fighting was not yet ended. Next morning, October 24, the Union forces resumed pursuit, Blunt in advance, Pleasonton following, with Moonlight's brigade on the right flank across the Kansas line. The road was littered with the debris of a routed army—broken wagons, caissons, rifles, blankets, harness, and an occasional sick or wounded Confederate soldier.

On the previous evening, after a consultation in a farmhouse, Curtis and Pleasonton had agreed that Price's army must be overtaken and destroyed. At first Pleasonton had expressed a desire to withdraw; his men had been in their saddles for several days and they and their mounts were nearing exhaustion. After Curtis explained that his militiamen were eager to return home and vote in the important election, Pleasonton agreed to send his soldiers back into the chase.

Had it not been for the wagon train, Price's experienced horse soldiers probably would have outrun their pursuers. But at dawn on the twenty-fourth the train was a confused collection of covered wagons, carriages, ambulances, tents, cattle, and foot soldiers. Precious hours were lost getting the train into motion, and then it moved, said one of Shelby's disgusted cavalrymen, "as slowly as a gorged anaconda dragging its huge body over the prairie."

Rain began falling soon after they crossed the Kansas line and turned southward. Although the roads became slippery with mud, the continued presence of Federal skirmishers in their rear spurred the Confederates to superhuman efforts. They drove the train across thirty-three miles of prairie, camping that night near the Marais-des-Cygnes River, under a dark and rainy sky. During the night Federal cavalry drove in some of Price's pickets, but "Old Pap" was so confident he had saved his train that he made plans to send Shelby ahead next morning to raid Fort Scott and capture what military supplies might be there.

Shelby never reached Fort Scott. Early the next afternoon he received an urgent summons from Price to turn back and save the army from destruction. As Shelby galloped back he met Fagan's and Marmaduke's men "retreating in utter and indescribable confusion, many of them having thrown away their arms." Shelby could not rally them, although some slowed their flight long enough to shout that Marmaduke and all the army's artillery had been captured.

To slow the pursuing Federals, Shelby formed three lines. The first line would fire a volley, then wheel and gallop back through the second and third to dismount and reload; then the second and third lines would repeat the maneuver. "Slowly, slowly my old brigade was melting away," he wrote afterwards. But he held off the attackers until the routed divisions could re-form behind him. Sunset ended the action.

The day's fighting had begun along the Marais-des-Cygnes with a dawn attack by Pleasonton's cavalry. This had started a running fight of several miles to Mine Creek, where Price was crossing his wagon train. To save the train, Marmaduke and Fagan deployed their men on horseback, Marmaduke's division formed in the first line of defense.

Philips and Benteen, who had battled Marmaduke forty-eight hours earlier along the Big Blue, led their brigades across the plain at a thundering gallop. Marmaduke ordered a charge to meet them, and with bugles blaring, blue and gray lines closed at full speed. They clashed with terrific impact, and the fighting was hand-to-hand, on horseback and on foot. In a matter of minutes the Federals had captured Marmaduke, Brigadier General William Cabell, four colonels, a thousand men, and ten pieces of artillery.

Both Pleasonton and Curtis again raced after Price's army, but Shelby's stubborn rear guard kept them off the train, and the Confederate column did not halt until midnight. At last Price realized that he could not escape with both his army and his train. He ordered most of the wagons corraled and burned, and once again his army became a column of cavalry. The next day's march covered almost sixty miles.

For twelve more days the Federals continued the pursuit, fighting the Confederates hard at Newtonia, Missouri, but Price at last escaped with 5,000 men across the Arkansas River. There ended one of the war's most wide-ranging movements of Union and Confederate troops—across hundreds of miles of plains, mountains, and rivers. The climax had been the Battle of Westport, and except for guerrilla activity it virtually closed out the war in the Kansas-Missouri border country.

Confederate President Jefferson Davis, although viewed as stubborn and aristocratic, was actually a sensitive and warm individual who believed strongly in the Southern cause. From Frank Leslie's Illustrated History of the Civil War, 1861–65, page 81.

14

No More Bugles

*I*t seemed providential to the 2nd Kentucky boys in south-western Virginia that Basil Duke should have been exchanged in the same week they lost (General) John Morgan. "I hear this morning Colonel Duke is exchanged," one of them wrote from Abingdon. "If so, we are all *all right*."

Duke joined the brigade* at Jonesboro, Tennessee, immediately following John Morgan's death. Colonel D. Howard Smith graciously offered to relinquish command of the 2nd Kentucky Battalion and other elements of the old Morgan regiments, and once again Duke was leading the alligator horses. There were not many of the veterans left, less than 300—most of them so poorly armed he wondered how they had been able to fight at all, the calibers of their rifles so varied that it was impossible to keep enough ammunition in supply.

During the two weeks they camped outside Jonesboro, he devoted most of his time to collecting weapons, supplies and equipment. Private George Mosgrove, who was serving under him at this time, described him as being nervous and impatient, "restlessly turning in his saddle, his dark eyes flashing."

[*Remnants of Brigadier General John Hunt Morgan's cavalry were reorganized in early 1864 into the 1st, 2nd, 3rd, and 4th Special Cavalry Battalions. These battalions were disbanded on April 12, 1865, by Brigadier General John Echols, Commanding, Department of Southwestern Virginia and East Tennessee. Part of these battalions, however, then joined President Jefferson Davis and his escort as they fled Richmond toward Georgia.]

General John Echols, now in active command of the department, suggested that the fragmented Morgan regiments be brought together and reorganized along new lines, a move which Duke agreed would bring more efficiency to his command. In the new organization, most of the 2nd Kentucky boys ended up under their commander of the Indiana-Ohio raid, Major Thomas Webber. On official rolls they were listed as 4th Battalion, Kentucky Cavalry, but in all private communications they continued to call themselves 2nd Kentucky Cavalry.

The entire brigade was now officially Duke's Cavalry, the young commander receiving his brigadier general's commission late in September. By October he had brought his command to a strength of 578 officers and men present for duty, and was ready to march against the enemy in eastern Tennessee.

But this last autumn and winter of the Civil War was not to be a season of victories for twenty-six-year-old General Duke. In his first fight at Bull's Gap, November 13, he won the decision but lost too many men; and men lost now could not be replaced. It was a night attack, fought on foot in the mountains. "The night was cloudless," he wrote, "and the moon at its full and shedding a brilliant light. The dark lines of troops could be seen almost as clearly as by day. Their positions were distinctly marked, however, by the flashes from the rifles, coming thick and fast, making them look, as they moved along, bending and oscillating, like rolling waves of flame, throwing off fiery spray. When my brigade had moved far around upon the left, and had taken position, obliquely toward the enemy's rear, it suddenly opened. The Federal line recoiled, and closed from both flanks toward the road, in one dense mass, which looked before the fighting ceased and the rout fairly commenced, like a huge Catherine wheel spouting streams of fire."

Duke's men captured all the enemy artillery, a wagon train, and an ambulance filled with much-needed medical supplies. They also took 300 prisoners, but the Federals' firepower, improved considerably since Duke had last faced the enemy, had riddled his brigade. Major Webber, for instance, leading twenty-eight men in one charge, had sustained fourteen casualties.

They withdrew with their wounded to the base camp at Abingdon and began a winter of defensive operations, fighting off enemy patrols probing for weaknesses in the lines guarding the salt and lead deposits. On December 21, the Federals under General Stephen Burbridge massed their forces and broke through the Confederate lines, wrecking the vital salt works at Saltville, demolishing buildings, kettles, machinery, pumps, wells and stores.

(That very same day General Hardee was evacuating Savannah; Sherman had completed his march to the sea, cutting the South in half.)

Duke's brigade, brought up as reinforcements, drove Burbridge's cavalrymen out of Saltville and pursued them through a blinding snowstorm all the way to the Kentucky line. Major William J. Davis, who had been captured in Indiana after his command was split at Twelve Mile Island, had recently been exchanged, and was a member of the pursuing expedition. "As we ascended the steep mountain road leading from Saltville," he wrote, "the cold intensified so as to test the greatest power of endurance. Men beat their breasts to promote a more vigorous circulation, or, dismounting, limped on benumbed feet beside their hobbling horses. The necks, breasts and forelegs of the horses were covered with clinging sheets of frozen breath or blood that had oozed from the fissures in their swollen nostrils. Often their lips were sealed by the frost to the steel bits, or protruded livid and rugged with icicles of blood. Soon we met indications of the still greater suffering of our foes. Horses dead from cold were seen along the road, frozen stiff in every imaginable attitude; some leaned against the perpendicular cliff on the right, with legs swollen to an enormous size and split open to the bone from knee to hoof; some knelt with muzzles cemented to the hard earth by blood; others lay prone but with heads upraised. . . . These corpses actually impeded our pursuit; sometimes six or eight lay in one heap; once I counted 200 in one mile. . . . You may think the sight of hundreds of horses, dead, as I have said, horrible; what think you—you who have never seen war, but have read of its 'pomp and circumstance,' and perchance have glorified the butchery of it—what think you of men lying on bed or floor, some of them in the article of death, frozen, as were their dumb beasts by the road side? The hands of some of these gallant men were swollen and cracked with bleeding fissures a quarter of an inch wide. Their legs, from which pantaloons have been ripped, looked as if affected by elephantiasis; their feet, from which boots had been cut, were a shapeless mass; legs and feet seemed red like the shells of boiled lobsters and were split into bloody cracks like the hands."

Returning from this ordeal, the brigade settled into winter quarters at Abingdon. The men built huts against the continuing cold, but most of the time they were half-famished and half-clothed. "Many men are badly in need of clothing," Duke reported on New Year's Day of 1865, "and all are clamorous for their pay. Guns, saddles, and cartridge boxes are all needed."

In worse condition than the men were their horses. Southwestern Virginia had been stripped of fodder and grain, and as the South's transportation system had virtually collapsed no supplies could be shipped in. Duke could not bear to watch the last of his horses die of starvation; reluctantly he ordered the brigade dismounted and sent the animals overland to North Carolina. One of the men assigned to this horse detail was Sergeant Henry Stone, who had returned on a blockade runner from his Canadian exile. From Mecklenburg County, North Carolina, young Stone reported briefly: "I am now for the first time at a convalescent camp; not for the improvement of myself but for the health of my horse. Weather pleasant."

(About the same time, General Sherman, after reorganizing his army around Savannah, was starting north through the Carolinas.)

At Abingdon the icy winter dragged on through February, keeping the enemy away but making life miserable for the boys cooped up in their wooden huts. An army inspector reporting on the condition of Duke's Brigade, February 15, noted that "about one-fourth of the men need arms and one-third lack accoutrements. There were present at the date of my inspection 328 men and their discipline seemed better than that of the other commands of the department."

This favorable military comparison, however, did not mean that morale was especially high among the Kentucky boys; it merely indicated that their morale was not quite as low as that of some of the others.

For doom was in the chill winter air; no one could deny it. It was foreshadowed in the lack of arms and ammunition no longer replenished, in their rations of worm-eaten peas, rancid mess-pork, and unbolted corn meal. It showed itself in the fluttering rags they wore for uniforms, their soleless boots, the thin bedding blankets taken from horses sent southward, in the absence of the horses themselves. It could be heard in songs they sang in the huts of evenings—no more rollicking ditties of carefree cavaliers, but sad songs of lost Lorenas, of angels marching in the sky, of grief-stricken mothers and sweethearts. Basil Duke composed no more lilting poems of galloping raiders, no poems at all. The chivalry they cherished was gone with the old world of their youth, a world dying with each passing day.

Yet not one of them spoke of defeat, or dared think of it in the loneliness of the winter nights. "Two strange features characterized the temper of the Southern people in the last days of the Confederacy," Duke would recall a year or so later. "Crushed and dispirited as they were, they still seemed unable to realize the fact that the cause was utterly lost. Even when their fate stared them in the face, they could not recognize it."

In the first warm days of spring the exchanged prisoners of war began returning from Camp Douglas, pale-skinned and soft-muscled, in sharp contrast to their lean and weathered comrades. But there was something in the spirit of these returned men that was communicated to the others, a mood of desperate revenge. By the first of April, Duke's Brigade was at its highest strength, more than 600 men—almost half of them former prisoners who had seen their last fighting during the Indiana-Ohio raid of 1863.

They arrived just in time to help stand off Federal columns moving out of east Tennessee. Although they were disappointed at having to march and fight on foot (the horses were still in North Carolina) they complained less than those who had not been in prison, and were the last to yield ground when ammunition ran out.

Duke's men held on stubbornly to their little corner of south-western Virginia, but every day the news was bad. Sherman was already into North Carolina, and Lee's thinning lines were retreating in Virginia. After Richmond fell on April 3, the Confederacy's last hope was for Lee and Johnston to effect a junction of their forces at Danville, Virginia. As a part of this strategy, Duke's Brigade received orders to march eastward and join Lee's crippled army.

They marched out toward Roanoke—cavalrymen without horses —but with an occasional plume still thrust into a ragged slouch hat. Boots and shoes were cracked and worn through to the rocky road on which they marched, and before the first day's ending some had thrown away the worthless shells of cheap leather, walking barefooted.

En route up the valley toward Roanoke on April 9, Duke received the news of General Lee's surrender at Appomattox. "If the light of heaven had gone out," he said, "a more utter despair and consternation would not have ensued. When the news first came, it perfectly paralyzed every one. Men looked at each other as if they had just heard a sentence of death and eternal ruin passed upon all."

During the next twenty-four hours, General Echols struggled vainly to hold the troops of his department together. Entire companies of infantrymen threw down their arms and walked away, heading for home. But most of the cavalrymen—mounted and dismounted— clung together, and at Christiansburg, on April 12, Echols held a final council of war. He announced that he would take all the mounted men to North Carolina to join General Joe Johnston and continue the fighting. He would issue sixty-day furloughs to infantrymen and dismounted cavalrymen; if the war was still going on at the end of that time, these men would be recalled to duty.

Only about ten of Duke's dismounted men elected to take furloughs. With Duke's approval the others mounted themselves on mules taken from abandoned infantry wagons, determined to ride these slow-footed, barebacked animals with blind bridles and rope halters to the Mississippi River, if necessary, rather than surrender.

The march south began at four o'clock that afternoon in a torrent of April rain, four generals leading about 1,200 men. Echols was in command, the others being Duke, George Cosby, and John C. Vaughn. "The gloomy skies seemed to threaten disaster," wrote Duke. "But braver in the hour of despair than ever before, my men never faltered or murmured. The trial found them true. To command such men was the proudest honor that an officer could obtain."

Not all the Morgan men who had been in Northern prisons were exchanged in time to reach Duke's Brigade before the fall of Richmond. Among these were Lieutenants Winder Monroe and Leeland Hathaway, and Private Jack Messick—three young men who were about to enter upon their most exciting adventure of the war.

At the time of their capture at Buffington Island, they were with Dick Morgan's 14th Kentucky, but Monroe was one of the original members of the 2nd Kentucky, both he and Jack Messick having served with Tom Quirk's scouts. Hathaway had been transferred from the 11th Kentucky immediately before the raid.

Released in northern Virginia early in April, Monroe, Hathaway and Messick found themselves cut off from Richmond. Taking a roundabout route, they started on foot for southwestern Virginia, hoping to find Duke's command. After crossing the James River they were caught up in the stream of Lee's retreating columns. The three returning cavalrymen were shocked by the appearance of these ragged troops—their anguished yet resolute faces, their utter fatigue. "No man saw them," Hathaway noted, "except with uncovered head and reverential greetings."

At Danville, where they had been told they might find Duke, they found instead another Kentuckian, General John C. Breckinridge, acting as Secretary of War. "We were worn out with our tramp of 150 miles," said Hathaway. "My boots had lost their soles and I had walked barefoot for the last fifty miles. Altogether we were in rather a sad plight. We walked into the General's office, Monroe, Messick and I. General Breckinridge rose to meet us, calling me and Winder by name."

After they learned that Duke was marching his troops south to join General Johnston's army, they told Breckinridge they would like to offer their services for this same venture. "General Breckinridge called an aide, gave him verbal orders to have our requirements met. I soon had a pair of red *leather* Confederate shoes—we all had bridles and saddles and a written order to take such horses as we could find."

The only horses apparent in all Danville were some blind coach animals, but they mounted up and started for North Carolina, exchanging the blind horses a day or so later for better ones.

For three days they rode steadily, finding no trace of Duke's outfit. Several times they sighted Federal patrols moving on the roads, but managed to elude them, dodging into bushes and woods. "Winder Monroe told us that his grandfather, Judge Thomas Monroe* and family were at Abbeville, South Carolina, and suggested that we head for that place. We agreed to go."

On April 28, the three adventurers rode into Abbeville. It was a sunny, summery day, the air lazy and fragrant with honeysuckle, yellow jasmine and wistaria winding over the fences and galleries of the houses. After their long months of prison life and the rains and grim events of Virginia, it was like entering into Heaven.

"We found the Judge and his family as we expected very hospitable and much pleased to see Winder. They were living on the barest necessities. Not to burden them we drew the rations of musty meal and salt meat (very little of either, too) to which as soldiers we were entitled and this proved a very welcome addition to their scant larder."

Abbeville was filled with rumors that Johnston had surrendered his army to Sherman in North Carolina, but no one could be certain of anything. The boys decided to wait and see what would happen next. Two days after their arrival in Abbeville they learned that President Jefferson Davis's wife, fleeing from Richmond, had just reached the town and was in need of assistance. "After consulting with Winder and Jack," Hathaway recorded, "I went to see her and found her very much disturbed and at a loss what to do."

[*Thomas Bell Monroe, a U. S. district judge of Confederate sympathies, left Lexington, Kentucky, on the same day his grandson, Winder, rode away with John Morgan for Green River in September 1861. After the fall of Nashville, Judge Monroe took his family to South Carolina.]

Varina Howell Davis, according to young Hathaway, "was then a rather heavy dark woman about forty years old—not at all handsome or pretty, but very bright and entertaining." Her traveling party consisted of herself; her four children; her sister, Maggie Howell; two servants; and Burton N. Harrison, the President's private secretary. Harrison, who was in charge of the little caravan, did not impress the Kentucky boys with his capabilities. "Harrison was sick and utterly demoralized," Hathaway said.

Mrs. Davis was impatient to leave Abbeville and start for the Florida coast, where she hoped to board a ship and take her children to safety. Her plans were quite vague; she had no exact point of departure or any certain vessel in mind. She told Hathaway that nobody seemed to have authority or the discipline to give her transportation out of Abbeville.

"It is now about three o'clock," Hathaway said to her. "Can you be ready to move at sunrise tomorrow?"

"I am ready now," she replied.

"What do you want to take?" he asked.

The young Lieutenant was overwhelmed when she showed him her baggage, "a discouraging mass of every kind of household goods and other paraphernalia pertaining to her and her family in their personal and official capacities. I said, 'It is impracticable to attempt to move this mass of stuff.' She then consented to select but when the selection was made not a little was left. I insisted on taking only clothing but she was decided so I went to work with Winder and Jack. There was a Quartermaster camp near the town. We fitted out two ambulances with two mules to each and two first-class U.S. wagons with four mules to each. To each four bright true soldiers at once volunteered to drive by daylight on the morning of the 2nd of May. We began putting in the loads and promptly about sunrise we were on the road."

This strange hegira southward across Carolina and Georgia would last for eight days, and to the three Kentucky boys it was a dreamlike existence, sometimes frantic, often bewildering. As cavalrymen and prisoners of war, they had learned to be surprised at nothing, but an experience such as this was unimaginable—Morgan's alligator horses escorting the First Lady of the Confederacy on a mad flight to nowhere!

As they approached the Savannah River, they heard rumors of a smallpox epidemic, and Varina Davis began worrying because one of her children had not been vaccinated. She insisted that her escorts stop and find a physician. But in none of the sleepy little towns could a doctor be found. Mrs. Davis then asked them to make inquiries at the larger plantations. "Halting at a house near the road," Burton Harrison recorded, "Mrs. Davis had the operation performed by the planter, who got a fresh scab from the arm of a little negro called up for the purpose."

With such delays as this, and the excessive burden of luggage they were hauling, they made very slow progress. Hathaway, Monroe and Messick in turn attempted to persuade Mrs. Davis to permit them to store her goods in some plantation house along the way and start traveling lightly and rapidly both day and night. Harrison stubbornly opposed this plan, evidently considering it necessary for the wife of his chief to be surrounded by a fully equipped retinue. "We did not entirely conceal our contempt," Hathaway admitted, "for the private secretary, who was the cause of this dawdling in the face of danger."

By day the forested river bottoms were filled with bright-feathered song birds. Sweet-scented magnolias were in full bloom; grape and scuppernong vines festooned the trees. At nights mosquitoes swarmed in clouds, but Mrs. Davis was able to supply preventive netting from her adequate stores. After they moved into the pinewoods, the nights were more pleasant. "This great forest of stately long-leaved pines stretched above and around us and our nights were the most delightful camping parties." Every evening before bedtime, the three boys heaped up piles of brown pine needles to soften the blanket pallets of Mrs. Davis, her sister and her children.

As a gesture of gratitude toward her soldier escorts, Mrs. Davis presented each one with a twenty-dollar gold piece, and then another gift to be shared among them—"a bottle of rare old brandy which had been sent to her by Louis Napoleon." They planned to keep the gold pieces forever, but the Napoleon brandy they considered expendable, and at night after their civilian charges were fast asleep, the trio of Kentuckians shared precious sips of the delightful liquid. Under soughing pines that towered to the stars, they pondered the wonders of chance in human destiny, and savored the French Emperor's brandy.

At Washington, Georgia, they finally persuaded Mrs. Davis to leave the heavily laden wagons in the care of friends. They dismissed the drivers, but picked up two additional members—Major Victor Maurin and Captain George Moody, who volunteered to strengthen Mrs. Davis's armed escort of three.

From Washington they headed straight south, traveling more rapidly now through an almost trackless extent of pines broken only by occasional swamps and sluggish streams. They saw no more plantation houses, but only ramshackle cabins. Food supplies ran short, and as they neared the Ocmulgee River bad weather caught up with them.

Although they were unaware of it, the pelting rains probably saved them from immediate capture, obliterating tracks of the ambulance wheels soon after they passed over the sandy roads. Union patrols were searching actively in the area, not for Varina Davis but for her husband, President Jefferson Davis, who for several days had been attempting to join his family.

On May 9, along a small creek in the pinewoods near Irwinville, President Davis and his escort overtook his wife's little cavalcade. It was an emotion-filled reunion for the President and his wife. Hathaway, Monroe and Messick stood aside, slightly awed by the presence of this fellow Kentuckian who had led the Confederacy through four years of war.

Then Monroe suddenly stared hard at one of the three colonels who had arrived with the President. He was William Preston Johnston, the officer who had sworn Winder Monroe into John Morgan's squadron at Woodsonville, Kentucky, on that long ago October day of 1861—in that time when war was all knighthood and romance, campfires in the autumn woods, dashing raids by moonlight—in a time when none dreamed of death, imprisonment, or defeat.

At that moment of recognition and remembrance, Lieutenant Monroe must have reflected again on the chance and coincidence of war; but after more than three years of it he had learned to expect the unexpected.

A few days before Winder Monroe and his two companions had arrived in Abbeville, South Carolina, the band of troopers for which they had been searching—Duke's Brigade—rode into Charlotte, North Carolina. Somewhere along the danger-filled Carolina roads, the trio had passed their old comrades and pushed ahead of them.

In mid-April, Charlotte was a stronghold of Confederate cavalry units which had escorted President Davis and his Cabinet from Richmond, and the arrival of Duke's troopers added to the jam of horses and men in the dusty streets. Informed that President Davis was staying at the Bates House, Duke drew his column up in front of the door. After all, Jeff Davis was an original Kentucky alligator horse, and this was the first opportunity they had had to do him honor in person since the wedding of John Morgan. They cheered and waved hats and flags until he came to the door and made them a little speech.

Davis thanked the Kentucky boys for their cordial greeting, complimented them on their gallantry as fighting men, and urged them not to despair of the Confederacy but to remain with their last organized band, upholding the flag. While he was speaking, some of them dismounted and walked up on the porch steps, crowding around the President, hoping to shake his hand. As he concluded his remarks, a courier pushed through the group, handing Davis a message.

"I was standing just inside the hall door," Sergeant Will Dyer recalled afterward, "and when the President opened and read the dispatch, I noticed that he was greatly affected by it. Turning to Mr. Reagan,* who was by his side, he handed him the paper with the remark, 'This is very unfortunate, read it to the men.'" The message told of the assassination of Abraham Lincoln. For several minutes, according to Dyer, "a solemn stillness, approaching awe, settled over the crowd, then the terrible deed was discussed in whispers among the men." Abe Lincoln, they remembered, had been born a Kentucky alligator horse.

[*John H. Reagan, the Confederate Postmaster-General.]

Jefferson Davis, with tears in his eyes, bids farewell to his cavalry escort in the square in Washington, Georgia, and begs them to seek their own safety. This sketch was done by a special artist for the foreign publication who traveled with Davis during the retreat southward until forty-eight hours before Davis's capture. From Illustrated London News, July 22, 1865.

The boys of the 2nd Kentucky found several old friends in Charlotte, former regimental members who had transferred long ago to Billy Breckinridge's 9th Cavalry. Breckinridge's outfit, with three other skeleton brigades, formed the President's escort, and when Duke learned that Davis was planning to move his Cabinet farther south he went to see him and offered the services of his Kentucky cavalry to strengthen the escort force.

Davis agreed that this would be desirable, and volunteered to help the Kentuckians obtain saddles. (En route to Charlotte, Duke had picked up the brigade's horses which had wintered in Mecklenburg County, but only a few of them had saddles.)

The Confederate President's inability to comprehend the full disaster which had befallen his armies is indicated by a message which he sent on April 20 to General Beauregard at Greensboro; "General Duke's brigade is here without saddles. There are none here or this side of Augusta. Send to this point 600, or as many as can be had." In late April of 1865 a Confederate general would have required supernatural powers to produce 600 saddles.

On the day Davis sent this message, General Johnston was negotiating for surrender to Sherman, and a day or two later his Secretary of War, John C. Breckinridge, arrived in Charlotte to inform the President that all hope was gone for continuing the war. Even then, Davis refused to believe the end had come. He declared that he would go on to Alabama, join General Forrest, and if necessary fight the war from across the Mississippi.

That afternoon Breckinridge, who had served as Vice President of the United States under Buchanan and had run for President against Lincoln and Douglas, went out to Basil Duke's camp to be with old friends from Kentucky. "He seated himself at the foot of a large tree and talked for more than an hour with the men who crowded around him," Duke said. "Great curiosity was, of course, felt to learn something of the terms of the agreement with Sherman, and he answered all questions with perfect frankness." All Confederate soldiers east of the Mississippi were to surrender their arms as soon as arrangements could be completed, Breckinridge explained. The terms were honorable. They had fought bravely, but they had lost the war.

Like Jefferson Davis, however, there were still many who refused to accept the inevitability of defeat, some who felt as did one of Duke's boys who declared he would "sooner march to the Rio Grande than surrender to any Yankee."

In the last week of April, Davis issued orders to abandon Charlotte, and with Duke's Kentuckians and other units of his cavalry escort started for Abbeville. The column moved slowly down into South Carolina, through York and Union, crossing Broad River at Smith's Ford on April 29.

While on this march Duke recorded an encounter which some of his troopers had with an old lady who bitterly reproached them for taking forage from her barn. "You are a gang of thieving, rascally Kentuckians," she cried, "afraid to go home, while our boys are surrendering decently."

"Madam," one of them replied politely, "you are speaking out of your turn. South Carolina had a good deal to say in getting up this war, but we Kentuckians have contracted to close it out."

Their officers attempted to "close it out" on May 2, the day the President and his escort rode into Abbeville. On that afternoon they held the Confederacy's last council of war, with Davis presiding. Besides Generals Breckinridge and Bragg, the council consisted only of Basil Duke and the four other brigade commanders. By one of those odd coincidences of war, this last meeting of the Confederate government was held in the same town where the first secession meeting had been held five years earlier.

At the beginning of the discussion, Davis was affable, dignified, gave no sign of apprehension. He suggested that the South was suffering from unwarranted panic, that it yet had resources to continue the war, and therefore it was the duty of those who remained with arms in their hands to give an example to inspire others so that the Confederacy might be saved.

One by one, Breckinridge, Bragg, Duke, and the others reluctantly disagreed. The war was hopeless; they could not support prolonging it with useless bloodshed. Yet all agreed they would not disband their men until they had guarded the President to a place of safety.

"No," Davis cried, "I will listen to no propositions for my safety. I appeal to you for the cause of the country." For a minute or so the President lost his composure, bitterly accusing his generals of being willing to consent to the degradation of the South they had sworn to defend.

"We were silent," Duke wrote afterward, "for we could not agree with him, and respected him too much to reply. . . . When he arose to leave the room, he had lost his erect bearing, his face was pale, and he faltered so much in his step that he was compelled to lean on General Breckinridge. It was a sad sight to men who felt toward him as we did."

Resigned now to defeat, Davis's thoughts turned to the safety of his family. Determined to join them and escape from the country, he told his generals to be prepared to march at midnight for Washington, Georgia, where his family had last been reported.

The President had one more assignment for Basil Duke's Kentuckians. At ten o'clock that evening, Duke was summoned to the house where Davis and Breckinridge were staying, and was informed that his brigade had been selected to guard and transport the funds of the Confederate Treasury from Abbeville to Georgia. The Secretary of the Treasury, G. A. Trenholm, had fallen ill and could not accompany the column. Postmaster-General Reagan would act as treasurer, but Duke himself would be the responsible custodian until the money was delivered to Washington, Georgia.

It was not an assignment to Duke's liking. In the first place no one seemed to know how much treasure there was. Davis believed it consisted of about half a million dollars in gold and silver, but he had no official accounting in his possession.

Shortly before the abandonment of Richmond the treasure had been brought out by rail under guard of Captain William H. Parker and sixty midshipmen of the Confederate States Naval Academy. It was packed in sacks and boxes—double-eagle gold pieces, Mexican silver dollars, copper coins, silver bricks, gold ingots and nuggets. At

Greensboro, North Carolina, Captain Parker detached two boxes of gold sovereigns, about $35,000 for expenses of the President and his Cabinet, and $39,000 to pay off General Johnston's troops.

When Parker's train reached Chester, South Carolina, he discovered the railroad was impassable beyond that point. He had to commandeer wagons, transfer his precious cargo, and haul it forty miles to Newberry, where it was loaded aboard another railroad train.

On April 16, Parker brought the treasure into Abbeville, ran the boxcars containing it upon a siding, and set up a vigilant guard. He was waiting there when President Davis and the cavalry arrived on May 2, and was immensely relieved when he received orders to transfer the burden of responsibility to General Basil Duke.

It was pitch dark when Duke reported to Captain Parker with the President's transfer order. He had brought six wagons and a detail of fifty men, and without preliminaries the work of loading the treasure began.

Duke was anxious to obtain an exact statement of the sum he was to guard, but Parker had no listing whatsoever. He knew only that the bulk of the treasure was in Mexican dollars packed in nail kegs; the sacks of gold double-eagles supposedly contained 5,000 dollars each; there was an undetermined number of gold ingots and some hundreds of pounds of copper cents.

"It was packed in money belts, shot bags, a few small iron chests and wooden boxes, some of them of the frailest description," Duke said afterward. "I searched through the cars by the light of a few tallow candles, and gathered up all that was shown me or that I could find. More than an hour was occupied in transferring the treasure from the cars to the wagons, and after the latter had been started off and had gotten perhaps half a mile away, Lieutenant John Cole, one of the officers of the guard, rode up to me and handed over a pine box which apparently contained between two or three thousand dollars in gold. After the rest of us had left the cars he had remained and continued the search, and in a car which we thought we had thoroughly examined he had discovered this box, stuck in a corner and covered up with a piece of brown sacking."

Although Duke had hoped to keep the nature of his cargo a secret confined to the boys of the loading detail, it was far too big a secret to conceal for long. By the time his column reached the Savannah River, the entire cavalry escort knew what was in the wagons guarded by Duke's Kentuckians.

Naturally, the boys began wondering what was going to happen to all this gold and silver. There were rumors that Jeff Davis had promised to use it to pay off all men who accompanied him to the Mississippi River, but from talk they heard among the junior officers they guessed the President had abandoned his plans to march west. Suppose the enemy overtook them before they could get the treasure out of the country; the Federals would seize all the money, give them paroles, send them home, and they would never receive their final pay.

Delegations from the ranks went to see Duke, and asked him if they could not be paid off immediately. Duke sympathized with their point of view, but passed the decision to General Breckinridge. Late on May 3, Breckinridge ordered the column halted, asked the quartermasters of each brigade to submit payrolls, and there in the pinewoods of Georgia the last armed troops of the Confederacy lined up for their final pay.

Each of the 4,166 cavalrymen received about twenty-six dollars, carefully counted out in gold and silver. Duke kept an exact accounting, recording $108,322.90 paid out. Before midnight his wagons had been lightened by one fourth and the troopers had hard money in their jeans pockets for the first time in many months.

Early the next afternoon when Duke halted his wagons outside Washington, Georgia, he was pleased to learn that President Davis, who had arrived ahead of the column, had appointed a new acting treasurer to assume responsibility for the government funds. The man was Captain Micajah H. Clark, former chief clerk of the Confederate executive office.

The transfer was arranged at Duke's camp about a mile outside Washington. "Selecting the shade of a large elm tree as the 'Treasury Department,'" Micajah Clark later wrote, "I commenced my duties as Acting Treasurer, C.S.A." His first order of business was to count his holdings, and according to his records the amount totaled $288,022.90.

For years afterward there would be many lurid stories published about the mystery of what happened to the Confederate treasure, tales of buried gold in Georgia and Florida. In some of the early stories, amounts usually were estimated at from two million to as much as thirty million dollars in coin, bullion and gold nuggets.

As late as 1881, Captain Clark was still vainly attempting to quiet these rumors and to deny charges that he knew more about the treasure than he ever told. He prepared a detailed listing showing how he disposed of the funds entrusted to his care, item by item.

Like Duke, he was eager to be rid of the treasure as quickly as possible, handing out in a few hours large amounts to commissary officers for purchase of rations, and to trusted officials who were to transport the money to points where troops might be paid off before surrendering. In each case, Clark always required a signed receipt. But what happened to these "boxes of silver bullion" and "kegs of Mexican silver dollars" after they left Clark's office under the elm tree is not easy to determine.

The Captain's last payment before leaving Washington, Georgia, was $86,000 in gold coin and silver bullion to "a trusted officer of the Navy," Clark taking a receipt "for its transmission out of the Confederacy." What happened to this money is still a real mystery. Not long after Clark published his accounts in 1881, the young naval officer, William H. Parker, who escorted the treasury from Richmond to Abbeville, made a critical reply. Parker claimed that no naval officer had taken this money out of the country, and that the $86,000 had never been reported afterward. Parker also intimated that the amount which he took out of Richmond was at least $100,000 more than Clark's records showed.

One other aspect of the mystery is an official report of Major Charles M. Betts, 15th Pennsylvania Cavalry, describing the capture on May 8 of seven wagons hidden in the woods near the fork of the Appalachee and Oconee rivers, about thirty-five miles from Washington, Georgia. Major Betts discovered in these wagons four million dollars in Confederate paper money and $188,000 in coin. Whether this was a part of the treasure brought from Richmond, probably no one will ever know.

One of Duke's boys, Will Dyer, was inclined to scoff at all the furor over the mystery in later years. "There has been much written about the buried Confederate Treasure," he said, "but this is all moonshine. We got all the money there was in the treasury and the only wonder is that we got to keep it. The Yankees didn't know we had it or they would have prowled us sure." Of the $26.25 he received in final pay, he declared: "This was more money than I had seen for three years and I felt rich."

While Captain Clark was making his payments and taking his receipts on May 4, President Davis was preparing to leave Washington and continue south in hopes of overtaking his fleeing family. Aware by now that Federal cavalry patrols were in earnest pursuit of him, Davis decided to dress as a plain country farmer and travel in a covered wagon. On the insistence of his officers, however, a small military escort was formed to ride in the vicinity to insure his personal safety.

The escort consisted of Colonels William Preston Johnston, Francis R. Lubbock and John Taylor Wood, with a detail of "ten trusty men" under command of Captain Given Campbell. Captain Campbell had been with Colonel W. C. P. Breckinridge's 9th Kentucky Cavalry, but at one time he had served in the 2nd Regiment as an enlisted man. Eight of the "ten trusty men"—all carefully selected volunteers for this mission—were also from the old 2nd Kentucky.

A few hours after Davis's departure, General Breckinridge began ordering the cavalry brigades to march out in various directions from Washington. This was a scheme to divert the Federals so as to give the President time to be well on his way south before all the escort surrendered. Commanders of the different brigades were instructed not to offer battle; if confronted by Federal forces they were to surrender and take paroles.

As part of this plan, Basil Duke was ordered to march his brigade to Woodstock, Georgia, and it was there that the survivors of the 2nd Kentucky Cavalry stood their last formation on May 8, 1865.

Duke made no solemn ceremony of this disbanding of the old Morgan command.

He advised the boys to return to their homes. For almost four years they had fought against heavy odds in manpower and resources, and he assured them that there was no disgrace in being released from service which they had worthily discharged. They left Woodstock in small parties, most of the Kentuckians going toward Chattanooga, a few to Augusta. The Mississippians and Texans rode off to the west.

As they came to Federal camps along the way they surrendered voluntarily, and in most cases met with no recrimination from the victors. These men who had faced each other in battle respected each other's courage. Each Confederate soldier signed a parole, a form not standardized but varying according to the issuing officer, sometimes quite brief, sometimes elaborate with a sworn statement not to bear arms against the United States, a description of the height, and the hair, eye, and complexion coloration of the parolee. Most statements included a reassuring phrase, such as "not to be disturbed by the authorities of the United States so long as he observes this parole and obeys the laws in force where he may reside."

The disarmed Confederates treasured these fragile bits of paper above all other possessions; many would preserve them carefully to the ends of their lives. They could go home now, knowing they were free men *not to be disturbed,* losers in war, unvanquished in spirit.

But there were still, on May 8, twelve Morgan men—eleven of them originally from the old 2nd—who were very much involved in the pursuance of their military obligations. These were Captain Given Campbell and eight of the ten troopers riding with Jefferson Davis; and Winder Monroe, Leeland Hathaway and Jack Messick, who had been escorting the President's wife.

After Davis rejoined his family in the pinewoods near Irwinville, the journey was temporarily delayed for a happy reunion. It was late in the day; orders were given to unhitch mules and horses for a night camp.

Hathaway and his two companions were appalled that the President had no intention of resuming travel during the night. Being

veteran cavalrymen they felt that safety now lay only in rapid movement—as John Morgan had taught them on their raids—rapid
movement and light equipment.

Unable to restrain himself, Hathaway made bold to approach the
President and offer some polite advice. "Mr. President," he said in
his slow Kentucky speech, "don't you know that the Yankees know
you are traveling this course and that you are burdened with all this
stuff?"

Before Davis could reply, Burton Harrison interrupted. "Not
necessarily so," the secretary said coldly.

"You evidently underestimate your enemy then," Hathaway
retorted, "which is always dangerous. If a regiment of Morgan's old
command were in the neighborhood of such a train as this it would
know to a dot everything about it."

If Davis made any comment during this conversation, Hathaway
failed to record it. "I couldn't change their programme," he wrote,
"and I couldn't cut loose from them situated as were Mrs. Davis and
her children, so I staid—and the catastrophe came, about daylight on
the morning of the 10th of May."

They bedded down that last night under tall long-needled pines,
the moonlit forest quiet but for the gentle brushing of a warm spring
wind in the pluming treetops. There were twenty-one men, Varina
Davis and her sister, the four Davis children, and two servants—all
that was left of the power and glory of the Confederate States of
America. Curiously, of the twenty-one men fourteen were Kentuckians—representatives of a state which had been divided in loyalties.

The Yankees came at dawn, as Lee Hathaway had warned they
would, two different cavalry regiments, each unaware of the other's
presence, both eager to win credit for capturing Jeff Davis. Lieutenant Colonel Benjamin D. Pritchard's 4th Michigan arrived a few
minutes ahead of Lieutenant Colonel Henry Harnden's 1st Wisconsin, charging in and throwing a cordon around the camp.

Awakened by their approach, William Preston Johnston arose and
pulled on his boots. As he started toward the campfire he saw eight
or ten mounted men riding like ghosts out of the morning mist. In

the shadowy light he could not determine their uniforms, but he turned back to his saddle, which he had been using as a pillow, and was searching for his revolver when three men in Union blue dashed up and ordered him to surrender. They took his weapon and ordered him over to the campfire. A moment later a burst of rifle fire crackled out of the forest, echoing, increasing in rapidity. The guards hesitated a minute or so, then remounted and rode quickly away.

Johnston hurried toward the Davis tent, some fifty yards from the fire. The President was seated calmly on a camp stool, getting into a pair of cavalry boots. Varina Davis was weeping; she was both frightened and angry. She told Johnston that the intruders had taken her husband's waterproof coat; she believed they were only thieving guerrillas. But Johnston shook his head. "This is bad business, sir," he said to Davis, then noticing the President was shivering from cold, he turned to go and find a coat for him. The rifle fire was continuing off to one side of the camp, but he knew now that none of the Confederate escort was involved. They were all gathered around the campfire under guard of a Yankee captain and a squad of dismounted troopers.

As Johnston came up to the group, he said mildly: "Captain, your men are fighting each other over yonder." The Yankee Captain looked startled; he said he thought his men were fighting Jeff Davis's escort.

"You have our whole camp," Johnston assured him. "I know your men are fighting each other. We have nobody on that side of the slough."

It was as Johnston said. Harnden's 1st Wisconsin had blundered into Pritchard's 4th Michigan, and for several minutes they fought among the thick pines, each believing the other was Confederate cavalry. Not until the Wisconsin troopers captured one of the Michigan men was the error discovered. Two Michigan men were already dead; several Wisconsin men severely wounded. Until long after the war there would be ill-feeling between these two regiments, each blaming the other for the error, each claiming credit for finding Jeff Davis.

The actual business of capturing the Confederate Chief of State was a simple matter, although there are almost as many versions of the affair as there were witnesses. One story has it that Davis was preparing to mount his horse and escape when a Federal soldier halted him and demanded: "Are you armed?"

"If I were armed," replied Davis, "you would not be living to ask the question."

Much was made of the costume worn by the President at the time of his capture, the Northern press publishing colorful descriptions of how he was disguised as a woman, with accompanying caricatures showing him in outlandish female garb. From all official accounts of the Federal officers present, however, it is clear that he was wearing trousers, cavalry boots, and a lady's shawl or waterproof wrapper thrown over his shoulders by his wife.

After the President and his party were taken into custody, Lieutenant Colonel Pritchard carefully recorded their names, first listing the officers and then adding the following: "Private Sanders, 2nd Kentucky Cavalry; Private Walbert, 2nd Kentucky Cavalry; Private Baker, 2nd Kentucky Cavalry; Private Smith, 2nd Kentucky Cavalry; Private Heath, 2nd Kentucky Cavalry; Private Elston, 2nd Kentucky Cavalry; Private J. W. Farley, 2nd Kentucky Cavalry."

All the captives were searched, their baggage opened and examined for arms and valuables. Monroe, Hathaway and Messick managed to conceal the precious $20 gold coins which Varina Davis had given them, but the others lost everything. Captain Given Campbell and his ten men had to surrender their last pay, more than $300 in gold. Johnston gave up $1,500 in personal funds. In a pair of saddlebags, Pritchard's men found about three thousand dollars which had been assigned by Micajah Clark for the President's expenses in fleeing the country. Johnston vainly protested the seizure of his pair of pistols: they had been worn by his father, Albert Sydney Johnston, during the battle of Shiloh.

Lee Hathaway also lost a prized pistol, presented to him only a few hours before by the President as a token of appreciation for what the young lieutenant had done for his family. "We were then placed under heavy guard," Hathaway said, "for the melancholy march to Macon, Georgia."

On the second day of the prisoners' four-day journey to Macon, Hathaway told of being "much shocked and grieved at sight of a large streamer bearing the ominous words: *$100,000 Reward For the Capture of Jeff Davis*. This was carried aloft on a flag staff and was borne by one of a body of cavalry which came from the direction of Macon."

The legend on this banner was the first knowledge Lieutenant Colonel Pritchard and his 4th Michigan cavalrymen had of such a reward, and its immediate effect was to set in motion a number of rival claims among the men. Pritchard resolved the controversy by suggesting that the reward be distributed among all the men present at the time of Jefferson Davis's capture.

The banner's effect upon the captured Confederates was to create uneasiness among them for the President's safety. Now that it was known that Davis was worth $100,000, they feared the Yankees might shoot him to make certain he could not escape.

But their fears were groundless. In fact, when Pritchard brought his prisoners into Macon on May 13, to turn them over to Major General James H. Wilson, the latter greeted Davis by ordering his troops drawn up in double lines facing inward, and they presented arms to the Confederate President as he passed between them.

This would be the last recognition of Jefferson Davis's office, however. After the Union Army passed him on to the vindictive Secretary of War, Edwin M. Stanton, his life would become a hell of miseries and indignities.

From Macon the prisoners were taken to Augusta, where they were marched aboard a gunboat and transported to Savannah and up the coast to Hilton Head. On May 20, they were in Hampton Roads, surrounded by a cordon of warships. Hathaway, Monroe and Messick were the last of the Morgan men in captivity, the others having been paroled in Georgia, and they thought surely that now they would be released. But when Jeff Davis was taken off to Fortress Monroe, the three young men were transferred to another vessel. This ship sailed north, and although they were told nothing of their destination, the boys were more confident than ever that at the end of the voyage they would be set free.

Instead, the ship docked off Fort McHenry and they were hustled ashore without ceremony and imprisoned in an old brick stable. They were locked into separate cells with heavy double oak doors, the only ventilation and light coming from a tiny slit in the outer wall. No one would tell them why they were there.

By raising their voices they could talk to one another through the walls of the adjoining cells. For several days they kept each other's spirits up by shouting encouragements back and forth; they fought bedbugs day and night; they carefully cultivated one of the friendlier guards. When they asked this guard why they were being held as prisoners, he told them frankly that he did not know, but would try to find out. The guard made inquiries, but no one at Fort McHenry seemed to know why the three young Confederates were there. When they sent the guard to bring pencil and paper so that they might write to relatives, he returned and informed them that they would not be allowed to communicate with relatives or anybody else outside.

After nearly two months of this maddening uncertainty, Hathaway decided to risk his precious twenty-dollar gold piece, the present from Varina Davis. He showed the coin to the friendly guard and told him he could have it if he would take a letter into Baltimore and mail it. When the guard agreed to do this, Hathaway tore a leaf from his Bible, and with a stub of pencil scrawled a note to his father in Kentucky. He had to rely on the guard to furnish an envelope and address it, and to make certain this was done, Hathaway refused to release his gold coin until the guard returned with a receipt showing the letter had been mailed.

The letter reached its destination, and as soon as the boys' relatives in Kentucky learned where they were, representatives from their families journeyed to Baltimore—only to be refused admittance to Fort McHenry. Nor would the commandant give them any reason why their boys were still being held as prisoners.

Acting as spokesman for the group, Hathaway's father went

directly to President Andrew Johnson in Washington and showed him the note which his son had written on the torn Bible leaf.

"What is your boy doing in Fort McHenry?" Johnson asked.

"I don't know. That's what I've been trying to learn. I've come to you for help."

"Are there charges against him?"

The elder Hathaway did not know; apparently his son did not know either. President Johnson sent him to see Secretary Stanton to find out what the charges were. Stanton seemed to be quite familiar with the names Hathaway, Monroe, and Messick. They had been captured with Jeff Davis, Stanton said. He admitted there were no charges against the young men, but he declared that he eventually expected to link them directly with the assassination plot against President Lincoln. He hoped to prove that Jeff Davis had arranged the assassination, and he suspected that these three boys were in-volved in it. Therefore, he could not release them.

Frustrated and considerably alarmed after his interview with Stanton, Hathaway's father returned to the White House and told Andrew Johnson what he had learned. Johnson, who was already be-ginning to distrust Stanton, sent off a messenger to the Secretary, ordering him either to bring charges against his three prisoners or to release them. Stanton returned the messenger with a note of refusal.

In the presence of the elder Hathaway, Johnson exploded verbally. "I will show Stanton who is President!" he shouted, and wrote out an order instructing the commandant at Fort McHenry to free the prisoners Leeland Hathaway, Winder Monroe, and Jack Messick.

And so it was that the last troopers of John Morgan's command—and the last representatives of the 2nd Kentucky Cavalry—returned to their homes in the Bluegrass during the peaceful summer of 1865.

Others like them were still finding their different ways back to a world that looked much the same, but was not the same, and never again would be anything like the world they left in 1861 to join John Morgan's cavalry. They were not certain how they would be received by neighbors, cousins, brothers—who had fought on the other side of the great conflict.

It was Basil Duke, their last leader, who most eloquently expressed their unspoken emotions: "There was no humiliation for these men," he wrote. "They had done their part and served faithfully, until there was no longer a cause and a country to serve. They knew not what their fate would be, and indulged in no speculation regarding it. They had been taught fortitude by the past, and, without useless repining and unmanly fear, they faced the future."

Suggested Readings

CHAPTER 1: WILSON'S CREEK

Bearss, Edwin C. *The Battle of Wilson's Creek*. Bozeman, Montana: Artcraft Printers, 1975.

Holcombe and Adams. *An Account of the Battle of Wilson's Creek or Oak Hills Fought Between the Union Troops, Commanded by Gen. Lyon, and the Southern, or Confederate Troops, Under Command of Gens. McCulloch and Price, on Saturday, August 10, 1861, in Greene County, Missouri.* (Centennial Edition Reprint). Springfield, Missouri: Springfield Public Library and the Greene County Historical Society, 1961.

CHAPTER 2: PEA RIDGE

Cunningham, Frank. *General Stand Watie's Confederate Indians*. San Antonio, Texas: The Naylor Company, 1959.

Josephy, Alvin M. *War on the Frontier: The Trans-Mississippi West*. Alexandria, Virginia: Time-Life Books, 1986.

Shea, William L. and Earl J. Hess. *Pea Ridge: Civil War Campaign in the West*. Chapel Hill: The University of North Carolina Press, 1992.

CHAPTER 3: A CIVIL WAR LOVE STORY

Chetlain, Augustus Louis. *The Recollections of 70 Years*. Galena, Illinois: Gazette Publishing Co., 1899.

CHAPTER 4: MORGAN'S CHRISTMAS RAID

Brewer, James D. *The Raiders of 1862*. Westport, Connecticut: Praeger, 1997.

Brown, Dee Alexander. *The Bold Cavaliers*. Philadelphia: J. B. Lippincott Company, 1959.

Duke, Basil W. (edited with an introduction and notes by Cecil Fletcher Holland). *A History of Morgan's Cavalry*. Bloomington: Indiana University Press, 1960.

_____. *Reminiscences of General Basil W. Duke*. Garden City, New York: Doubleday, Page and Co., 1911.

Holland, Cecil Fletcher. *Morgan and His Raiders*. New York: The Macmillan Company, 1942.

Metzler, William E. *Morgan and His Dixie Cavaliers*. n. p., Beaver Press, Inc., 1976.

Ramage, James A. *Rebel Raider: Life of General John Hunt Morgan*. Lexington: University Press of Kentucky, 1986.

Swiggett, Howard. *The Rebel Raider: A Life of John Hunt Morgan*. Indianapolis: The Bobbs-Merrill Company, Inc., 1934.

CHAPTER 5: BATTLE AT CHICKASAW BLUFFS

Bearss, Edwin Cole. *Vicksburg Is the Key: The Campaign for Vicksburg*. Vol. I. Dayton, Ohio: Morningside House, Inc., October 1991 (Reissued).

CHAPTER 6: GRIERSON'S RAID

Brown, Dee. *Grierson's Raid*. Urbana: University of Illinois Press, 1954.

CHAPTER 7: THE GREAT RAID BEGINS

Brown, Dee Alexander. *The Bold Cavaliers*. Philadelphia: J. B. Lippincott Company, 1959.

Duke, Basil W. (edited with an introduction and notes by Cecil Fletcher Holland). *A History of Morgan's Cavalry*. Bloomington: Indiana University Press, 1960.

_____. *Reminiscences of General Basil W. Duke*. Garden City, New York: Doubleday, Page and Co., 1911.

Holland, Cecil Fletcher. *Morgan and His Raiders*. New York: The Macmillan Company, 1942.

Keller, Allan. *Morgan's Raid*. Indianapolis: The Bobbs-Merrill Company, Inc., 1961.

Metzler, William E. *Morgan and His Dixie Cavaliers*. n. p., Beaver Press, Inc., 1976.

Ramage, James A. *Rebel Raider: Life of General John Hunt Morgan*. Lexington: University Press of Kentucky, 1986.

Swiggett, Howard. *The Rebel Raider: A Life of John Hunt Morgan*. Indianapolis: The Bobbs-Merrill Company, Inc., 1934.

CHAPTER 8: FARTHEST POINT NORTH

Brown, Dee Alexander. *The Bold Cavaliers*. Philadelphia: J. B. Lippincott Company, 1959.

Duke, Basil W. (edited with an introduction and notes by Cecil Fletcher Holland). *A History of Morgan's Cavalry*. Bloomington: Indiana University Press, 1960.

_____. *Reminiscences of General Basil W. Duke*. Garden City, New York: Doubleday, Page and Co., 1911.

Holland, Cecil Fletcher. *Morgan and His Raiders*. New York: The
Macmillan Company, 1942.
Keller, Allan. *Morgan's Raid*. Indianapolis: The Bobbs-Merrill Company,
Inc., 1961.
Metzler, William E. *Morgan and His Dixie Cavaliers*. n. p., Beaver Press,
Inc., 1976.
Ramage, James A. *Rebel Raider: Life of General John Hunt Morgan*.
Lexington: University Press of Kentucky, 1986.
Swiggett, Howard. *The Rebel Raider: A Life of John Hunt Morgan*.
Indianapolis: The Bobbs-Merrill Company, Inc., 1934.

CHAPTER 9: OATHS AND ALLEGIANCES

Brown, Dee. *The Galvanized Yankees*. Urbana: University of Illinois Press,
1963.

CHAPTER 10: BATTLE OF BRICE'S CROSS ROADS

Bearss, Edwin C. *Forrest at Brice's Cross Roads and in North Mississippi in
1864*. Dayton, Ohio: Morningside House, Inc. 1987 (Reissued).

CHAPTER 11: THE NORTHWEST CONSPIRACY

Karamanski, Theodore J. *Rally 'Round the Flag: Chicago and the Civil War*.
Chicago: Nelson-Hall Publishers, 1993.
Levy, George. *To Die In Chicago*. Evanston, Illinois: Evanston Publishing,
Inc., 1994.

CHAPTER 12: THE MILLION-DOLLAR WAGON TRAIN RAID

Cunningham, Frank. *General Stand Watie's Confederate Indians*. San
Antonio, Texas: The Naylor Company, 1959.

CHAPTER 13: THE BATTLE OF WESTPORT

Josephy, Alvin M. *War on the Frontier: The Trans-Mississippi West*.
Alexandria, Virginia: Time-Life Books, 1986.
Monnett, Howard N. *Action Before Westport 1864*. Rev. ed. Niwot,
Colorado: University Press of Colorado, 1995.

CHAPTER 14: NO MORE BUGLES

Brown, Dee Alexander. *The Bold Cavaliers*. Philadelphia: J. B. Lippincott
Company, 1959.
Clark, James C. *Last Train South: The Flight of the Confederate Government
from Richmond*. Jefferson, North Carolina: McFarland & Company
Publishers, Inc., 1984.
Davis, Jefferson. *The Rise and Fall of the Confederate Government*. New
York: Carleton Publishers, 1866.

Duke, Basil W. (edited with an introduction and notes by Cecil Fletcher Holland). *A History of Morgan's Cavalry.* Bloomington: Indiana University Press, 1960.

_____. *Reminiscences of General Basil W. Duke.* Garden City, New York: Doubleday, Page and Co., 1911.

Fox, John A. *The Capture of Jefferson Davis.* New York: n. p., 1964. (A Collection of Letters and Reports Placed for Auction).

Hanna, A. J. *Flight Into Oblivion.* Richmond, Virginia: Johnson Publishing Co., 1938.

Bibliography

(Pertaining only to identification of individual participants in each chapter)

Amann, William Frayne (ed.). *Personnel of the Civil War.* Vol. I, *The Confederate Armies.* Vol. II, *The Union Armies.* New York: Thomas Yoseloff, 1961.

Andreas, A. T. *History of Chicago* (reprint). Vol. II. New York: Arno Press, 1975.

Bancroft, Frederic. *The Life of William H. Seward.* Vol. II. New York: Harper & Brothers Publishers, 1990.

Bates, Samuel P. *History of Pennsylvania Volunteers 1861–65.* Vol. IV. Harrisburg: B. Singerly, State Printer, 1870.

Bearss, Edwin C. *The Battle of Wilson's Creek.* 4th ed. Cassville, Missouri: Wilson's Creek National Battlefield Foundation, 1992.

———. *Forrest at Brice's Cross Roads and in North Mississippi in 1864.* Dayton, Ohio: Press of Morningside Bookshop, 1979.

———. *Vicksburg Is the Key: The Campaign for Vicksburg.* Vol. I. Dayton, Ohio: Morningside House, 1985.

Biographical Directory of the American Congress 1774–1961. Washington, D.C.: Government Printing Office, 1961.

Brown, Dee Alexander. *The Bold Cavaliers.* Philadelphia: J. B. Lippincott Company, 1959.

———. *The Galvanized Yankees.* Urbana: University of Illinois Press, 1963.

Castleman, John B., Major C.S.A., B. Gen. U.S.A. *Active Service.* Louisville, Kentucky: Courier-Journal Job Printing Co., 1917.

Commanders of Army Corps, Divisions & Brigades, United States Army 1861–1865. Washington: Quartermaster General of the Army, 1887.

Connelley, William Elsey. *Quantrill and the Border Wars.* Cedar Rapids, Iowa: The Torch Press, Publishers, 1910.

Cullum, Bvt. Major General George W. *Biographical Register of the Officers and Graduates of the U.S. Military Academy, at West Point, N.Y., from its Establishment, March 16, 1802 to the Army Re-Organization of 1866–67.* Vol. I, 1802–1840. Vol. II, 1841–1867. New York: D. Van Nostrand, 1868.

Duke, Brigadier General Basil, Brigadier General Orlando B. Willcox, and Captain Thomas H. Hines. *The Great Indiana-Ohio Raid by Brig. Gen.*

John Hunt Morgan and His Men July 1863. Louisville, Kentucky: The Book-Nook Press, 1955.

Eastman, Francis S. *Chicago City Manual 1911.* Chicago: Bureau of Statistics and Municipal Library, 1911.

Encyclopedia of Indiana (a volume of *Encyclopedia of the United States*). 2d ed. New York: Somerset Publishers, Inc., 1993.

Funk, Arville E. *The Morgan Raid in Indiana and Ohio (1863).* Rev. ed. Mentone, Indiana: Superior Printing Company, 1978.

Gibson, Charles Dana, and E. Kay. *Dictionary of Transports and Combatant Vessels Steam and Sail Employed by the Union Army 1861–1868.* Camden, Maine: Ensign Press, 1995.

Holland, Cecil Fletcher. *Morgan and His Raiders.* New York: The Macmillan Company, 1942.

House Executive Documents, 39th Congress, 2nd Session, No. 50, 1866–67. Washington, D.C.: Government Printing Office.

Johnson, Robert Underwood, and Clarence Cough Buel (ed.). *Battles and Leaders of the Civil War: Being For the Most Part Contributions by Union and Confederate Officers.* Based upon "The Century War Series." Vol. III. New York: The Century Company, 1887–88.

Karamanski, Theodore J. *Rally 'Round the Flag: Chicago and the Civil War.* Chicago: Nelson-Hall, 1993.

Levy, George. *To Die in Chicago: Confederate Prisoners at Camp Douglas 1862–1865.* Evanston, Illinois: Evanston Publishing Inc., 1994.

Merrifield, Charles Warren. *The Chicago Conspiracy: A Study of the Insurrectionary Phase of the Civil War Peace Movement in the Old Northwest.* Chicago: The University of Chicago, 1935.

Monnett, Howard N. *Action Before Westport 1864.* Rev. ed. Niwot, Colorado: University Press of Colorado, 1995.

Newman, Ralph, and E. B. Long. *The Civil War.* Vol. II, *The Picture Chronicle of the Events, Leaders and Battlefields of the War.* New York: Grosset & Dunlap, Inc., 1956.

Official Army Register of the Volunteer Force of the United States Army for the Years 1861, '62, '63, '64, '65. Part VII. Missouri, Wisconsin, Iowa, Minnesota, California, Kansas, Oregon, Nevada. (Reprint). Gaithersburg, M.D.: Ron R. Van Sickle Military Books, 1987.

Peterson, Richard C., James E. McGhee, Kip A. Lindberg, and Keith I. Daleen. *Sterling Price's Lieutenants: A Guide to the Officers and Organization of the Missouri State Guard 1861–1865.* Shawnee Mission, Kansas: Two Trails Publishing, 1995.

Ramage, James A. *Rebel Raider: Life of General John Hunt Morgan.* Lexington: University Press of Kentucky, 1986.

Report of the Adjutant General of the State of Illinois. Vol. I. Springfield: Phillips Bros, State Printers, 1900.

_____. Vol. IV. Springfield: Phillips Bros, State Printers, 1901.

_____. Vol. VIII. Springfield: Journal Company, Printers and Binders, 1901.

Report of the Adjutant General of the State of Indiana. Vol. I. Indianapolis: Alexander H. Conner, State Printer, 1869 (?).

_____. Vol. III. Indianapolis: Samuel M. Douglass, State Printer, 1866.

Report of the Adjutant General of the State of Kentucky: Confederate Kentucky Volunteers War 1861–1865. 2 vols. Frankfurt, Kentucky: The State Journal Company, 1915–1918.

Republican Congressional Committee. *Copperhead Conspiracy in the Northwest.* 1864.

Rostor Commission. *Official Rostor of the Soldiers of the State of Ohio in the War of the Rebellion 1861–1866.* Vol. XI. Akron, Ohio: Werner Ptg. & Litho. Co., 1891.

Secretary of the Interior (compiled and printed under direction of). *Register of Officers and Agents, Civil, Military and Naval in the Service of the United States on the Thirtieth September, 1863.* Washington, D.C.: Government Printing Office, 1864.

Settle, Jr., William A. *Jesse James Was His Name.* Columbia, Missouri: University of Missouri Press, 1966.

Shea, William L., and Earl J. Hess. *Pea Ridge: Civil War Campaign in the West.* Chapel Hill: The University of North Carolina Press, 1992.

Sifakis, Stewart. *Kentucky, Maryland, Missouri, the Confederate Units and the Indian Units: Compendium of the Confederate Armies.* New York: Facts On File, 1995.

_____. *Who Was Who in the Civil War.* New York: Facts on File Publications, 1988.

Smith, George B. *Official Army List of the Volunteers of Illinois, Indiana, Wisconsin, Minnesota, Michigan, Iowa, Missouri, Kansas, Nebraska, Colorado.* Chicago: Tribune Book and Job Printing Establishment, 1862.

Spiller, Roger J. (ed.). *Dictionary of American Military Biography.* Vols. I & III. Westport, Connecticut: Greenwood Press, 1984.

Starr, Stephen Z. *The Life of a Soldier of Fortune: Colonel Grenfell's Wars.* Baton Rouge: Louisiana State University Press, 1971.

Terrell, W. H. H., Adjutant General. *Indiana in the War of the Rebellion.* Indianapolis: Douglass & Conner, Journal Office, Printers, 1869.

Tunnard, W. H. *A Southern Record: The History of the Third Regiment Louisiana Infantry.* Baton Rouge, Louisiana: Printed for the Author, 1866.

The War of the Rebellion: A Compilation of the Official Records of the Union and Confederate Armies. Series I, vol. III. Washington, D.C.: Government Printing Office, 1881.

_____. Series I, vol. VIII. Washington, D.C.: Government Printing Office, 1883.

_____. Series I, vol. XIII. Washington, D.C.: Government Printing Office, 1887.

_____. Series I, vol. XX (parts I and II). Washington, D.C.: Government Printing Office, 1887.

_____. Series I, vol. XXIII (parts I and II). Washington, D.C.: Government Printing Office, 1889.

_____. Series I, vol. XXXIV (parts I and IV). Washington, D.C.: Government Printing Office, 1891.

_____. Series I, vol. XLI (parts I and III). Washington, D.C.: Government Printing Office, 1893.

Warner, Ezra J. *Generals in Blue*. Baton Rouge: Louisiana State University Press, 1964.

Whaley, Elizabeth J. *Forgotten Hero: General James B. McPherson*. New York: Exposition Press, 1955.

Reference Identification Guide
of Participants Cited in Chapters
Killed in Action

CHAPTER 1: WILSON'S CREEK (August 10, 1861)

CONFEDERATE

Major General **Sterling Price,** Commanding, Missouri State Guard.

Brigadier General **John Bullock Clark, Sr.,** Commanding, 3rd Division, Missouri State Guard.

Brigadier General **James H. McBride,** Commanding, 7th Division, Missouri State Guard.

Brigadier General **Benjamin McCulloch,** Commanding, McCulloch's Brigade, and Commanding, all Southern Forces at Wilson's Creek.

Brigadier General **Mosby M. Parsons,** Commanding, 6th Division, Missouri State Guard.

Brigadier General **Nicholas Bartlett Pearce,** Commanding, 1st Division, Army of Arkansas, and Commanding, all Arkansas State Forces.

Brigadier General **James S. Rains,** Commanding, 2nd Division, Missouri State Guard.

Brigadier General **William Y. Slack,** Commanding, 4th Division, Missouri State Guard.

Colonel **Thomas J. Churchill,** Commanding, 1st Arkansas Mounted Rifles.

Colonel **John Gratiot,** Commanding, 3rd Arkansas State Infantry Regiment.

Colonel **Elkanah Greer,** Commanding, South Kansas–Texas Cavalry Regiment.

Colonel **Louis Hébert,** Commanding, 3rd Louisiana Infantry Regiment.

Colonel **James McIntosh,** Commanding, 2nd Arkansas Mounted Rifles.

Lieutenant Colonel **Dandridge McRae,** Commanding, McRae's Arkansas Infantry Battalion.

Captain **Henry Guibor,** Commanding, Guibor's Battery, Missouri State Guard.

Captain **John Vigilini,** Commanding, Company K, 3rd Louisiana Infantry Regiment.

Captain **William E. Woodruff,** Commanding, Woodruff's Battery (also known as Pulaski Battery, Arkansas State Troops).

Lieutenant **William P. Barlow,** Guibor's Battery, Missouri State Guard.

Sergeant **William Watson,** Company K, 3rd Louisiana Infantry Regiment.

Corporal **Henry Gentles,** Company K, 3rd Louisiana Infantry Regiment.

UNION

Major General John C. Frémont, Commanding, Western Department, Headquartered in St. Louis, Missouri.

Major General Henry W. Halleck, although named in the article, played no role in the Battle of Wilson's Creek. He was reappointed in the U.S. Army on August 19, 1861, with the rank of major general and did not assume command of the Department of the Missouri until November 9, 1861.

Brigadier General Nathaniel Lyon,* Commanding, Army of the West.

Colonel Franz Sigel, Commanding, 2nd Brigade, Army of the West.

Major Peter J. Osterhaus, Commanding, 2nd Missouri Volunteer Infantry (often referred to as Osterhaus's Battalion).

Major John M. Schofield, 1st Missouri Volunteer Infantry, Acting Adjutant-General, Army of the West, and Adjutant to Brigadier General Nathaniel Lyon.

Major Samuel D. Sturgis, 1st U.S. Cavalry, Commanding, 1st Brigade, Army of the West, and Commanding Army of the West following the death on the battlefield of Brigadier General Nathaniel Lyon.

Captain Gordon Granger, Regiment of Mounted Rifles, Acting Assistant Adjutant-General to Major Samuel D. Sturgis.

Captain Joseph Plummer, Commanding, 1st U.S. Infantry Regiment, and Commanding Plummer's Battalion of U.S. Regular Infantry.

Captain James Totten, Commanding, Battery F, 2nd U. S. Artillery.

Second Lieutenant John V. Du Bois, Regiment of Mounted Rifles, Commanding, Du Bois' Artillery (a temporary organization disbanded after Battle of Wilson's Creek).

Wild Bill Hickok was an unlikely participant in the Battle of Wilson's Creek. If he participated at all, it was in the role as a civilian teamster and not as a soldier.

Frank James claimed to have been present during the Battle of Wilson's Creek. If correct, it is reasonable to believe he was a member of a Clay County company in the 5th Division, Missouri State Guard.

William Quantrill was more than likely present during the Battle of Wilson's Creek. If so, he probably served as a member of Captain Joel Mayes's company of Cherokees.

Cole Younger claimed to have participated in the Battle of Wilson's Creek on his Missouri Confederate pension application. If this is true, he probably served in an unknown Missouri State Guard unit.

CHAPTER 2: PEA RIDGE (March 7–8, 1862)

CONFEDERATE

Major General Sterling Price, Commanding, Price's Division, Army of the West.

Major General Earl Van Dorn, Commanding, Army of the West and Trans-Mississippi District.

Brigadier General Ben McCulloch,* Commanding, McCulloch's Division, Army of the West.

Brigadier General Albert J. Pike (Provisional Army), Commanding, Pike's Indian Brigade, McCulloch's Division, Army of the West.

Brigadier General William Y. Slack,* Commanding, 2nd Missouri Brigade, Price's Division, Army of the West, and upon death was succeeded in command by Colonel Thomas H. Rosser.

Colonel Elijah Gates, Commanding, 1st Missouri Cavalry Regiment, 1st Missouri Brigade, Price's Division, Army of the West.

Colonel Elkaneh Greer, Commanding, 3rd Texas Cavalry Regiment, McCulloch's Division, Army of the West, and assumed temporary command of the Division on the field upon learning of the deaths of Brigadier General Ben McCulloch and Colonel James M. McIntosh.

Colonel Louis Hébert, Commanding, Hébert's Infantry Brigade, McCulloch's Division, Army of the West, until captured and succeeded in command by Colonel Evander McNair.

Colonel Henry Little, Commanding, 1st Missouri Brigade, Price's Division, Army of the West.

Colonel James M. McIntosh,* (promoted to brigadier general January 24, 1862), Commanding, McIntosh's Cavalry Brigade, McCulloch's Division, Army of the West.

Colonel Benjamin A. Rives,* Commanding, 3rd Missouri Infantry Regiment, 1st Missouri Brigade, Price's Division, Army of the West.

Colonel Stand Watie, Commanding, 2nd Cherokee Mounted Rifles.

Captain S. Churchill Clark,* Commanding, Clark's Battery, 1st Missouri Brigade, Price's Division, Army of the West, and grandson of Capt. William Clark, noted explorer.

Captain Henry Guibor, Commanding, Guibor's Battery, Missouri State Guard, and president, court of inquiry investigating conduct of members of Hart's Arkansas Battery Light Artillery, commanded by Captain William Hart, at Battle of Pea Ridge (Elkhorn Tavern), and concluding they were "guilty of no misconduct on field of battle" and "relieved of censure."

Captain Joseph O. Shelby, Commanding, Shelby's Cavalry Company, 8th Division, Missouri State Guard.

UNION

Brigadier General Alexander Asboth, Commanding, 2nd Division, Army of the Southwest.

Brigadier General Samuel R. Curtis, Commanding, Army of the Southwest.

Brigadier General Jefferson C. Davis, USV, Commanding, 3rd Division, Army of the Southwest.

Brigadier General Franz Sigel, Commanding, 1st and 2nd Divisions, Army of the Southwest.

Colonel Eugene A. Carr, Commanding, 4th Division, Army of the Southwest.

Colonel Grenville M. Dodge, Commanding, 1st Brigade, 4th Division, Army of the Southwest.

Colonel Peter J. Osterhaus, Commanding, 1st Division, Army of the Southwest.

Colonel William Vandever, Commanding, 2nd Brigade, 4th Division, Army of the Southwest.

Lieutenant Colonel George Currie (should be Captain George Currie), Company F, 59th Illinois Volunteer Infantry Regiment (changed from 9th Regiment Infantry Missouri Volunteers by order of War Department on February 12, 1862), 3rd Division, Army of the Southwest.

Lieutenant Colonel Henry H. Trimble, 3rd Iowa Cavalry Regiment, Unassigned Command (Headquarters Unit), Army of the Southwest.

Captain Philip H. Sheridan, Chief Quartermaster and Chief Commissary of Subsistence, Army of the Southwest.

Private Peter Pelican, Company B, 36th Illinois Infantry Regiment, 2nd Brigade, 1st Division, Army of the Southwest.

Private Thomas Welch, Company M, 3rd Illinois Cavalry Regiment, 1st Brigade, 4th Division, Army of the Southwest.

CHAPTER 3: A CIVIL WAR LOVE STORY (1862–February 18, 1864)

CONFEDERATE

General Joseph E. Johnston, Commanding, Department of Northern Virginia (October 22, 1861–May 31, 1862); Commanding, Department of the West (December 4, 1862–December 1863); Commanding, Army of Tennessee (December 27, 1863–July 18, 1864).

UNION

Brigadier General Oliver O. Howard, USV, Commanding, 1st Brigade, 1st Division, II Corps, Army of the Potomac (March 13, 1862–June 1, 1862); Commanding, 2nd Brigade, 2nd Division, II Corps, Army of the Potomac (August 27, 1862–September 17, 1862); Commanding, 2nd Division, Army of the Potomac (September 17, 1862–January 26, 1863); Promoted to major general, USV (November 29, 1862); Commanding, II Corps, Army of the Potomac (January 26, 1863–February 5, 1863); Commanding, 2nd Division, Army of the Potomac, (February 7, 1863–April 1, 1863); Commanding, XI Corps, Army of the Potomac (April 2, 1863–September 25, 1863); Commanding XI Corps, Army of the Cumberland (September 25, 1863–January 21, 1864 and February 25, 1864–April 18, 1864); Commanding, IV Corps, Army of the Cumberland (April 10, 1864–July 27, 1864); appointed Commanding, Department and Army of the Tennessee (July 27, 1864, to succeed Major General James B. McPherson).

Brigadier General James B. McPherson, USV, * Commanding, Engineer Brigade, Army of the Tennessee (June 4, 1862–October 4, 1862); promoted to major general, USV (October 8, 1862); Commanding, Right Wing, XIII Army Corps,

Army of the Tennessee (November 1, 1862–December 18, 1862); Commanding, XVII Corps, Army of the Tennessee (December 18, 1862–April 23, 1864); Promoted to brigadier general, USA (August 1, 1863); Commanding, Department and Army of the Tennessee (March 26, 1864–until killed in action during Battle of Atlanta, July 22, 1864).

Brigadier General William T. Sherman, USV, Commanding, District of Cairo, Department of the Missouri (February 14, 1862–March 1, 1862); Commanding, 5th Division, Army of the Tennessee (March 1, 1862–July 21, 1862); promoted to major general, USV (May 1, 1862); Commanding, 5th Division, District of Memphis, Army of the Tennessee (July 21, 1862–September 24, 1862); Commanding, 1st Division, District of Memphis, Army of the Tennessee (September 24, 1862–October 26, 1862); simultaneously Commanding, District of Memphis (July 21, 1862–October 26, 1862); Commanding, District of Memphis, XIII Corps, Army of the Tennessee (October 24, 1862–November 25, 1862), Commanding, Yazoo Expeditionary Force, Army of the Tennessee (December 18, 1862–January 4, 1863); Commanding, II Corps, Army of the Mississippi (January 4, 1863–January 12, 1863); Commanding, XV Corps, Army of the Tennessee (January 12, 1863–October 29, 1863); promoted brigadier general, USA (July 4, 1863); Commanding Department and Army of the Tennessee (October 24, 1863–March 26, 1864).

Captain Henry Van Sellar, 12th Illinois Volunteer Infantry Regiment (commissioned a second lieutenant on August 1, 1861, in Company E, promoted to captain on October 18, 1861, in Company E, bypassed the rank of major, promoted to lieutenant colonel on February 19, 1864, as a field and staff officer, and promoted to colonel July 10, 1865, but mustered out as lieutenant colonel on that same date).

CHAPTER 4: MORGAN'S CHRISTMAS RAID
(December 22, 1862–January 3, 1863)

CONFEDERATE

Jefferson Davis, President and Commander-in-Chief, The Confederate States of America.

General Braxton Bragg, Commanding, Army of Tennessee.

Brigadier General Nathan Bedford Forrest, Commanding, Cavalry Brigade, Army of Tennessee.

Brigadier General John Hunt Morgan, Commanding, 2nd Cavalry Brigade, 3rd Division, Department of East Tennessee.

Colonel Roy S. (Leroy) Cluke, Commanding, 8th Kentucky Cavalry Regiment, 2nd Cavalry Brigade, Department of East Tennessee.

Colonel Basil W. Duke, Commanding, 2nd Kentucky Cavalry Regiment, 2nd Cavalry Brigade, Department of East Tennessee.

Lieutenant Colonel William C. P. Breckinridge, Commanding, Kentucky Battalion, 2nd Cavalry Brigade, Department of East Tennessee.

Captain Thomas Quirk, Chief of Scouts.

Lieutenant James B. McCreary, 11th Kentucky Cavalry Regiment.

Ordinance Sergeant Kelion F. Peddicord, Quirk's Scouts.

Ordnance Sergeant Henry L. Stone, 9th Kentucky Cavalry Regiment.

Scout Thomas Berry, Quirk's Scouts.

Scout Johnny Wyeth, Independent Member, Quirk's Scouts

Scout Bennett S. Young, Quirk's Scouts

UNION

Major General Ulysses S. Grant, Commanding, Department and Army of the Tennessee.

Major General William S. Rosecrans, Commanding, XIV Corps, Army of the Cumberland.

Major General Horatio G. Wright, Commanding, Department of the Ohio.

Brigadier General Jeremiah T. Boyle, Commanding, District of Western Kentucky.

Colonel John M. Harlan, 10th Kentucky Infantry, Commanding, 2nd Brigade, District of Western Kentucky.

Lieutenant Colonel H. S. Smith, Commanding, U.S. Forces (seven or eight unidentified companies of U.S. troops), Elizabethtown, Kentucky.

CHAPTER 5: BATTLE AT CHICKASAW BLUFFS

(December 27, 1862–January 3, 1863)

NOTE: For more than one hundred years, many historians and writers have referred to the Battle of Chickasaw Bayou as the Battle of Chickasaw Bluffs. This is incorrect, but it is easy to understand why this misconception would exist. The line of bluffs towering above Chickasaw Bayou caused soldiers to refer to that engagement as the Battle of Chickasaw Bluffs. However, Chickasaw Bluffs is a specific geographic area located north of Memphis, Tennessee. The bluffs north of Vicksburg overlooking Chickasaw Bayou are known as the Walnut Hills. In fact, some accounts refer to this engagement as the Battle of Walnut Hills. The official name of the engagement as established by the U.S. War Department is the Battle of Chickasaw Bayou.

CONFEDERATE

Lieutenant General John C. Pemberton, Commanding, Department of Mississippi and Eastern Louisiana.

Major General Martin L. Smith, Commanding, 2nd Military District, including Vicksburg, Mississippi, until December 30, 1862.

Major General Carter L. Stevenson, Commanding, 2nd Military District, including Vicksburg, Mississippi, after December 30, 1862, succeeding Major General Martin L. Smith.

Major General Earl Van Dorn, Commanding, Army of the West, Trans-Mississippi District (Department No. 2).

Brigadier General Seth M. Barton, Commanding, Barton's Brigade, consisting of 40th Georgia Infantry, 42nd Georgia Infantry, 43rd Georgia Infantry, 52nd Georgia Infantry, and Detachment of Botetourt Virginia Artillery.

Brigadier General Nathan Bedford Forrest, Commanding, Cavalry Brigade, Army of Tennessee (reported in chapter as holding rank of Major General).

Brigadier General Stephen D. Lee, Commanding, Provisional Division through December 30, 1862.

Brigadier General John C. Vaughn, Commanding, Vaughn's Brigade, consisting of 60th Tennessee Infantry, 61st Tennessee Infantry, and 62nd Tennessee Infantry.

Colonel Winchester Hall, Commanding, 26th Louisiana Infantry.

Colonel C. H. Morrison, Commanding, 31st Louisiana Infantry.

Colonel C. D. Phillips, Commanding, 52nd Georgia Infantry.

Lieutenant J. A. Tarleton, Commanding, Battery D, 1st Mississippi Light Artillery.

UNION

Major General Frank P. Blair, Jr., Commanding, 1st Brigade, consisting of 13th Illinois Infantry, 29th Missouri Infantry, 30th Missouri Infantry, 31st Missouri Infantry, 32nd Missouri Infantry, 58th Ohio Infantry, 4th Company, Ohio Light Artillery, and Company C, 10th Missouri Cavalry.

Major General Ulysses S. Grant, Commanding, Department and Army of the Tennessee.

Major General John A. McClernand, USV, although named in the article, did not play any role in the Battle at Chickasaw Bluffs. He was between major assignments until being appointed to command Army of the Mississippi, Department of the Tennessee, on January 4, 1863.

Major General William T. Sherman, Commanding, Yazoo Expeditionary Force, Army of the Tennessee (December 18, 1862–January 4, 1863).

Brigadier General Charles E. Hovey, Commanding, 2nd Brigade, consisting of 25th Iowa Infantry, 31st Iowa Infantry, 3rd Missouri Infantry, 12th Missouri Infantry, 17th Missouri Infantry, 76th Ohio Infantry, and Company F, 2nd Missouri Light Artillery.

Brigadier General George W. Morgan, Commanding, 3rd Division, consisting of 1st Brigade, consisting of 118th Illinois Infantry, 69th Indiana Infantry, and 120th Ohio Infantry.

Brigadier General Andrew J. Smith, Commanding, 1st Division, consisting of Company C, 4th Indiana Cavalry as Escort, 1st and 2nd Brigades and Artillery.

Brigadier General Morgan L. Smith, Commanding, 2nd Division, consisting of 1st and 4th Brigades until being wounded and succeeded by Brigadier General David Stuart.

Brigadier General Frederick Steele, Commanding, 4th Division, consisting of 1st Brigade and including 13th Illinois Infantry, 29th Missouri Infantry, 30th Missouri Infantry, 31st Missouri Infantry, 32nd Missouri Infantry, 58th Ohio Infantry, 4th Company, Ohio Light Artillery, and Company C, 10th Missouri Cavalry.
Brigadier General John H. Thayer, Commanding, 3rd Brigade of 4th Division.
Acting Rear Admiral David D. Porter, Commanding, Mississippi River Squadron.
Colonel John F. DeCourcy, Commanding, 3rd Brigade of 3rd Division, consisting of 54th Indiana Infantry, 22nd Kentucky Infantry, 16th Ohio Infantry, and 42nd Ohio Infantry.
Colonel J. A. Williamson, Commanding, 4th Iowa Infantry of 3rd Brigade, 4th Division.
Lieutenant Colonel James H. Blood, Commanding, 6th Missouri Infantry of 1st Brigade, 2nd Division.
Captain Charles McDonald, Adjutant to Brigadier General Morgan L. Smith.
Private Albert H. Sibley, Company H, 13th Illinois Volunteer Infantry Regiment.

CHAPTER 6: GRIERSON'S RAID (April 17–May 2, 1863)

CONFEDERATE
Lieutenant General John C. Pemberton, Commanding, Department of Mississippi and Eastern Louisiana.
Brigadier General James R. Chalmers, Commanding, Western part of Confederate forces, headquartered at Panola, Mississippi, in a district that extended approximately from New Albany, Mississippi, on the east to the Coldwater River on the west.
Brigadier General Daniel Ruggles, Commanding, Eastern part of Confederate forces, headquartered at Columbus, Mississippi, in a district that extended approximately from New Albany, Mississippi, on the west to the Mississippi-Alabama state line on the east.
Colonel Wirt Adams, Wirt Adams's, Mississippi Cavalry Regiment (Unattached) and Commanding, Mississippi Cavalry.
Lieutenant Colonel Clark R. Barteau, Commanding, 2nd Tennessee Cavalry Regiment.

UNION
General Henry W. Halleck, General-in-Chief, U.S. Army, Washington, D.C.
Major General Ulysses S. Grant, USV, Commanding, Army and Department of the Tennessee.
Major General William T. Sherman, USV, Commanding, XV Corps, Army of the Tennessee.
Colonel Benjamin H. Grierson, Commanding, 1st Brigade, 1st Cavalry Division, XVI Army Corps, Department of the Tennessee.
Colonel Edward Hatch, Commanding, 2nd Iowa Cavalry Regiment.

Lieutenant Colonel William D. Blackburn,* 7th Illinois Cavalry Regiment.

Major Henry C. Forbes (held rank of Captain during raid), Commanding, Company B, 7th Illinois Cavalry Regiment.

Major Hiram W. Love, 2nd Iowa Cavalry Regiment, Commanding and leading "Quinine Brigade" (consisting of sick and wounded horse soldiers) back to LaGrange, Tennessee.

First Sergeant Stephen A. Forbes, Company B, 7th Illinois Cavalry Regiment (although identified with this rank by Dee Brown in his book *Grierson's Raid,* "The Report of the Adjutant General of the State of Illinois" lists Stephen A. Forbes as a private September 5, 1861, a second lieutenant February 10, 1863 and a captain March 28, 1865. There is no official mention of him as a first sergeant with this unit). However, Stephen A. Forbes, in his address before the Illinois State Historical Society, at its Eighth Annual Meeting, in Springfield, Illinois, January 24, 1907, stated: "It was my good fortune to make this ride, a youth of 18 at the time, first sergeant of a company of the 7th Illinois, of which my brother H. C. Forbes, was captain."

Sergeant Richard M. Surby, Company A, 7th Illinois Cavalry Regiment, quartermaster sergeant, 7th Illinois Cavalry Regiment, and first leader of the Butternut Guerrillas.

CHAPTER 7: THE GREAT RAID BEGINS (July 2–26, 1863)

CONFEDERATE

General Braxton Bragg, Commanding, Department No. 2.

General Joseph E. Johnston, Commanding, Army of the West.

General Robert E. Lee, Commanding, Army of Northern Virginia.

Major General Simon Bolivar Buckner, Commanding, Army of East Tennessee.

Brigadier General Nathan Bedford Forrest, Commanding, Cavalry Division, Army of Tennessee.

Brigadier General Roger Hanson,* Commanding, 4th (Kentucky) Brigade, 1st (Breckinridge's) Division, Hardee's Corps, Army of Tennessee (November 20, 1862–January 2, 1863), was promoted to brigadier general December 13, 1862, mortally wounded at Murfreesboro, Tennessee, on January 2, 1863, and died two days later.

Brigadier General John Hunt Morgan, Commanding, Morgan's Division, Cavalry Corps, Department No. 2.

Colonel James W. Bowles, a field officer with the 2nd Kentucky Cavalry Regiment.

Colonel William C. P. Breckinridge, Commanding, 9th Kentucky Cavalry Regiment, 1st Brigade, Morgan's Division, Department No. 2.

Colonel David W. Chenault,* Commanding, 7th (Chenault's) Cavalry Regiment (later named 11th Kentucky Cavalry Regiment), 2nd Brigade, Department No. 2.

Colonel Roy S. Cluke, Commanding, 2nd Brigade, and Commanding, 8th Kentucky Cavalry Regiment, 2nd Brigade, Morgan's Division, Department No. 2.

Colonel Basil W. Duke, Commanding, 1st Brigade, Morgan's Division, Department No. 2.

Colonel Adam R. Johnson, Commanding, 10th Kentucky Cavalry Regiment, 2nd Brigade, Morgan's Division, Department No. 2.

Colonel Richard C. Morgan, Commanding, 14th Kentucky Cavalry Regiment, and serving as advance guard, 2nd Brigade, Morgan's Division, Department No. 2.

Colonel D. Howard Smith, Commanding, 5th Kentucky Cavalry Regiment, 1st Brigade, Morgan's Division, Department No. 2.

Colonel W. W. Ward, Commanding, Ward's (9th Tennessee) Regiment, 1st Brigade, Morgan's Division, Department No. 2.

Lieutenant Colonel Robert Alston, Adjutant to Brigadier General John Hunt Morgan.

Major James B. McCreary, a Field Officer with the 11th Kentucky Cavalry Regiment.

Major Thomas B. Webber, Commanding, 2nd Kentucky Cavalry Regiment, 1st Brigade, Morgan's Division, Department No. 2.

Captain (should be Major) **Edward P. Byrne,** Commanding, Kentucky Battery (Light Artillery), Morgan's Division, Department No. 2.

Captain Thomas M. Coombs, Commanding, Company K, 5th Kentucky Cavalry Regiment (no rolls on file), unit was consolidated with Company G, 5th Kentucky Cavalry Regiment, circa November 1, 1862.

Captain William C. Davis, Acting Assistant Adjutant General, 1st Brigade.

Captain William J. Davis, reported as Commanding a Company but unable to locate and confirm any listing of person with this rank, first name, middle initial, and last name in the *Report of the Adjutant General of the State of Kentucky Confederate Kentucky Volunteers War 1861–1865.*

Captain Thomas B. Franks, Company I, 2nd Kentucky Cavalry Regiment, and serving later with Quirk's Scouts (second commander).

Captain Thomas Henry Hines, Commanding, Company E, 9th Kentucky Cavalry Regiment, and serving later with Quirk's Scouts (third commander).

Captain W. J. Jones, reported as Commanding a Company but unable to locate and confirm any listing of person with this rank, initials, and last name in the *Report of the Adjutant General of the State of Kentucky Confederate Kentucky Volunteers War 1861–1865.*

Captain H. Clay Meriwether, Commanding, Company H, 10th Kentucky Cavalry Regiment.

Captain Calvin "Cally" Cogswell Morgan, 2nd Kentucky Cavalry Regiment.

Captain Thomas Quirk, Commanding, Quirk's Scouts as of November 15, 1862 (first commander), until wounded at Burksville, Kentucky, July 2, 1863.

Captain Samuel B. Taylor, Commanding, Company E, 10th Kentucky Cavalry Regiment.

Captain Alexander Tribble, * Company B, 11th Kentucky Cavalry Regiment, killed at Green River bridge on July 4, 1863.

First Lieutenant George B. Eastin, D Company, 2nd Kentucky Cavalry Regiment (Private George Donald when captured).

First Lieutenant Josiah B. Gathright, Company H, 8th Kentucky Cavalry Regiment.

First Lieutenant Thomas H. Morgan,* 2nd Kentucky Cavalry Regiment. (Killed during an attack near Lebanon, Kentucky, July 5, 1863.)

First Lieutenant Ashley S. Welch, Company L, 2nd Kentucky Cavalry Regiment.

Lieutenant Leland Hathaway, Adjutant of 9th Kentucky Cavalry Regiment but later transferred to 8th Kentucky Cavalry Regiment.

Lieutenant Joe Tucker (unable to locate and confirm any listing of person with this rank, first name, and last name, in the *Report of the Adjutant General of the State of Kentucky Confederate Kentucky Volunteers War 1861–1865*).

Sergeant Kelion Peddicord, enlisted October 11, 1861, and was appointed first sergeant, Company C, 2nd Kentucky Cavalry Regiment.

Ordnance Sergeant Henry L. Stone, 9th Kentucky Cavalry Regiment, serving as a scout under Captain Thomas Henry Hines until captured at Buffington Island, Ohio, becoming a prisoner at Camp Douglas, escaping and returning to duty.

Private Thomas Boss, Company C, 2nd Kentucky Cavalry Regiment.

Private John "Jack" Messick, Company A, 2nd Kentucky Cavalry Regiment, a member of Quirk's Scouts, captured at Buffington Island, Ohio, July 19, 1863.

Private Winder W. Monroe, promoted to second lieutenant, Company I, 4th Kentucky Cavalry Regiment, a member of Quirk's Scouts, captured at Buffington Island, Ohio, July 19, 1863.

Private George D. Mosgrove, Company K, 4th Kentucky Cavalry Regiment.

Private Bennett H. Young, Company B, 8th Kentucky Cavalry Regiment, and a member of Quirk's Scouts.

George "Lightning" Ellsworth, telegrapher attached to the 2nd Kentucky Cavalry Regiment.

John T. Shanks, commissioned as a captain on the field but had no direct command and often served under Colonel Richard C. Morgan according to his own statements on page 14 of *House Executive Documents*, 39th Congress, 2nd Session, No. 50, 1866–67, but no listing could be found of his service in the records on file as of June 30, 1863, and December 31, 1864, at Camp Bowen, Virginia.

NOTE: Command assignments to the 1st and 2nd Brigades of Morgan's Division "appear to have been the composition of Morgan's Command when he set out on the raid." *The War of the Rebellion: A Compilation of the Official Records of the Union and Confederate Armies.* Series I, vol. XXIII, part II, p. 944. Washington, D.C.: Government Printing Office, 1889.

UNION

Major General Ulysses S. Grant, USV, Commanding, Army and Department of the Tennessee.

Brigadier General John Love, Commanding with rank of major general, Indiana Legion from September 10, 1861, until resigning January 1, 1863. Appointed acting brigadier general on orders from Brigadier General O. B. Willcox during General John Hunt Morgan's raid into Indiana and commanded volunteer troops at Seymour, Indiana, which included "two regiments of U.S. volunteers, about 300 Minute-Men and a small force of citizens."

Colonel Dennis J. Halisey,* Commanding, 6th Kentucky Cavalry Regiment.

Colonel Lewis Jordan, Sr., Commanding, 6th Regiment, 2nd Brigade, 2nd Division, Indiana Legion—Corydon, Indiana—Harrison County.

Colonel Orlando H. Moore, Commanding, 25th Michigan Infantry Volunteers.

Colonel Frank L. Wolford, Commanding, Wolford's Cavalry (1st Kentucky Union Cavalry Regiment).

Lieutenant Colonel Charles S. Hanson, Commanding, 20th Kentucky Infantry Regiment.

Captain Ballard, served as first master or captain of the steamboat *John T. McCombs* but no first name, middle initial, or reference of any kind could be located for Captain Ballard.

Captain Pepper, served as first master or captain of the 700-ton steamboat *Alice Dean,* which was chartered May 26, 1863–June 6, 1863, and is alleged to have been burned on July 25, 1863, but no first name, middle initial, or reference of any kind could be located for Captain Pepper.

Governor Oliver P. Morton, Governor of Indiana, January 16, 1861–January 24, 1867.

CHAPTER 8 : FARTHEST POINT NORTH (July 2–26, 1863)

CONFEDERATE

General Braxton Bragg, Commanding, Department No. 2.

General Robert E. Lee, Commanding, Army of Northern Virginia.

Brigadier General John Hunt Morgan, Commanding, Morgan's Division, Cavalry Corps, Department No. 2.

Colonel Roy S. Cluke, Commanding, 2nd Brigade, and Commanding, 8th Kentucky Cavalry Regiment, 2nd Brigade, Morgan's Division, Department No. 2.

Colonel Basil W. Duke, Commanding, 1st Brigade, Morgan's Division, Department No. 2.

Colonel J. Warren Grigsby, Commanding, 6th Kentucky Cavalry Regiment, 1st Brigade, Morgan's Division, Department No. 2.

Colonel Adam R. Johnson, Commanding, 10th Kentucky Cavalry Regiment, 2nd Brigade, Morgan's Division, Department No. 2.

Colonel Richard C. Morgan, Commanding, 14th Kentucky Cavalry Regiment, and serving as advance guard, 2nd Brigade, Morgan's Division, Department No. 2.

Colonel D. Howard Smith, Commanding, 5th Kentucky Cavalry Regiment, 1st Brigade, Morgan's Division, Department No. 2.

Major James B. McCreary, a field officer with the 11th Kentucky Cavalry Regiment.

Major Thomas B. Webber (appointed acting colonel in field by Brigadier General John Hunt Morgan), Commanding, 2nd Kentucky Cavalry Regiment, 1st Brigade, Morgan's Division, Department No. 2.

Captain (should be Major) **Edward P. Byrne,** Commanding, Kentucky Battery (Light Artillery), Morgan's Division, Department No. 2.

Captain John Cooper, Company L, 2nd Kentucky Cavalry Regiment.

Captain Thomas Henry Hines, Commanding, Company E, 9th Kentucky Cavalry Regiment, and serving later with Quirk's Scouts (third commander).

Captain N. M. Lea, Company F, 2nd Kentucky Cavalry Regiment.

Captain Ralph Sheldon, Company C, 2nd Kentucky Cavalry Regiment.

Captain Samuel B. Taylor, Commanding, Company E, 10th Kentucky Cavalry Regiment.

Sergeant Kelion Peddicord, enlisted October 11, 1861, and was appointed first sergeant, Company C, 2nd Kentucky Cavalry Regiment.

Ordnance Sergeant Henry L. Stone, 9th Kentucky Cavalry Regiment, serving as a scout under Captain Thomas Henry Hines until captured at Buffington Island, Ohio, becoming a prisoner at Camp Douglas, escaping, and returning to duty.

Private Bennett H. Young, Company B, 8th Kentucky Cavalry Regiment, and a member of Quirk's Scouts.

George "Lightning" Ellsworth, telegrapher attached to the 2nd Kentucky Cavalry Regiment.

George St. Leger Grenfell, a British soldier of fortune who retained the rank of colonel from his service in the British Army and many other foreign assignments, had served in 1862 as assistant adjutant general to Colonel John Hunt Morgan, left Colonel Morgan for General Braxton Bragg on December 20, 1862, was appointed to the rank of lieutenant colonel (May 28, 1863, with seniority to May 2, 1863) in the Confederate Army, and was assigned inspector of cavalry on the staff of General Bragg.

NOTE: Command assignments to the 1st and 2nd Brigades of Morgan's Division "appear to have been the composition of Morgan's Command when he set out on the raid." *The War of The Rebellion: A Compilation of the Official Records of the Union and Confederate Armies.* Series I, vol. XXIII, part II, p. 944. Washington, D.C.: Government Printing Office, 1889.

UNION

General Winfield Scott, a career soldier who retired from the U.S. Army on November 1, 1861, but kept an active interest in the war effort.

Major General Ambrose E. Burnside, Commanding, Department of the Ohio.

Major General Ulysses S. Grant, USV, Commanding, Army and Department of the Tennessee.

Major General James Birdseye McPherson, USV, Commanding, XVII Corps, Army of the Tennessee.

Major General William S. Rosecrans, USV, Commanding, Army and Department of the Cumberland.

Major General William Tecumseh Sherman, USV (Brigadier General, USA, July 4, 1863), Commanding XV Corps, Army of the Tennessee.

Brigadier General Edward H. Hobson, Commanding, 2nd Brigade, 3rd Division, XXIII Army Corps.

Brigadier General Henry M. Judah, Commanding, 3rd Division, XXIII Army Corps.

Brigadier General Mahlon D. Manson, Commanding, 1st Brigade, 3rd Division, XXIII Army Corps.

Brigadier General James M. Shackleford, Commanding, 1st Brigade, 2nd Division, XXIII Army Corps.

Colonel James Collier, leader of approximately 500 Minute-Men, Steubenville, Ohio.

Colonel Israel Garrard, Commanding, 7th Ohio Cavalry Regiment, 3rd Brigade, 1st Division, XXIII Army Corps.

Colonel Frank L. Wolford, Commanding, Wolford's Cavalry (1st Kentucky Union Cavalry Regiment).

Major George W. Rue, 9th Kentucky Cavalry Regiment.

Major W. B. Way, 9th Michigan Cavalry Regiment.

Captain Theodore F. Allen, Company D, 7th Ohio Cavalry Regiment.

Acting Captain James Burbick, New Lisbon, Ohio (Local Militia)

CHAPTER 9: OATHS AND ALLEGIANCES
(December 21, 1863–November 13, 1866)

CONFEDERATE

Brigadier General John Hunt Morgan, Commanding 2,460 men in the raid through southern Indiana and Ohio, July 2–26, 1863.

Henry M. Stanley, a wealthy Southern businessman who gave his name to the former John Rowlands.

Henry Morton Stanley (John Rowlands), Union prisoner of war (April 16–June 4, 1862) at Camp Douglas who had the distinction of having served in the Union Army and Navy, and Confederate Army, but is most noted for discovering David Livingstone, near Lake Tanganyika, in southern Africa, in 1871.

UNION

Major General Benjamin Butler USV, Commanding, Department of Virginia and North Carolina (November 11, 1863–May 2, 1864) with responsibility for Point Lookout prison camp, and Commanding, Army of the James (April–August 27, 1864, September 7–December 14, 1864, and December 24, 1864–January 8, 1865).

Major General Henry W. Halleck, Commanding, Department of Missouri (November 19, 1861–March 11, 1862); Commanding, Department of the Mississippi (March 13, 1862–September 19, 1862); Commander-in-Chief (July 11, 1862–March 12, 1864).

Major General George B. McClellan, Commander-in-Chief (November 5, 1861–March 11, 1862).

Major General John Pope USV, Commanding, Department of the Northwest (September 16, 1862–November 28, 1862, and February 13, 1863–February 13, 1865).

Brigadier General Gilmon Marston, Commandant, Point Lookout Prison, Maryland, when established August 1, 1863, remaining under his jurisdiction while Commanding, District of St. Mary's, XVIII Corps, Department of Virginia and North Carolina (December 1, 1863–April 28, 1864). Prison was closed July 13, 1865.

Colonel James A. Mulligan, Commandant, Camp Douglas (February 26–June 14, 1862), who initiated the concept of enlisting Confederate prisoners in the Union Army.

Lieutenant Colonel William Hoffman, Commissary General of Prisoners (circa August 27, 1862–November 3, 1865).

U.S. Marshall Robert Murray, Southern District, New York State.

Edwin M. Stanton, Secretary of War (January 15, 1862–May 26, 1868).

Lorenzo Thomas, Adjutant General (circa March 7, 1861–March 13, 1863), promoted to rank of brigadier general (circa August 3, 1861) and assigned to duties in the West on March 13, 1863.

W. H. Wilkes, a Confederate soldier, prisoner at Camp Douglas, and nephew of Union Commodore Charles Wilkes.

Little Crow, leader of Sioux uprising in Minnesota, including unsuccessful attack on Ft. Ridgely (August 21–22, 1862), commanded force of Indians defeated by Colonel Henry H. Sibley at Wood Lake (September 23, 1862), and died July 8, 1863.

David Livingstone, Scottish missionary, traveler, and explorer of southern Africa, who sought the origin of the Nile River and was discovered in good health by Henry Morton Stanley, near Lake Tanganyika, in 1871.

CHAPTER 10: BATTLE OF BRICE'S CROSS ROADS (June 10, 1864)

CONFEDERATE

Major General Nathan Bedford Forrest, Commanding, Forrest's Cavalry Corps, and operating in western Tennessee and northern Mississippi.

Major General Stephen D. Lee, Commanding, Department of Alabama, Mississippi, and Eastern Louisiana. Headquartered at Tupelo, Mississippi.

Brigadier General Abraham Buford, Commanding, Buford's Division, including 3rd Brigade, 4th Brigade, 6th Brigade, Johnson's Brigade, and Artillery.

Colonel Clark R. Barteau, Commanding, 2nd Tennessee Cavalry Regiment.

Colonel Tyree H. Bell, Commanding, 4th Brigade, including 2nd Tennessee Cavalry Regiment, 16th Tennessee Cavalry Regiment, 19th Tennessee Cavalry Regiment, and 20th Tennessee Cavalry Regiment.

Colonel William A. Johnson, Commanding, Johnson's Brigade, including 4th Alabama Cavalry Regiment, Moreland's Alabama Cavalry Regiment, Williams's Alabama Cavalry Battalion, and Warren's Alabama Cavalry Battalion.

Colonel Hylan B. Lyon, Commanding, 3rd Brigade, including 3rd Kentucky Mounted Infantry, 7th Kentucky Mounted Infantry, 8th Kentucky Mounted Infantry, and 12th Kentucky Cavalry Regiment.

Colonel Edmund Rucker, Commanding, 6th Brigade, including 8th Mississippi Cavalry Regiment, 18th Mississippi Cavalry Battalion, and 7th Tennessee Cavalry Regiment.

Captain John W. Morton, Commanding, Artillery, including Morton's Tennessee Battery and Rice's Tennessee Battery.

Captain T. W. Rice, Commanding, Rice's Tennessee Battery.

UNION

Major General William T. Sherman, Commanding, Army of the West.

Brigadier General Benjamin H. Grierson, USV, Commanding, 1st Cavalry Division, consisting of 1st Brigade and 2nd Brigade, XVI Corps, Army of the Tennessee.

Brigadier General Samuel D. Sturgis, Commanding, Sturgis's Expeditionary Force, District of West Tennessee, Department of the Tennessee.

Colonel Edward Bouton, Commanding 3rd Brigade, consisting of 55th U.S. Colored Infantry Regiment, 59th U.S. Colored Infantry Regiment, and Company F of the 2nd U.S. Colored Artillery.

Colonel George B. Hoge, Commanding, 2nd Brigade, consisting of 81st Illinois Infantry Regiment, 95th Illinois Infantry Regiment, 108th Illinois Infantry Regiment, 113th Illinois Infantry Regiment, 120th Illinois Infantry Regiment, and Company B of the 2nd Illinois Light Artillery.

Colonel William L. McMillen, Commanding, 1st Brigade, 1st Division, XVI Corps, Army of the Tennessee.

Colonel De Witt C. Thomas, Commanding, 93rd Indiana Infantry Regiment.

Colonel George E. Waring, Jr., Commanding, 1st Cavalry Brigade, consisting of 7th Indiana Cavalry Regiment, detachments from the 3rd and 9th Illinois Cavalry Regiments, 4th Missouri Cavalry Regiment, 2nd New Jersey Cavalry Regiment, and 19th Pennsylvania Cavalry Regiment.

Colonel Edward F. Winslow, Commanding, 2nd Brigade, consisting of a detachment from the 7th Illinois Cavalry Regiment, 3rd Iowa Cavalry Regiment, 4th Iowa Cavalry Regiment, a detachment from the 10th Missouri Cavalry Regiment, and a section from the 7th Wisconsin Battery.

Lieutenant Colonel Jefferson Brumback, Commanding, 95th Ohio Infantry Regiment.

Lieutenant Colonel George R. Clarke, Commanding, 113th Illinois Infantry Regiment.

Lieutenant Colonel Charles G. Eaton, Commanding, 72nd Ohio Infantry Regiment.

Lieutenant Colonel John W. Noble, Commanding, 3rd Iowa Cavalry Regiment.

Captain Henry S. Lee, Commanding, a section of the 7th Wisconsin Battery.

CHAPTER 11: THE NORTHWEST CONSPIRACY (August–November 1864)

CONFEDERATE

Jefferson Davis, President and Commander-in-Chief, The Confederate States of America.

Brigadier General Charles Walsh, Commanding, Sons of Liberty and Confederates in the Chicago Conspiracy who, in 1862, was a candidate for sheriff of Cook County.

Colonel George St. Leger Grenfell, a British soldier of fortune, who earlier served as adjutant general and chief of staff to Brigadier General John Hunt Morgan and later as inspector general on General Braxton Bragg's staff.

Colonel Vincent Marmaduke, of Saline County, Missouri, expelled from Missouri because of pro-Confederate sympathies, and brother of Confederate Major General John S. Marmaduke.

Major John B. Castleman, 2nd Kentucky Cavalry Regiment who enlisted Captain Thomas Henry Hines.

Captain George Cantrill, allegedly a former officer serving under Brigadier General John Hunt Morgan who was arrested with other alleged "Chicago Conspirators," petitioned for a separate trial January 12, 1865, as not being "subject to jurisdiction of a military tribunal," but unable to locate and confirm any listing of person with this rank, first name, and last name, in the *Report of the Adjutant General of the State of Kentucky Confederate Kentucky Volunteers War 1861–1865*.

Captain Thomas Henry Hines, a member of Brigadier General John Hunt Morgan's Division, Cavalry Corps, who escaped with General Morgan from the Ohio State Penitentiary, on November 28, 1863, and was appointed by Secretary of War James A. Seddon to command the expedition in Chicago.

Captain (field promotion) John T. Shanks, a former officer in the Confederate Army who joined Brigadier General John Hunt Morgan's cavalry, was assigned as a scout under the command of Captain Thomas H. Hines until captured July 19, 1863, at Buffington Island, Ohio, was transferred to Camp Douglas as a prisoner on August 17, 1863, and took the oath of allegiance to the U.S. Government to become a Galvanized Yankee.

First Lieutenant Ben Drake (promoted December 22, 1862), Company M, 2nd Kentucky Cavalry Regiment.

Lieutenant John J. Bettersworth (alias J. B. Fielding), one of the alleged conspirators, but unable to locate and confirm any listing of person with this rank, first name, middle initial, and last name in the *Report of the Adjutant General of the State of Kentucky Confederate Kentucky Volunteers War 1861–1865*.

Lieutenant George B. Eastin, Company D, 2nd Kentucky Cavalry Regiment.

Sergeant Maurice Langhorn, who served in an artillery unit as part of Brigadier General John Hunt Morgan's Cavalry Division, was a prisoner of war, and became an informer after taking the oath of allegiance to the U.S. Government.

Private Charles T. Daniel (alias Charles Travis), Company C, 14th Kentucky Cavalry Regiment, as stated in his plea on page 14 of *House Executive Document 50* regarding the trial of persons arrested in the "Chicago Conspiracy," but unable to locate and confirm any listing of his service as a member of this company and regiment as recorded on the rolls filed June 30, 1863, and December 31, 1864, at Camp Bowen, Virginia.

Clement C. Clay, Jr., a former U.S. Senator from Alabama and, after secession, a Confederate Senator, who was sent to Canada to assist Jacob Thompson to ascertain the extent of support in seeking a cessation of hostilities or continuing the war.

George (Lightning) Ellsworth, a telegrapher who accompanied Brigadier General John Hunt Morgan on his 1863 raid through Kentucky, Indiana, and Ohio.

Buckner S. Morris, treasurer of the Sons of Liberty, second mayor of Chicago, and a former circuit court judge, practicing law in Chicago at time of the alleged conspiracy.

Jacob Thompson, of Mississippi and a former secretary of the interior in the administration of President James Buchanan, was appointed a commissioner by President Jefferson Davis to ascertain the extent of support in seeking a cessation of hostilities or continuing the war. He also supervised the assembly in Toronto, Canada, as of August 24, 1864, of rebel sympathizers, soldiers, and escaped prisoners to plan the release of prisoners of war at various military camps.

Ware, one of approximately 150 alleged conspirators arrested and believed to be from central or southern Illinois, but no first name or any other information was given about him during the trial of the alleged Chicago Conspirators.

UNION

Lieutenant General Ulysses Simpson Grant, Commanding, Armies of the United States, and establishing headquarters in the field with the Army of the Potomac.

Major General George B. McClellan, General-in-Chief of the Armies (November 6, 1861–March 11, 1862), Commanding Army of the Potomac (August 20, 1861–November 9, 1862), resigning from the Army (November 8, 1864) to become Democratic Party candidate for president in 1864.

Major General William Tecumseh Sherman, Commanding, Military Division of the Mississippi, including the Army of the Tennessee, the Army of the Cumberland and the Army of the Ohio.

Brigadier General Henry B. Carrington, Commanding, District of Indiana.

Brigadier General John Cook, Commanding, District of Illinois, with headquarters in Springfield.

Colonel Benjamin J. Sweet, Commander of Camp Douglas (July 1, 1864–September 29, 1865), and promoted to brigadier general on December 20, 1864.
Thomas H. Keefe, Chief of Detectives, Northwest Department, War Department Secret Service.
William H. Seward, Secretary of State (March 5, 1861–March 4, 1869).
Horatio Seymour, presided over a session at the 1864 Democratic convention which was heavily stacked with pro-Confederates.
Clement Laird Vallandigham, former Democratic U.S. representative from Ohio (May 25, 1858–March 3, 1863) and delegate to the 1864 Democratic National Convention in Chicago.

CHAPTER 12: THE MILLION-DOLLAR WAGON TRAIN RAID
(September 19, 1864)

CONFEDERATE
General E. Kirby Smith, Commanding, Trans-Mississippi Department, head-quartered at Shreveport, Louisiana.
Major General Sterling Price, Commanding, Army of Missouri.
Brigadier General Richard M. Gano, Commanding, 5th Texas Brigade, consisting of 29th Texas Cavalry Regiment, 30th Texas Cavalry Regiment, 33rd Texas Cavalry Regiment, 1st Texas-Arizona Battalion, 1st (5th) Texas Partisan Rangers, Good's (Texas) Battalion, and Wells' (Texas) Battalion.
Brigadier General Stand Watie, Commanding, 1st Confederate Indian Cavalry Brigade.
Colonel Charles DeMorse, Commanding, 29th Texas Cavalry Regiment.
Lieutenant Colonel John Jumper, Commanding, Battalion of Seminoles.
Lieutenant Colonel C. N. Vann, Commanding, 1st Cherokee Regiment.
Major E. M. Stackpole, a member of the staff of Brigadier General Richard M. Gano, Commanding, 5th Texas Brigade.
Captain Sylvanus Howell, Commanding, Howell's (Texas) Battery.
Captain George Washington, Commanding, Reserve Squadron, 2nd (Indian) Brigade, Indian Cavalry Division.

UNION
Major Henry Hopkins, 2nd Kansas Cavalry, Commanding detachment from the 2nd, 6th, and 14th Kansas Cavalry Regiments.
Captain Henry Ledger, Commanding, 6th Kansas Cavalry Regiment.

CHAPTER 13: BATTLE OF WESTPORT (October 22–24, 1864)

CONFEDERATE
Major General James F. Fagan, Commanding, Fagan's Division, consisting of Cabell's Brigade, Dobbin's Brigade, Slemon's Brigade, McCray's Brigade, and

three unattached units consisting of Anderson's Arkansas Cavalry Battalion, Lyle's Arkansas Cavalry, and Rogan's Arkansas Cavalry.

Major General John S. Marmaduke, Commanding, Marmaduke's Division, consisting of Company D of the 5th Missouri Cavalry as escort, Marmaduke's Brigade, two artillery units under command of Major Joseph H. Pratt, and Freeman's Brigade.

NOTE: During the period between April 21 and May 17, 1864, Brigadier General John S. Marmaduke was advanced in rank to major general although no official documentation could be found. However, in his correspondence from the field on May 17, 1864 to Lt. Col. J. F. Belton, assistant adjutant general, District of Arkansas, he signed as major general. This would substantiate his listing as major general in the Order of Battle for the engagement at Westport and again in a report on October 25, 1864, of his capture as a major general. According to some references, he was not officially promoted to the rank of major general by the Confederate government until March 18, 1865, with rank to the previous day.

Major General Sterling Price, Commanding, Army of Missouri.

Brigadier General William L. Cabell, Commanding, Cabell's Brigade, consisting of Gordon's Arkansas Cavalry, Gunter's Arkansas Cavalry Battalion, Harrell's Arkansas Cavalry Battalion, Hill's Arkansas Cavalry, Monroe's Arkansas Cavalry, Morgan's Arkansas Cavalry, Witherspoon's Arkansas Cavalry Battalion, and Hughey's Arkansas Battery.

Brigadier General Joseph O. Shelby, Commanding, Shelby's Division, consisting of Shelby's Iron Brigade, Jackman's Brigade, Tyler's Brigade, and an unattached unit of the 46th Arkansas Infantry (mounted).

Brigadier General M. Jeff Thompson, Commanding, Shelby's Iron Brigade, consisting of the 5th Missouri Cavalry, 11th Missouri Cavalry, 12th Missouri Cavalry, Crisp's Cavalry Battalion, Elliott's Missouri Cavalry Regiment, Johnson's Cavalry Battalion, Slayback's Missouri Cavalry Battalion, and Collins's Missouri Battery.

Thomas C. Reynolds, former lieutenant governor of Missouri, attached to the staff of Brigadier General Joseph O. Shelby until claiming the governorship of Missouri.

Colonel Sidney D. Jackman, Commanding, Jackman's Brigade, consisting of Hunter's Missouri Cavalry Regiment, Jackman's Missouri Cavalry Regiment, Schnable's Missouri Cavalry Battalion, Williams's Missouri Cavalry Battalion, and Collins's Missouri Battery.

Colonel James H. McGhee,* Commanding, McGhee's Arkansas Cavalry, until wounded on October 23 and succeeded in command by Lieutenant Colonel Jesse S. Grider.

UNION

Major General James G. Blunt, Commanding, 1st Provisional Cavalry Division.

Major General Samuel R. Curtis, Commanding, Department of Kansas, Army of the Border.

Major General George W. Dietzler, Adjutant General of State of Kansas, Commanding, Kansas State Militia Division.

Major General Alfred Pleasonton, Commanding, Provisional Cavalry Division (often called the 2nd Division, Army of the Border, by Major General Samuel R. Curtis).

Major General William S. Rosecrans, USV, Commanding, Department of the Missouri.

Brigadier General M. S. Grant, Kansas State Militia Division, reporting to Major General George W. Dietzler.

Brigadier General John McNeil, Commanding, 2nd Brigade, consisting of 2nd Missouri Cavalry Regiment (Merrill's Horse), 13th Missouri Cavalry Regiment, 7th Kansas Cavalry Regiment, 17th Illinois Cavalry Regiment, 3rd Missouri State Militia, 5th Missouri State Militia, 9th Missouri State Militia, Battery B of the 2nd Missouri Light Artillery, and a battery of four 12-pound mountain howitzers.

Brigadier General John B. Sanborn, Commanding, 3rd Brigade, consisting of 2nd Arkansas Cavalry Regiment, 6th Missouri State Militia, 8th Missouri State Militia, 6th Provisional Enrolled Missouri Militia, 7th Provisional Enrolled Missouri Militia, Battery H of the 2nd Missouri Light Artillery, and Battery L of the 2nd Missouri Light Artillery.

Colonel Charles W. Blair, Commanding, 3rd Brigade, consisting of 6th Kansas Militia Cavalry Regiment, Eves. Battalion Kansas Militia Cavalry Regiment, right section of the 2nd Kansas State Artillery, and the 9th Wisconsin Battery.

Colonel James H. Ford, Commanding, 4th Brigade, consisting of 2nd Colorado Cavalry Regiment, a detachment of the 16th Kansas Cavalry Regiment and Captain W. D. McLain's Independent Colorado Battery.

Colonel Charles R. Jennison, Commanding, 1st Brigade, consisting of 15th Kansas Cavalry Regiment, 3rd Wisconsin Cavalry Regiment (five companies), Foster's Battalion, P.E.M.M., and a battery of five 12-pound mountain howitzers.

Colonel Thomas Moonlight, Commanding, 2nd Brigade, consisting of 11th Kansas Cavalry Regiment, 5th Kansas Cavalry Regiment (Company L and Company M), 16th Kansas Cavalry Regiment (Company A and Company D), a battery of four 12-pound mountain howitzers manned by Company E of the 11th Kansas Cavalry Regiment, and the 11th Kansas Militia Cavalry Regiment.

Colonel John F. Philips, Commanding, 1st Brigade, consisting of 1st Missouri State Militia, 4th Missouri State Militia, and 7th Missouri State Militia.

Lieutenant Colonel Frederick W. Benteen, Commanding, 4th Brigade, consisting of 3rd Iowa Cavalry Regiment, 4th Iowa Cavalry Regiment, 10th Missouri Cavalry Regiment, 7th Indiana Cavalry Regiment and 4th Missouri Cavalry Regiment combined.

Captain Edward W. Dee, 4th Iowa Cavalry.

Captain James H. Dodge, Commanding, 9th Wisconsin Battery.

Captain Curtis Johnson, Commanding, Company E, 15th Kansas Cavalry, District of South Kansas, Department of Kansas.

Captain W. D. McLain, Commanding, Captain W. D. McLain's Independent Colorado Battery.

CHAPTER 14: NO MORE BUGLES (October 1864–July 1865)

CONFEDERATE

Jefferson Davis, President and Commander-in-Chief, The Confederate States of America (February 18, 1861–May 10, 1865).

General Pierre G. T. Beauregard, Commanding, all troops in South Carolina, reporting to General Joseph E. Johnston, and second in command of Army of Tennessee.

General Braxton Bragg, Commanding, defense of Wilmington, North Carolina, relieving Major General W. H. C. Whiting.

General Joseph E. Johnston, having no major assignment July 18, 1864–February 25, 1865, received the appointment, Commanding, Army of Tennessee and Department of Tennessee and Georgia, and Commanding, Department of South Carolina, Georgia, and Florida (February 25, 1865–April 26, 1865), and Commanding, Department of North Carolina (March 16, 1865–April 26, 1865).

General Robert E. Lee, Commanding, Army of Northern Virginia until February 6, 1865, when appointed General-in-Chief, all Confederate armies (February 6, 1865–April 9, 1865).

Lieutenant General W. J. Hardee, Commanding, Department of South Carolina, Georgia, and Florida (October 5, 1864–February 16, 1865), reporting to headquarters, Division of the West.

Major General John C. Breckinridge, Commanding, Departments of East Tennessee and Western Virginia until being appointed Acting Secretary of War (February 6, 1865).

Major General Nathan Bedford Forrest, Commanding, District of Mississippi and East Louisiana (January 27, 1865).

Brigadier General George B. Cosby, Commanding Hodge's (old) Brigade, Department of Western Virginia and East Tennessee (September 5, 1864–circa April 1865).

Brigadier General Basil Duke, Commanding, remnants of the Cavalry Division of Brigadier General John Hunt Morgan that guarded President Jefferson Davis during his attempted retreat from Richmond, Virginia, to Georgia, and succeeded command of improvised remnant companies of Morgan's Division following Morgan's death on September 4, 1864, in Greenville, Tennessee.

Brigadier General John Echols, Commanding, a brigade in Wharton's Division, Army of Valley District, Department of Northern Virginia (January 31, 1865), and appointed to command 3rd Military Sub-District of Texas, Trans-Mississippi Department (March 29, 1865).

Brigadier General John C. Vaughn, Commanding, Cavalry Brigade, Department of Western Virginia and East Tennessee (fall 1864–circa April 1865).

Colonel William C. P. Breckinridge, Commanding, 9th Kentucky Cavalry Regiment.

Colonel Burton N. Harrison, private secretary to President Jefferson Davis who accompanied the Confederate States president on his retreat southward.

Colonel William Preston Johnston, aide-de-camp to President Jefferson Davis who accompanied the Confederate States president on his retreat southward.

Colonel Francis R. Lubbock, aide-de-camp to President Jefferson Davis who accompanied the Confederates States President on his retreat southward.

Dick Morgan (Colonel Richard C. Morgan), Commanding, Morgan's Cavalry Regiment, also known as the 14th Kentucky Cavalry Regiment.

Colonel D. Howard Smith, Commanding, 5th Kentucky Cavalry Regiment earlier, was captured and exchanged, rejoined remnants of the command at Saltville, Virginia, in 1864, assumed temporary command of improvised companies of Morgan's Division, relinquished command to Brigadier General Basil Duke upon his arrival, and ultimately surrendered at Columbus, Mississippi, on May 18, 1865.

Colonel John Taylor Wood, aide-de-camp to President Jefferson Davis who accompanied the Confederate States president on his retreat southward.

Captain William H. Parker, a naval officer who escorted the national archives and remaining treasures of The Confederate States of America during the retreat southward with President Jefferson Davis.

Major William J. Davis, Assistant Adjutant General for Major General John C. Breckinridge.

Major Victor Maurin, Richardson's Battalion, Confederate Light Artillery, Louisiana, who was a member of the escort southward for Varina Howell Davis.

Major Thomas B. Webber, a field officer with the 4th Kentucky Special Cavalry Battalion.

Captain Given Campbell, Company B, 2nd Kentucky Cavalry Regiment.

Captain Micajah H. Clark, former chief clerk of the Confederate Executive Office and acting treasurer, Confederate States of America, succeeding Acting Treasurer John H. Reagan.

Captain George V. Moody, Chief of Artillery, Capt. Moody's Company (Madison Light Artillery, Louisiana Artillery).

Captain Tom Quirk, although named in this chapter, did not participate in the retreat southward of President Jefferson Davis and his escort, but Colonel Joseph T. Tucker and seven other officers in a letter dated September 12, 1864, petitioned Colonel Basil Duke to use his influence with the Confederate War Department to have Captain Thomas Quirk, Company A, 2nd Battalion, reinstated.

Lieutenant Leeland Hathaway, 14th Kentucky Cavalry Regiment.

Lieutenant Winder W. Monroe, at times a member of Companies A, G, and I, 2nd Kentucky Cavalry Regiment, and later a member of Colonel Richard C. Morgan's 14th Kentucky Cavalry Regiment.

Second Lieutenant John B. Cole, Company K, 2nd Kentucky Cavalry Regiment.

Sergeant (John) Will Dyer, 4th Sergeant of Company G, 1st Kentucky Cavalry Regiment.

Ordnance Sergeant Henry L. Stone, 9th Kentucky Cavalry Regiment, and a member of the Kentucky Brigade that escorted President Jefferson Davis and his Cabinet southward from Greensboro, North Carolina, to Washington, Georgia, where it was disbanded.

Private Baker, allegedly with the 2nd Kentucky Cavalry Regiment, but unable with this incomplete information to locate and confirm any listing of person with this rank and last name in the Report of the *Adjutant General of the State of Kentucky Confederate Kentucky Volunteers War 1861–1865.*

Private Elston, allegedly with the 2nd Kentucky Cavalry Regiment, but unable with this incomplete information to locate and confirm any listing of person with this rank and last name in the *Report of the Adjutant General of the State of Kentucky Confederate Kentucky Volunteers War 1861–1865.*

Private John W. Farley, Company D, 2nd Kentucky Cavalry Regiment.

Private Heath, allegedly with the 2nd Kentucky Cavalry Regiment, but unable with this incomplete information to locate and confirm any listing of person with this rank and last name in the *Report of the Adjutant General of the State of Kentucky Confederate Kentucky Volunteers War 1861–1865.*

Private John "Jack" Messick, Company A, 2nd Kentucky Cavalry Regiment.

Private George D. Mosgrove, Company K, 4th Kentucky Cavalry Regiment.

Private B. F. Sanders, Company G, 2nd Kentucky Cavalry Regiment.

Private Smith, allegedly with the 2nd Kentucky Cavalry Regiment, but unable with this incomplete information to locate and confirm any listing of person with this rank and last name in the *Report of the Adjutant General of the State of Kentucky Confederate Kentucky Volunteers War 1861–1865.*

Private J. A. Walbert, Company B, 15th Kentucky Cavalry Regiment also known as 2nd (Woodward's) Kentucky Cavalry Regiment.

Varina Howell Davis, second wife of Jefferson Davis, president of The Confederate States of America.

Margaret "Maggie" Howell, sister of Varina Howell Davis.

Judge Thomas Bell Monroe, a U. S. District Judge who lived in Abbeville, South Carolina, and grandfather of Lieutenant Winder Monroe.

John H. Reagan, Postmaster General, The Confederate States of America, who accompanied President Jefferson Davis on his retreat southward and assumed the temporary duties of Secretary of the Treasury George A. Trenholm due to his absence because of illness.

G. (George) A. Trenholm, Secretary of the Treasury, The Confederate States of America, who was too ill to accompany President Jefferson Davis on his retreat southward, leaving Postmaster General John Reagan to assume his duties on a temporary basis.

UNION

Major General William T. Sherman, Commanding, Military Division of the Mississippi.

Major General James H. Wilson (promoted to major general May 6, 1865), Commanding, Cavalry Corps, Military Division of the Mississippi.

Brigadier General Stephen G. Burbridge, Commanding, District of Kentucky, XXIII Army Corps. Unit transferred to Department of the Cumberland (January 17, 1865).

Lieutenant Colonel Henry Harnden, 1st Wisconsin Cavalry Regiment.

Lieutenant Colonel Benjamin D. Pritchard, Commanding, 4th Regiment Michigan Volunteer Cavalry.

Major Charles M. Betts, originally commanding Company F, 15th Pennsylvania Cavalry Regiment until promoted to Lieutenant Colonel as of March 13, 1865, as a field and staff officer, 15th Pennsylvania Cavalry Regiment.

James Buchanan, President of the United States (March 4, 1857–March 4, 1861).

President Andrew Johnson, assumed presidency April 15, 1865, upon death of Abraham Lincoln, served as president through noon, March 4, 1869, and wrote note ordering release of prisoners Lieutenant Leeland Hathaway, Lieutenant Winder Monroe, and Private Jack Messick from Fort McHenry.

Edwin M. Stanton, Secretary of War, (January 15, 1862–May 26, 1868).

Index

Page references in **boldface** type refer to illustrations.